THE LAW IN ACTION

THE LEGAL SYSTEM
OF NORTHERN IRELAND

THE LAW IN ACTION

Small Claims :
The New Procedure in Northern Ireland (3rd ed, 1988)
D. S. Greer

Industrial Tribunals in Northern Ireland (2nd ed, 1989)
P. Bateson and J. McKee

Family Breakdown, Children and the Law (1985)
G. Kerr

Wardship in Northern Ireland (1988)
K. O'Halloran

Servicing the Legal System

The Servicing the Legal System programme was inaugurated in August 1980 in the Faculty of Law of the Queen's University of Belfast to promote the publication of commentaries on various aspects of the law and legal system of Northern Ireland. Generous financial and other support for the Programme has been provided by the Northern Ireland Court Service, the Inn of Court of Northern Ireland, the Bar Council of Northern Ireland, the Law Society of Northern Ireland, the Northern Ireland Bankers' Association, TSB Northern Ireland plc and Queen's University. This publication is one of a series primarily designed to explain the law and its procedures to people who are not lawyers. Other books in this series and details of all SLS publications may be obtained from the SLS Office, Faculty of Law, Queen's University, Belfast BT7 1NN.

THE LEGAL SYSTEM
OF NORTHERN IRELAND

Brice Dickson

Belfast
1989

© Brice Dickson 1989

All rights reserved. No part of this publication may be reproduced, stored in a retrieval system or transmitted in any form or by any means, including photocopying and recording, without the prior written permission of the publishers.

First edition published in 1984 by SLS Legal Publications (NI), Faculty of Law, Queen's University, Belfast BT7 1NN.
Second Printing 1985
Third Printing 1986
Second Edition 1989
Second Printing 1991
Third Printing 1992

ISBN 0 85389 300 4

Printed in Northern Ireland for SLS
by Northern Whig Ltd

For Patricia M.

CONTENTS

PREFACE

The main purpose of this book is to supply basic information about the legal system to the general public. It provides for Northern Ireland what other books already provide for the legal systems of England, Scotland and the Republic of Ireland. Such a short and general work obviously cannot be a substitute for more scholarly examinations of particular aspects of the legal system, but it is hoped that the bringing together under one cover of information derived from a wide variety of sources will prove helpful and interesting. Guidance on where to find more information about particular matters is supplied in Appendix 1.

A further purpose of the book is to "demystify" the legal system, that is, to make its workings easier to understand. To that end the style has deliberately been kept simple. Words and phrases with a particular significance in legal circles are explained, but otherwise the text is completely non-technical. Even a person who has no previous knowledge of the law should be able to read the book with full understanding. It must be stressed, however, that the book does not set out to give concrete advice on particular legal issues. Chapters 2 and 3 provide background information for people with legal problems, but information about the actual content of the law still needs to be looked for in other sources. Chapters 4 and 5, similarly, deal primarily with criminal and civil *procedure*, not with criminal and civil *law*. Chapter 7 has a section on social security appeal tribunals, but gives no advice on entitlement to benefits.

The book does not attempt to give a critique of the legal system. It is purely descriptive. A great deal could indeed be written about the system's merits and demerits, but in this case readers are left to draw their own conclusions as to whether the various features of the legal system make sense. Furthermore, a book of this size cannot cover every conceivable aspect of the legal system. It concentrates instead on what is most common and most typical, without going into great detail.

This second edition follows the order of treatment adopted in its predecessor, but I have taken the opportunity to update the statistics, insert more tables, substitute new paragraphs for some that had become outmoded (especially in Chapters 1,4,7 and 8) and revise the Appendices. I have tried to ensure that the information supplied is up-to-date as of 1st February 1989.

Many colleagues and friends assisted with the preparation of the first edition and the same is true for the second. I wish to thank in particular Miss Brigid Hadfield, Dr Michael Knight, Mr Steven McBride, Mr Gerry McCormack and Mr Robert Millar. The staff of SLS Legal Publications (NI), in particular Dr Peter Ingram, have been extremely supportive throughout. My indebtedness to others who have written about aspects of the Northern Ireland legal system, especially Professor Desmond Greer, is obvious for all to see. After so much help, whatever faults survive in the work must remain entirely my own responsibility. I shall be very pleased to hear from anyone who discovers mistakes.

Copyright material in Appendices 3 and 4 is reproduced by permission of the Comptroller of Her Majety's Stationery Office, with the exception of the application form for legal advice and assistance, reproduced by permission of the Law Society of Northern Ireland, and the report of *Campbell v. Armstrong and others*, reprinted by permission of the Editor of the Northern Ireland Law Reports.

BRICE DICKSON
The Queen's University of Belfast
March 1989.

1

The History and Administration of the Legal System

1.1 The Early Legal History of Northern Ireland

The history of a legal system is inevitably bound up with the political history of the territory in which the legal system has operated. For that reason alone the legal history of Northern Ireland is long and complex. A true appreciation of it is essential, however, if the workings of the legal system today are to be properly understood. As well as throwing light on why things are as they are, the history also helps us, to some extent, to identify those aspects of the system which are overdue for change. The importance of an historical approach will be made particularly apparent in Chapter 2. The first three sections of this opening chapter provide a brief sketch of the history, while the fourth, fifth and sixth sections describe the bodies and persons who have inherited the political or professional responsibility for operating the legal system in Northern Ireland.

The Brehon law system

Before the arrival of the Normans in 1169 Ireland was governed by Brehon law. This was a legal system based on traditional custom, the laws being formulated and applied by respected native jurists called Brehons. Brehon law continued to apply after 1169 in areas outside the Normans' control, and even in areas within their control it continued to govern the native Irish. The Normans themselves were subject to the English "common law" system, which at that time was already unifying the various local law systems throughout England.

As the Normans extended their influence English law slowly became more important in Ireland. In 1171 King Henry II is said to have held a Council at Lismore, near Waterford, "where the laws of England were by all freely received and confirmed," but it is more likely in actual fact that the English laws were only gradually accepted during the course of the following century. By 1300 English law applied in most of Ireland, and some 30 years later the policy of leaving the native Irish to be governed by Brehon law was reversed. By this time, however, the Irish were beginning to regroup, with the object of repelling the Norman invaders. Consequently, the influence of English law went into a gradual decline. By 1500 English law extended only to the area around Dublin known as the Pale; the rest of Ireland had returned to Brehon law.

All this changed again with the Tudor reconquest, which culminated in the Flight of the Earls in 1607 and the Plantation of Ulster in the early years of the seventeenth century. The whole of Ireland was then under English control and Brehon law completely ceased to apply. In a famous piece of litigation known as *The Case of Tanistry* (1607), Brehon law was declared to be incompatible with and contrary to the common law of England and could not, therefore, remain any part of the law in Ireland. Since then the provisions of Brehon law have been referred to by judges in a few cases concerning ancient fishing rights, but otherwise Brehon law has played no part at all in the modern legal history of Ireland.

The common law system

The system of law which has existed throughout Ireland since the seventeenth century is called the common law system, though it is important to note that this is only one sense in which the expression "common law" can be used. We will encounter its other meanings in due course. The most fundamental feature of the common law system is the doctrine of binding precedent. According to this doctrine, which is explained more fully in 2.4, once a court has made a decision on a particular point of law, that decision is a binding authority on lower courts in subsequent cases concerned with the same legal point. Now that many more laws are being created by Parliament than was the case a century or so ago, there is not so much scope for judge-made law, with the result that the force of the doctrine of precedent is diminishing. It is still much stronger, however, than in countries such as France and West Germany where a "civil law" system operates. The law there is laid down almost exclusively in codes and even when judges interpret these codes their decisions are not binding for later cases.

After the reconquest of Ireland in the sixteenth and seventeenth centuries the law in Ireland and England developed along much the same lines for about 300 years. The countries were administered differently, but the actual content of the law was almost identical. Some significant differences were created during the nineteenth century in an attempt to solve the intractable land problem in Ireland, and the two jurisdictions got out of step as regards the law on marriage and divorce and some other matters, but generally the laws remained very similar. Even since the partition of Ireland in 1920 the law throughout the two islands (with the exception of Scotland, which has more of a civil law system) has been based on the same fundamental common law concepts. The creation of separate Parliaments, though, which is described in the next section, has inevitably caused some divergences.

1.2 Parliaments

Just as the Parliament in England developed out of the King's Council (the "Curia Regis"), a Parliament in Ireland evolved, during the thirteenth century, out of the jurisdiction of the Justiciar, the King's official representative in Ireland. For two centuries there were Parliaments in both England and Ireland claiming the power to make laws for Ireland, and not until 1494-5 was it declared at a gathering at Drogheda that only legislation approved by the English Council could be passed by the Parliament in Ireland (Poynings' Law). The Irish Parliament continued to exist until 1800 and it purported to make some unapproved laws. Between 1783 and 1800 it even regained some of its former pre-eminence, because Poynings' Law was repealed in 1782. From the Act of Union in 1800, until 1921, the only legislative body for Ireland was the Parliament of the United Kingdom sitting in London. But not all of the legislation enacted by that Parliament applied automatically throughout the kingdom: some Acts were applied to Ireland only at a later date (and sometimes in a piecemeal fashion), some were specifically enacted for Ireland and never applied in England, and some were not extended to Ireland at all.

With the partitioning of Ireland in 1920 separate legal systems were established for North and South. The North consisted of six of the nine counties comprising the province of Ulster. Each part of the island was given its own Parliament as well as its own system of courts. In the South the old law continued to apply only when it was not inconsistent with the Constitution of the new state. For many years this resulted in few alterations, though in the past 15 years or so the Irish Constitution of 1937 has played an increasingly important role in the law's development in the Republic.

The Stormont Parliament

In Northern Ireland some scope for legal development distinct from that occurring in England was created by the transfer to a new local Parliament of the right to enact legislation "for the peace, order and good government" of the province. From 1932 this Parliament was located at Stormont, near Belfast. The matters which were transferred included local government matters, many aspects of civil and criminal law, agriculture, education and planning. Certain "excepted" and "reserved" matters, though, could be dealt with only by the Parliament at Westminster. Excepted matters were those which were of imperial or national concern (for which it would be undesirable to enact local variations), while reserved matters were those which were to be the preserve of the proposed Council of Ireland (which in fact was never created).

The Northern Ireland Parliament consisted of two chambers - the House of Commons and the Senate - but people were also elected to represent Northern Ireland constituencies at Westminster. The Monarch was represented in Northern Ireland by the Governor, residing at Hillsborough in County Down. The general policy of the Stormont Parliament was to keep in step with legislation enacted for Great Britain, although in certain areas (land law and family or personal matters again being prominent) Northern Ireland either failed to follow changes or introduced new laws of its own devising.

Northern Ireland under direct rule

This devolution of powers in the North continued until March 1972, when the Stormont Parliament was suspended. "Direct rule" was introduced, with laws on transferred matters being made by Order in Council (see 2.3) and executive powers being exercised by the Secretary of State for Northern Ireland. Under the Northern Ireland Constitution Act 1973 the Northern Ireland Parliament was abolished and a new system of devolution was tried. In January 1974 powers to make some laws (called "Measures") were vested in a one-chamber elected Assembly, but this experiment collapsed in May 1974 and since then direct rule has applied again, the arrangements being renewed annually under the Northern Ireland (Temporary Provisions) Act 1974.

In 1982 a new 78-member Northern Ireland Assembly, again with only one chamber and sitting at Stormont, was elected under the Northern Ireland Act 1982. It did not have any law-making powers - only "scrutiny, consultative and deliberative powers" - but the United Kingdom Government hoped that in due course some such powers could be transferred to it under the principle of so-called "rolling", or partial, devolution. Once again the experiment proved unsuccessful and the Assembly was dissolved in 1986. The signing of the Anglo-Irish Agreement in November 1985 led to the establishment of the Anglo-Irish Intergovernmental Conference, which convenes periodically to allow representatives from the Government of the Irish Republic to put forward their views on the governance of the province. The Agreement is a treaty between two sovereign states and does not have the force of internal domestic law.

Northern Ireland therefore continues to be controlled by the Parliament at Westminster, with the United Kingdom Government administering it through the Northern Ireland Office, a department headed by the Secretary of State for Northern Ireland (see 1.4). Northern Ireland constituencies elect 17 MPs to the Parliament at Westminster; the Northern Ireland Committee of that Parliament considers such matters affecting the province as may be referred to it. The various forms which Parliamentary law can take today are described in detail in 2.2 and 2.3.

During the period of direct rule the process of assimilation between the law in Northern Ireland and the law in England has, if anything, been fortified. Harmonization has also been fostered through the United Kingdom's membership both of the European Community (the Common Market) and of the Council of Europe (see 2.6).

1.3 Courts

The Four Courts

The Normans did not introduce a new system of law into England after the Battle of Hastings in 1066. William the Conqueror, in fact, declared that he did not wish to change the law at all. But in order to keep control over the whole country the Norman kings assumed responsibility for the administration of justice and created a new system of courts based at Westminster. These courts, supported by the royal power, gradually came to deal with the most important types of legal dispute, and it was from the rules devised by judges to settle disputes in these courts that there emerged a body of law which was common to the whole kingdom.

To begin with there were three courts to handle three broad categories of case. Cases involving the King's interest in the maintenance of law and order were dealt with by the Court of King's Bench; taxation cases were heard in the Court of Exchequer; and disputes involving only "common" (*i.e.* private) individuals went to the Court of Common Pleas. These courts met regularly at Westminster, but twice a year the justices would tour the country, on Assizes, to dispense the King's justice and reassert his authority in each of the counties. Each case was decided by one judge, usually sitting with a jury of 12 "true and honest"men.

There were many disputes which could not be dealt with in these three courts. Petitions sent to the King to settle such cases were referred by him to his Chancellor (at that time usually an influential cleric) for justice to be done "according to the conscience of the case." From this practice there emerged another court, the Court of Chancery. The convention developed that the justice dispensed by the Court of Chancery was "equity", while the justice dispensed by the King's three other courts was "common law" (another sense in which that phrase has been used). It was not until 1875 in England (1877 in Ireland) that common law and equity could be administered in one and the same court; until then the two types of law had to be kept quite separate.

When the Normans established themselves in Ireland they naturally introduced a system of courts modelled on the English system. Accordingly the Four Courts (of King's Bench, Exchequer, Common Pleas and Chancery) were set up in Dublin. As in England, the judges in most of these courts went on Assizes throughout those parts of Ireland under Norman control each spring and summer. Cases were therefore ordered to be tried in Dublin, unless before (in Latin, *nisi prius*) the given date of trial the Assize judge came to the county where the litigants lived.

These four courts formed the heart of the legal systems in England and Ireland until late in the nineteenth century. Over time other courts were established to deal with special types of case and with appeals. To the four "superior" courts in Dublin were added five more: a Court of Admiralty (to deal with shipping cases), a Court of Bankruptcy and Insolvency, a Court of Probate (to deal with disputes concerning wills), a Court for Matrimonial Causes, and a Landed Estates Court (part of the effort to solve the land problem). Two appeal courts called the Court of Exchequer Chamber and the Court of Appeal in Chancery were added. For cases involving smaller amounts there was created a system of "civil bill" or "county courts", and power to try less serious criminal cases was given to magistrates' courts. It can be seen that by the 1870s the court structure in Ireland had become exceedingly complicated and unmanageable.

The Supreme Court of Judicature

In 1877 a thorough reorganisation of the superior courts took place, again along English lines. The nine courts were amalgamated into one High Court which by 1900 came to have only two divisions - the Queen's Bench Division (which took over the work of seven of the old courts) and the Chancery Division (which took over the work of the other two - the Court of Chancery and the Landed Estates Court). The appeal courts were also amalgamated into one Court of Appeal. The new High Court and the Court of Appeal together constituted the Supreme Court of Judicature - a rather misleading title, since there could always be a second appeal from the Court of Appeal in Dublin to the real "supreme" court for the whole of the United Kingdom, the Appellate Committee of the House of Lords in London.

When the Government of Ireland Act of 1920 created separate court structures for the two parts of the island, the existing court system was closely followed in the North. A Supreme Court of Judicature of Northern Ireland was set up, comprising a High Court and a Court of Appeal. A Court of Criminal Appeal was added in 1930. The position remains much the same today, except that three important changes were made by the Judicature (Northern Ireland) Act 1978: a third division of the High Court (the Family Division) was created, the Crown Court replaced the old system of Assizes, and the Court of Criminal Appeal was merged with the Court of Appeal. The Supreme Court of Judicature in Northern Ireland now comprises the Crown Court, the High Court and the Court of Appeal. A further appeal still lies on many occasions from the Court of Appeal to the House of Lords.

The complete hierarchy of courts is set out in Table 1; their organisation and the precise location of the Crown Court and of the so-called inferior courts (magistrates' courts and county courts) are tabulated in Table 2. It can be seen that the province is divided into four circuits, seven county court divisions and 25 petty sessions districts. (The county courts for Londonderry and Belfast are called Recorder's courts.) The jurisdiction of these ordinary courts is more fully described in chapters 4 and 5, while chapters 6 and 7 examine the jurisdiction of some other specialized courts and certain tribunals. It should be mentioned that names are often given unofficially to courts whenever they are sitting to hear particular matters. Examples would be the companies court, the bankruptcy court, the bail court and the motions court. The motions court hears applications for interim court orders prior to the main trial of an action. The High Court also contans what is termed a Divisional Court, which is a sort of

THE HIERARCHY OF COURTS

The superior courts:

THE HOUSE OF LORDS
(London)

The Supreme Court of Judicature of Northern Ireland
THE COURT OF APPEAL
(Belfast)

THE HIGH COURT   THE CROWN COURT
(Belfast)   (8 towns in Northern Ireland)

Queen's   Family   Chancery
Bench   Division   Division
Division

The inferior courts:

COUNTY COURTS
including small claims courts
(19 towns in Northern Ireland)

MAGISTRATES' COURTS
including juvenile courts
(25 towns in Northern Ireland)

Table 1

ORGANISATION AND LOCATION OF COURTS IN NORTHERN IRELAND

Town/city	Circuit	County Court Division	Petty Sessions District	Court Sittings
Londonderry	Northern	Londonderry	Londonderry	Crown, Recorder's, Magistrates'
Limavady			Limavady	County, Magistrates'
Magherafelt			Magherafelt	County, Magistrates'
Strabane			Strabane	County, Magistrates'
Coleraine		N. Antrim	Coleraine	County, Magistrates'
Ballymena			Ballymena	Crown, County Magistrates'
Ballymoney			Ballymoney/ Moyle	County, Magistrates'
Antrim			Antrim	Magistrates'
Armagh	S. Western	Armagh	Armagh	Crown, County, Magistrates'
Craigavon			Craigavon	Crown, County Magistrates'
Omagh		Fermanagh & South Tyrone	Omagh	Crown, County Magistrates'
Cookstown			Cookstown	County, Magistrates'
Dungannon			Dungannon	County, Magistrates'
Clogher			Dungannon	Magistrates'
Enniskillen			Fermanagh	Crown, County Magistrates'
Killyleagh	S. Eastern	S. Down	Down	County, Magistrates'
Banbridge			Banbridge	County, Magistrates'
Newry			Newry and Mourne	County, Magistrates'
Kilkeel			Newry and Mourne	Magistrates'
Lisburn		Ards	Lisburn	County, Magistrates'
Bangor			North Down	Magistrates'
Newtownards			Ards	Crown, County
			Castlereagh	Magistrates'
Belfast	Eastern	Belfast	Belfast	Crown, Recorder's, Magistrates'
Newtownabbey			Carrickfergus and Newtownabbey	Magistrates'
Larne			Larne	Magistrates'

Table 2

appeal court *within* the Queen's Bench Division and which mainly hears applications for *habeas corpus* (see 4.4) or for judicial review (see 7.1); in England this Divisional Court plays a much more important part in the legal system since it also deals with appeals on pure points of law in criminal cases first heard in the magistrates' courts or the Crown Court. England also has Divisional Courts within the Family and Chancery Divisions of the High Court.

1.4 The Government Role

The overall shape of the legal system in Northern Ireland has been determined by Parliament, whether at Westminster or at Stormont, but the duty of supervising the administration of justice on a day-to-day basis falls in particular on three members of the British Government: the Lord Chancellor, the Secretary of State for Northern Ireland, and the Attorney-General. The actual operation of the system is the professional responsibility of officials such as the Director of Public Prosecutions, judges, magistrates and the police. A few words will be said in the next section about each of these officials, while the role of practising lawyers in the system will be fully described in 3.2. In this section we concentrate on the part played by Government in the adminstration of the legal system.

Central and local government

As already explained in 1.2, Northern Ireland is now governed directly from London, the relevant Government department being the Northern Ireland Office with the Secretary of State as its head and three or four Ministers as his assistants. The Northern Ireland Office has some divisions based in London and others in Belfast, so that most of the staff in the former belong to the United Kingdom civil service while those working in Belfast are usually seconded from the Northern Ireland civil service. The chief of the Northern Ireland civil service advises the Secretary of State on matters which were formerly the preserve of Parliament at Stormont and he co-ordinates the work of the six Northern Ireland departments. These departments are the Department of Agriculture, the Department of Economic Development, the Department of Education, the Department of the Environment, the Department of Finance and Personnel and the Department of Health and Social Services. Each of these obviously has a wide variety of matters to administer and each will encounter legal problems on very many points. Like any individual or organisation, they cannot defy the law, even though they may often be instrumental in having the law changed.

The present system of local government in Northern Ireland dates from 1973. There are 26 local authorities: two city councils (Belfast and Londonderry), 12 borough councils and 12 district councils. These are subdivided into 526 wards, with one councillor being elected under a single transferable vote system to represent each ward. City and borough councils may call the chairperson of their council the Mayor (in Belfast, the Lord Mayor) and may designate up to one quarter of their councillors as "aldermen"; they may also confer the freedom of the city or borough on distinguished persons. Otherwise the powers and functions of all 26 authorities are the same. These are by no means as extensive as those given to local authorities in Great Britain: education and housing, for instance, are no part of their concern. But they still have responsibilities regarding, amongst other things, environmental health, noise, nuisances, consumer protection, litter prevention, the enforcement of building regulations and the licensing of street-trading. Like central Government departments, local authorities are not above the law; their decisions can often be challenged in a court or tribunal. This has been made clear in several recent cases arising out of some councillors' opposition to the Anglo-Irish Agreement of 1985 (see 1.2).

The Privy Council

The Privy Council of the United Kingdom should be mentioned at this stage because, as will be further explained in 2.3, it is technically this body which today makes most of the important laws for Northern Ireland. These are called Orders in Council, which are simply one type of secondary legislation authorised by statute (in this case the Northern Ireland Act 1974). There used to be a separate Privy Council for Northern Ireland, but this no longer meets and no further appointments can be made to it: its functions have been transferred to the Secretary of State for Northern Ireland.

The Privy Council consists of advisers to the Queen. Appointment to it is a recognised reward for public and political service or for attaining high political office. The total membership exceeds 350, all of them entitled to the prefix "The Right Honourable . . ." and appointed for life, but the active section at any particular time mostly comprises the current Cabinet Ministers. Meetings are organised by the Lord President of the Council, who sometimes (but not always) is also the Minister in charge of organising Government business in the House of Commons as Leader of the House. Orders in Council are made when the Queen formally approves the draft Orders presented to her by the Government Ministers who happen to be closely involved with the matter in hand; they are signed by the Clerk of the Privy Council.

One part of the Privy Council is actually a court - its Judicial Committee. This was set up in 1833 with the task of acting as the last court of appeal for cases originating throughout the British Empire, whether civil or criminal. Vestiges of this role remain, as the Judicial Committee still hears appeals from places such as the Bahamas, the Channel Islands, the Falkland Islands, Gibraltar, Hong Kong, Jamaica, Malaysia, New Zealand and Singapore. In addition the court deals with appeals from certain professional disciplinary bodies within the United Kingdom, such as the General Medical Council and the equivalents for dentists, opticians and veterinary surgeons. This would be the only situation in which legal cases originating in Northern Ireland could find their way to the Privy Council, but the decisions taken by it on appeals from foreign jurisdictions can be of such persuasive influence that, although they do not bind judges in subsequent cases in Northern Ireland, they effectively alter the content of our common law (see 2.4).

The judges who sit in the Judicial Committee are Privy Councillors who are present or former senior judges in the United Kingdom or the Commonwealth. In most cases they are the same judges as those who sit as Law Lords in appeals to the House of Lords (see the next section). Five judges usually sit in each case, not wearing robes and using a room at 1, Downing Street in London. Their decisions take the form of "advice to Her Majesty", though dissenting opinions have been allowed since 1966.

From time to time an *ad hoc* committee of Privy Councillors is set up to consider specific matters. This is the way in which the matters leading up to the invasion of the Falkland Islands by Argentina in 1982 were investigated. Under the Northern Ireland Constitution Act 1973 the Secretary of State for Northern Ireland retains the power to ask the Judicial Committee of the Privy Council to decide whether provisions in an Act of the Stormont Parliament, in a Measure of the 1974 Northern Ireland Assembly, or in a "relevant subordinate instrument" are void because they discriminate on religious or political grounds. This power, however, has never been exercised.

The Lord Chancellor

The Lord Chancellor occupies a unique position in the United Kingdom: he (or she, for there have been one or two female Chancellors in the distant past) is not only a Minister in the Government, with a seat in the Cabinet, but also the Speaker of the House of Lords when it is acting in its legislative capacity as the second chamber of Parliament, and the senior judge when the House is acting in its judicial capacity (though he no longer participates in many cases). Nowadays the Lord Chancellor is a distinguished lawyer appointed by the Prime Minister of the day. Often he is a former Attorney-General. He exercises his executive functions in Northern Ireland through the Northern Ireland Court Service, which corresponds to the Lord Chancellor's Department in London. The civil servants in this office help to arrange the business of the courts, service the judges and magistrates, and advise the Lord Chancellor on legal policy issues. It is the Lord Chancellor who is in practice responsible for the organisation of the courts, the appointment of many judges and court officials, and the general efficiency of the legal system, including the legal aid schemes (see 3.3). From October 1988 his salary is £87,250 per annum. The present incumbent is a Scottish judge, Lord Mackay of Clashfern.

The Secretary of State for Northern Ireland

One of the main responsibilities of the Secretary of State, who is a member of the United Kingdom Cabinet, is the actual content of the law in Northern Ireland. It is he who must consider introducing into Parliament measures of law reform (see also 8.9) or updating social and welfare policies for the province. In addition he is generally in charge of the penal system and the treatment of offenders, a function performed in England by the Home Secretary. In this capacity he has power to refer the convictions of some criminals to the Court of Appeal for reconsideration (see 4.8), to release prisoners on licence or grant them special remission, and to grant pardons. He also has special functions under the province's emergency laws (see 4.9). In February 1989 the Secretary of State for Northern Ireland was Mr Tom King. He is the eighth person to have held the office since 1972.

The Attorney-General

The Attorney-General is the chief law officer of the Government, with responsibility for advising Government departments and representing the Government's interests in important legal disputes. Like the Lord Chancellor he is a political appointee (though not a member of the Cabinet) and he answers questions on legal matters in Parliament. By tradition he is meant to be non-political when giving legal advice or when acting in his capacity as head of the barristers' profession (the Bar). Before the abolition of the Stormont Parliament there was a separate Attorney-General for Northern Ireland; now the English Attorney-General acts for Northern Ireland as well. At the time of writing this is Sir Patrick Mayhew.

The Attorney-General has power to exercise some important discretions in selected matters involving the criminal law: his consent is required for the commencement of a wide range of prosecutions (though in most cases the consent can also be provided by the Director of Public Prosecutions) and he can decide that criminal proceedings which are already in progress should be terminated, by entering what is called a *nolle prosequi*. Under the emergency laws in Northern Ireland he can "de-schedule" certain offences (see 4.9). In matters concerned with the civil law (disputes between private individuals) his approval is needed for actions taken by private citizens to protect the public interest (relator actions), and exceptionally he can initiate proceedings himself. Sometimes he or his representative is asked to attend court as *amicus curiae*, that is, as a general legal adviser on points in issue in a case.

The Attorney-General's deputy is called the Solicitor-General, though he too is a barrister and a political appointee; currently he is Sir Nicholas Lyell. The Attorney-General appoints a Crown Solicitor for Northern Ireland, whose services are then available to any Northern Ireland executive authority or any United Kingdom Government department. The role of ordinary barristers and solicitors in Northern Ireland is explained in 3.2.

1.5 Legal Officials

The Director of Public Prosecutions

Prior to 1972 the majority of prosecutions in Northern Ireland were conducted by police officers, but prosecutions on behalf of Government departments, as well as all prosecutions for indictable (that is, serious) offences were the responsibility of Crown Solicitors and Crown Counsel. Following the recommendations of both the Hunt Report on the Royal Ulster Constabulary (1969) and the MacDermott Working Party on Public Prosecutions (1971), the role of the police in serious prosecutions was diminished and the involvement of Crown Solicitors was abolished. To take over these responsibilities the Office of the Director of Public Prosecutions was created. The relevant legislation is the Prosecution of Offences (Northern Ireland) Order 1972, as amended. Somewhat similar arrangements have recently been introduced in England by virtue of the Prosecution of Offences Act 1985, which created the Crown Prosecution Service. (The current DPP, in office since 1972, is Sir Barry Shaw.)

The DPP is appointed by the Attorney-General, who may also remove him from office on the grounds of inability or misbehaviour. He must be a barrister or a solicitor who has practised in Northern Ireland for not less than 10 years. He is assisted in his work by professional and other staff working in his office in the Royal Courts of Justice in Belfast and in offices in three other towns.

The chief function of the DPP in Northern Ireland is to bring prosecutions for indictable criminal offences, as well as for such less serious criminal offences as he considers should be dealt with by him. To date he has considered it right to control the prosecution of all offences arising out of incidents of a political nature as well as the prosecution of offences allegedly committed by police officers. The RUC continue to have responsibility for prosecuting minor cases. The procedures by which the DPP's Office becomes involved in conducting prosecutions are explained in more detail in 4.4.

The Director's Office will represent the Crown in all criminal cases in the Crown Court, the Court of Appeal and the House of Lords. It will also act for the Crown in appeals to a county court by defendants who have been convicted in a magistrates' court. It conducts many prosecutions on behalf of Government departments in magistrates' courts when requested in writing to do so, and if a proposed prosecution is a private one, or one to be brought by the police, the consent of the DPP (or of the Attorney-General) is very often required before the proceedings can officially be begun. The Director can step in to take over private prosecutions if this is in the public interest.

In addition to actually conducting prosecutions the Director can require the police to investigate incidents which appear to him to involve an offence, or to make further investigations into matters already referred to him. Whenever a defendant is applying for bail (see 4.4) the DPP's Office can make representations in such cases as the Director thinks fit, which goes some way to ensuring that uniform standards on this issue are applied throughout the province. Finally, if it appears to a coroner after an inquest (see 6.3) that a criminal offence may have been committed, the coroner must submit a written report on the case for consideration by the DPP.

Judges

Information about the judiciary in Northern Ireland is presented in tabular form in Tables 3 and 4. Details of the main types of case heard by the judges in each of the courts are supplied in Chapters 4 and 5. Apart from deciding cases, the main responsibility of the judges in Northern Ireland is to help make Rules of Court to govern the practice and procedure for dealing with cases in each of the various courts. There are, for instance, a Supreme Court Rules Committee, a Matrimonial Causes Rules Committee and a County Court Rules Committee. These Rules are a form of secondary legislation (explained in 2.3) and they are amended and updated at irregular intervals.

Like barristers and solicitors, judges enjoy what is called "immunity from suit" when they are performing in court; this means that you cannot sue a judge for compensation even if he or she has obviously taken a wrong decision which has caused you loss.

(1) House of Lords

The most senior judges in the United Kingdom are the Lords of Appeal in Ordinary, who hear appeals in the House of Lords whenever that body is sitting in its judicial capacity. They are appointed, as are all full-time senior judges, by the Queen acting by convention on the advice of the Prime Minister, who in turn consults the Lord Chancellor. They must already have held high judicial office for two years or be barristers of 15 years' standing, and they must retire at 75. There can be 11 Lords of Appeal at any one time. The best-known name at the present time is probably Lord Bridge. Usually a couple of incumbents are Scottish lawyers, and the former Lord Chief Justice of Northern Ireland, Lord Lowry, was appointed in August 1988.

Lords of Appeal - also called Law Lords - are assisted from time to time by the current and former Lord Chancellors, by other senior judges who have been appointed life peers and by retired Lords of Appeal (*e.g.* Lord Scarman). As an Appellate Committee the House of Lords usually sits as a bench of five judges, and never with a jury. Very important cases are sometimes heard by seven judges. Decisions on whether to grant permission for a case to be given a full hearing before the Appellate Commmittee are usually taken by only three Lords of Appeal (sitting as the Appeal Committee).

Many legal disputes which occur in Northern Ireland may in theory proceed as far as the House of Lords. In practice, of course, very few do - perhaps two or three a year. For most civil cases (see Chapter 5) the final court to which a case can be taken in Northern Ireland is the province's own Court of Appeal. In some instances it is possible to take a case beyond the House of Lords into Europe, but the courts there are not really hearing "appeals" (see 2.6).

(2) The Supreme Court

The judges of the Court of Appeal and the High Court are appointed by the Queen on the advice of the Lord Chancellor. In England the Prime Minister has a say in who should be appointed to the Court of Appeal, but not in Northern Ireland. These same judges, together with county court judges (see below), also sit in Northern Ireland's Crown Court (see 4.8). Since the Court of Appeal, the High Court and the Crown Court together make up the Supreme Court of Judicature of Northern Ireland, these judges are sometimes referred to as Supreme Court judges. Since 1921 there have been 30 Supreme Court judges; their names and periods of service can be found in Table 4.

Only barristers who have practised for at least 10 years are eligible for appointment. They must retire from the bench when they reach the age of 75; they can be removed from office before then if both Houses of Parliament so recommend, but this has not occurred in modern times.

The most important judge in Northern Ireland is the Lord Chief Justice of Northern Ireland. The office replaced that of the Lord Chancellor of Ireland in 1921. To date there have been six holders of the post: Sir Denis Henry (1921-25), Sir William Moore (1925-38), Sir James Andrews (1938-51), Lord MacDermott (1951-71), Lord Lowry (1971-88) and, from August 1988, Sir Brian Hutton. As a life peer the former "Chief" was a member of the House of Lords and on occasion he sat in the Appellate Committee of that House (though not in cases emanating from Northern Ireland).

The Lord Chief Justice is President of the Court of Appeal, the High Court and the Crown Court; in this capacity he assigns work to the judges of the various courts and has a number of other administrative responsibilities. (In England the Lord Chief Justice, Lord Lane, acts as President of the Criminal Division of the Court of Appeal, but the President of the Civil Division is called the Master of the Rolls. This latter post is the one from which Lord Denning retired after 20 years' service in 1982; the present office-bearer is Lord Donaldson.)

The Court of Appeal of Northern Ireland consists of the Lord Chief Justice and three other judges called Lords Justices of Appeal. At present these are Kelly LJ, MacDermott LJ and O'Donnell LJ and there have been 10 other Lords Justices since 1921. In criminal cases, moreover, all judges of the High Court are eligible to sit as judges of the Court of Appeal. The Lord Chief Justice can also ask a Lord Justice of Appeal to sit in the High Court, or a High Court judge to sit even in civil cases in the Court of Appeal. (For the distinction between criminal and civil cases, see 2.1 and 5.1.)

A case in the Court of Appeal will usually be heard by three judges, always sitting in Belfast, but some matters may be dealt with by a two-judge bench and some (incidental matters) by one judge sitting alone. A jury is never involved.

The High Court of Justice consists of the Lord Chief Justice and a total of six other judges. These judges are officially called puisne (pronounced "puny") judges and are referred to as "Mr Justice . . .". The six currently in post are Campbell J, Carswell J, Higgins J, McCollum J, Murray J, and Nicholson J. There have been five other men (apart from the Lords Chief Justices and the

THE JUDICIARY IN

	Number who can be appointed	Number now in office	Qualifications for office	Appointed by?
Justices of the Peace	Unlimited	approx. 1100	No formal qualifications	Lord Chancellor (on local advice)
Resident Magistrates (Deputies)	Unlimited	17 * (16)	At least 7 years in practice as a solicitor or barrister	The Queen, on recommendation of Lord Chancellor
County Court Judges (Deputies)	Unlimited	13 (34)	At least 10 years in practice as a solicitor or barrister **	The Queen, on recommendation of Lord Chancellor
Circuit Registrars (Deputies)	4	4 * (5)	At least 7 years in practice as a solicitor	Lord Chancellor, after consultations with Lord Chief Justice
High Court Masters	8	8	Generally, at least 10 years in practice as a solicitor or barrister	Lord Chancellor, after consultations with Lord Chief Justice
High Court Judges	6 + Lord Chief Justice	6	At least 10 years in practice as a barrister	The Queen, on advice of the Lord Chancellor
Court of Appeal Judges	3 + Lord Chief Justice	3	Served as High Court judge or at least 15 years in practice as a barrister	The Queen, on advice of the Lord Chancellor
House of Lords Judges (Lords of Appeal)	11 + Lord Chancellor	10	Held high judicial office for 2 years or at least 15 years in practice as a barrister	The Queen, on advice of the Prime Minister

* Apart from JPs, the only women among the judiciary in Northern Ireland are one female deputy RM and two female deputy circuit registrars.

Table 3

NORTHERN IRELAND

Removable how?	Retirement age	Addressed as	Salary (from Oct 1987)
By Lord Chancellor	In office for life	"Your Worship"	Expenses only
By Lord Chancellor for incapacity or misbehaviour	70	"Your Worship"	£33,500
By Lord Chancellor for incapacity or misbehaviour	72	"Your Worship"	£43,500
By Lord Chancellor for misbehaviour or inability to perform duties	72	"Mr Registrar"	£33,500
By Lord Chancellor for misbehaviour or inability to perform duties	72	"Master"	£33,500
Number of methods. Most likely is by the Queen on an address from both Houses of Parliament	75	"My Lord" or "Your Lordship"	£65,000 (LCJ: £74,750)
Number of methods. Most likely is by the Queen on an address from both Houses of Parliament	75	"My Lord" or "Your Lordship"	£71,750 (LCJ: £74,750)
Number of methods Most likely is by the Queen on an address from both Houses of Parliament	75	"My Lord" or "Your Lordship"	£74,750 (Lord Chancellor: £83,000)

** Deputy county court judges can be appointed from among solicitors of 10 years' standing or from the ranks of RMs. After 3 years they are eligible for appointment as full county court judges.

Table 3 (cont'd)

NORTHERN IRELAND'S SUPREME COURT JUDGES 1921 - 89

Sir James Andrews	LJ	1921 - 37	LCJ	1937 - 51
Sir Anthony Babington	LJ	1937 - 49		
Richard Best	LJ	1925 - 39		
Arthur Black	Ch	1943 - 49	LJ	1949 - 64
Thomas Brown	QB	1922 - 44		
Sir Anthony Campbell	QB	1988 -		
Sir Robert Carswell	QB	1984 -		
Sir Lancelot Curran	Ch	1949 - 56	LJ	1956 - 75
Sir Maurice Gibson	Ch	1968 - 75	LJ	1975 - 87
Sir Denis Henry	LCJ	1921 - 25		
Sir Iain Higgins	QB	1984 -		
Sir Brian Hutton	QB	1979 - 88	LCJ	1988 -
Sir Edward Jones	QB	1968 - 73	LJ	1973 - 84
Sir Basil Kelly	QB	1973 - 84	LJ	1984 -
William Lowry	QB	1947 - 49		
Lord Lowry	Ch/QB	1964 - 71	LCJ	1971 - 88
Lord MacDermott	QB	1944 - 47	LCJ	1951 - 71
Sir John MacDermott	QB/Fam	1973 - 87	LJ	1987 -
Sir Liam McCollum	QB	1987 -		
Sir Ambrose McGonigal	QB	1968 - 75	LJ	1975 - 79
Sir Herbert McVeigh	Ch	1956 - 64	LJ	1964 - 73
Robert Megaw	Ch	1932 - 43		
Sir William Moore	LJ	1921 - 25	LCJ	1925 - 38
Edward Murphy	LJ	1939 - 45		
Sir Donald Murray	QB/Ch	1975 -		
Sir Michael Nicholson	QB	1986 -		
Turlough O'Donnell	QB	1971 - 79	LJ	1979 -
Samuel Porter	LJ	1946 - 56		
Charles Sheil	QB	1949 - 68		
Daniel Wilson	Ch	1921 - 32		

Abbreviations: LJ - Lord Justice; Ch - Chancery; QB - Queen's Bench; LCJ - Lord Chief Justice; Fam - Family Division

Note: Knighthoods have been automatically conferred on Supreme Court Judges only since 1988

Table 4

Lords Justices) who have served as High Court judges in Northern Ireland since 1921. They may sit in any of the Divisions of the High Court, but some are seen as particularly expert in one or other Division, *e.g.* Murray J in the Chancery Division or MacDermott J in the Family Division. Except for hearings in the Divisional Court (see above, page 6) a High Court case will involve only one judge, always sitting in Belfast. Juries (of seven persons) are now used quite rarely; they are to be found mainly in libel cases. To ease the burden on High Court judges, the Lord Chancellor may from time to time request a county court judge to sit as a judge of the High Court.

(3) The inferior courts

County court judges, of whom there are now 13, with no fewer than 34 deputies, sit throughout Northern Ireland. Again, at least 10 years' practice as a barrister is required before a person can be considered for appointment, though deputy county court judges, who may after three years be made full county court judges, can be appointed from the ranks of resident magistrates (see below) or from solicitors of 10 years' standing. The retirement age is 72. County court judges are referred to as "His Honour Judge ...". The judges who sit for Belfast and Londonderry are called "Recorders" (Judges Pringle and Hart respectively).

Magistrates' courts are not staffed by judges at all but by resident magistrates, lay panellists or (occasionally) justices of the peace. All of these offices are described below.

Statutory officers

After consultations with the Lord Chief Justice of Northern Ireland the Lord Chancellor appoints certain "statutory officers" These include an Official Solicitor and eight Masters. The Official Solicitor represents the interests in a case which would not otherwise be adequately protected, such as those of children or of persons who are in custody for contempt: he must conduct such investigations and render such assistance as may be authorised by the Rules of the Supreme Court or required by any direction of a court for the purpose of assisting the court in the due administration of justice.

The Masters are former legal practitioners of 10 years' standing whose job it is to deal with a variety of procedural and relatively minor substantive issues before a dispute reaches a High Court judge. In effect they exercise the jurisdiction of a judge sitting in chambers, except in respect of certain specified matters. An appeal against their decisions usually lies to such a judge. The eight masters deal separately with matters relating to Queen's Bench and Appeals, Chancery, the High Court, Bankruptcy, Probate and Matrimonial, Care and Protection (for mental patients), Taxation (*i.e.* assessment of costs), and Enforcement of Judgments. There are Supreme Court Offices corresponding with each of the Master's roles, that for Queen's Bench and Appeals being called the Central Office.

There are also four circuit registrars, who assist the county court judges and exercise an important jurisdiction in the so-called "small claims courts" (see 5.4). The main administrators in county court divisions are called chief clerks (formerly Clerks of the Crown and Peace), while those in magistrates' courts are called clerks of petty sessions.

Resident magistrates

One of the major differences between the legal systems of Northern Ireland and England is that in Northern Ireland the responsibility for trying less serious criminal offences lies with full-time, legally qualified magistrates called "resident magistrates" (RMs). In England much of this work is still done by part-time justices who have no formal legal qualifications, though they undergo periodic training after they are appointed. The explanation for this difference is to be found in history: at the end of the eighteenth century there were parts of Ireland where there were not enough "proper" persons to act as ordinary part-time justices, so it was found necessary to appoint full-time magistrates (not necessarily lawyers) who were required to reside in these areas to assist the justices. This worked so well that during the nineteenth century the practice of appointing resident magistrates was extended throughout the whole of the island. Until 1935 the part-time justices could also sit with the RMs in magistrates' courts in Northern Ireland, but in that year this power was taken away, so that only resident magistrates can now sit in these courts, which deal mainly with minor criminal offences. The lay justices, who are called Justices of the Peace, do however retain an important role in the legal system (see below).

Today only barristers and solicitors of seven years' standing are eligible for appointment as RMs. They are appointed by the Queen on the recommendation of the Lord Chancellor. There are currently 17 in office, with 16 deputies. They must retire when they reach the age of 70. In court they are addressed as "Your Worship".

In addition to trying comparatively minor criminal offences, resident magistrates conduct committal proceedings in the more serious criminal cases (see 4.7). They also deal with some private (or civil) law disputes and are responsible for a number of matters which are more administrative in nature than judicial, such as the renewal of licences for public houses (see 5.2). They are immune from being sued for causing loss of litigants unless they act entirely beyond their powers (*i.e.* "without jurisdiction"): see *McC* v *Mullan* (1984), a Northern Ireland case that reached the House of Lords.

Justices of the Peace

The people who act as lay magistrates in Northern Ireland are called Justices of the Peace (JPs). The office is a very ancient one, first established in Ireland (as in England) in the fourteenth century. In England and Wales JPs still act as full-scale magistrates, but in Northern Ireland their powers have been severely limited since 1935.

Persons become JPs through appointment under the Queen's Commission of the Peace, which is issued for each county court division by the Lord Chancellor. They remain in office for life. The Lord Chancellor selects persons on the basis of recommendations made to him by local advisory committees in each county court division. The composition of these committees is secret, but the chairman is usually the Lord Lieutenant of the county (a representative of the Queen). Nominations can be submitted by any person or group and should be forwarded through the Assistant Secretary of Commissions in the Northern Ireland Court Service. Those appointed will invariably be respected people who, over the years, have gained the trust and the admiration of the local community. In Northern Ireland today there are approximately 1,100 JPs, of whom maybe 10 per cent are women. They receive no payment for their services, only out-of-pocket expenses.

Most of the powers which JPs have at the moment may be exercised only within the county for which they have been appointed. Their main task is the signing of summonses, warrants and various official forms (such as old-age pension forms). Summonses are documents which direct people to appear in court on a certain day in order to answer a particular allegation (see 4.2 and Appendix 4). Warrants are documents authorising the police to arrest someone who is suspected of having committed a crime or to search premises where, for instance, stolen goods are thought to be hidden; or they may take the form of written authorisation for committing a person for trial or to prison on remand. JPs have the power to conduct committal proceedings (see 4.7) and, provided the accused person consents, they can try summarily some minor criminal offences, such as vagrancy or poaching. Two justices must be appointed to every Board of Visitors for prisons in Northern Ireland (see below). They retain as well the somewhat controversial power to "bind over" persons to keep the peace or be of good behaviour. This power, which derives from the common law and the Justices of the Peace Act 1361, enables JPs (and RMs) to require people to forfeit a sum of money or serve a period of imprisonment if they break a promise to keep the peace or be of good behaviour during the stipulated period, which must not exceed two years. Strangely, such persons do not first have to be convicted of a criminal offence.

Other officials

There are several other officials whom you may encounter if you have a brush with the law. The Army, which includes the Ulster Defence Regiment, continues to assist the RUC in maintaining law and order in Northern Ireland and has been granted special powers to that end (see 4.9). The 131 traffic wardens have all the powers of police officers as regards the control of road traffic. Some organisations, such as the Ministry of Defence and port authorities, are empowered to set up their own police services for specific purposes.

Process servers and bailiffs are private individuals or firms who are engaged by both public and private bodies to deliver official documents or to enforce court orders. If you are forming a company you will have dealings with the office of the Registrar of Companies, and if you attempt to do your own conveyancing when moving house you will need to make use of the Land Registry, the Statutory Charges Register or the Registry of Deeds. The Registrar General, with his headquarters in Belfast and officers in every district council area, has responsibility for recording all births, deaths and marriages.

1.6 The Police, Probation and Prison Services

The police service

The police service in Northern Ireland is the Royal Ulster Constabulary. It was formed in 1922 to replace the Royal Irish Constabulary, which policed the island until partition. Following civil disturbances in 1968-69, an Advisory Committee was set up under the chairmanship of Lord Hunt to examine the recruitment, organisation, structure and composition of the RUC and to recommend as necessary whatever changes were required to provide for the efficient enforcement of law and order. Most of Lord Hunt's recommendations were subsequently implemented through the Police Act (NI) 1970.

The force, however, still has to work in exceptionally dangerous conditions and its members are therefore armed. Between 1969 and 1987, 164 police officers and a further 87 reservists were killed in terrorist incidents. Attacks on police patrols and police stations are still common, and they are not always carried out by republican paramilitaries. During 1986, following the signing of the Anglo-Irish Agreement in November 1985, there were well over 500 incidents of serious intimidation of RUC officers, and 121 police families had to be moved from their homes. For further details of the level of terrorist crime, see Table 7 in 4.2.

The RUC is currently organised on the basis of 12 divisions. In addition there is a traffic division, with headquarters in Belfast and four regional sub-divisions. There are 174 police stations throughout the province. The maximum permitted size of the service was increased during 1987 to 8,250 officers, with a further 4,900 in the Reserve (2,750 of them full-time). At the head of the force is the Chief Constable (Sir John Hermon), with one Deputy Chief Constable, three Senior Assistant Chief Constables and nine Assistant Chief Constables. A new Chief Constable will take over in 1989.

Police activities

As in other legal systems, the primary role of the RUC is to prevent and detect crime. Despite the troubles, the crime rate in Northern Ireland is comparatively low (see 4.2) and the detection rate is quite high - in 1987 it exceeded 43 per cent. The police have been assisted in their work during the past 19 years by the British army, though the avowed policy now is that the police have an independent responsibility in all areas and that the soldiers are merely there to give support when needed. The interrogation practices of the force were investigated in 1977 by the European Court of Human Rights (see 2.6) and in 1978 by a Committee of Inquiry headed by an English county court judge, Judge Bennett. Various recommendations for making the practices more acceptable were put forward and have since largely been implemented. Further inquiries have recently been undertaken into alleged shoot-to-kill incidents which occurred in 1982; these were the subject of the controversial Stalker-Sampson report in 1987, which has led to investigations of breach of discipline but not to any criminal prosecutions.

The RUC is accountable to the Police Authority for Northern Ireland, and complaints against its officers must be considered by the newly-created Independent Commission for Police Complaints; the role of both these bodies is described in more detail in 8.7. Her Majesty's Inspectorate of Constabulary for England and Wales acts as an advisory body to the Northern Ireland Office and the Police Authority regarding such matters as recruitment and equipment for the RUC; they also carry out *ad hoc* inspections of the force. The police officers' representative bodies in the province are the Superintendents' Association of Northern Ireland and, for lesser ranks, the Police Federation for Northern Ireland.

As part of its programme in community relations the RUC runs "Blue Lamp Discos" and "Blue Lamp Soccer" for young people. It organises a schools programme which embraces rambles, an inter-school quiz and sixth-form seminars. The police also try to deal with the problems of juveniles in a sympathetic manner through a Juvenile Liaison Scheme (see 6.1). The system for consulting with members of local communities is as yet somewhat underdeveloped: every district council has a liaison committee or a security committee (or both) involving the police, but these do not have much contact with community groups in the area. The neighbourhood policing scheme, on the other hand, is considered by the RUC to be most satisfactory, as are the support schemes set up to provide assistance to the victims of burglary.

In England the powers of prosecution which were formerly vested in the 43 police forces were transferred to the Crown Prosecution Service by the Prosecution of Offences Act 1985. The RUC still possesses such powers in minor cases but the Office of the Director of Public Prosecutions (explained at the start of 1.5) will deal with whichever of these offences he considers appropriate. The police's continuing monopoly over the investigation of crimes, however, is a limiting factor on the DPP's complete autonomy. In 1982 the practice emerged of using "supergrasses", or "converted terrorists", from some of whom evidence was obtained in exchange for immunity from prosecution ("turning Queen's evidence"); in these cases the evidence was collected by the police but the immunity was granted by the DPP. A total of 223 defendants had been tried on the word of a supergrass by the end of 1986; 53 convictions remained outstanding after appeals had been heard, but in all of these cases there was evidence to corroborate the testimony of the supergrass.

If the police decide not to prosecute someone for an alleged offence, any person with a sufficient interest (*locus standi*) in the matter can initiate a private prosecution instead. But private prosecutions are expensive and time-consuming, and the Attorney- General can always apply for them to be terminated if he does not feel that they are in the public interest (see 4.5). It is believed that only one private prosecution has actually reached the trial stage in Northern Ireland. As an alternative course of action, if an interested person feels aggrieved at the police's failure to investigate a crime or prosecute a suspect, an application can be made to the High Court for the prerogative order of *mandamus* which, if granted, will compel the police to carry out their duty (see 7.1). It is not possible to sue the police if one is the victim of a crime which the police negligently failed to forestall.

It is to the Chief Constable of the RUC that applications for firearm certificates must be made; an appeal against a refusal lies to the Secretary of State for Northern Ireland. At the end of 1987 there were 88,358 firearm certificates on issue, covering a total of 125,193 weapons.

The probation service

The probation service in Northern Ireland is now administered by the Probation Board. This was set up in 1982 with up to 18 members, appointed by the Secretary of State and drawn from a wide spectrum of the community. The present Chairman is Mr John Simpson. The Board is serviced by a small secretariat based at its headquarters in Belfast. There are probation offices throughout the province, all of which are listed in the telephone directory. In 1986-87 the cost of running the probation service was approximately £5.1 million.

The chief aim of the Probation Board is to prevent reoffending. In supporting the work of Northern Ireland's 160 or so probation officers it seeks to reduce the number of custodial sentences imposed by the courts. Probation officers, operating under the Probation Act (NI) 1950, write social enquiry reports (SERs) on offenders found guilty in a court. These reports are compulsory for offenders who are under 17; for older offenders they are provided only if the court so requests and if the offender consents. The reports attempt to give an objective assessment of the offender to the judge or magistrate, set out the courses of action available to the court, and make recommendations as to which would be most appropriate in the particular case. In 1986 nearly half of all SERs were written for adult offenders in magistrates' courts, a quarter concerned juvenile offenders, and the remainder dealt with Crown Court defendants or appellants.

A court can place an offender on probation for a period between six months and three years, although the majority of the thousand or so orders made each year are for two years. The order is not intended as a punishment but rather as an offer of rehabilitation. To that end the probation officer assigned to the case will befriend, give guidance to, and supervise the offender. This kind of supervision within the community is not only better for the offender, it is also vastly cheaper than containment in prison (the annual cost per offender is approximately £500 as opposed to £33,000 for imprisonment). The recidivism rate for those placed on probation (that is, the proportion of offenders who reoffend) is also quite low; at the moment it is running at about 33 per cent.

Probation officers also help to run the community service order scheme, whereby offenders aged 17 or over can be ordered to perform a set number of hours of community service (see 6.1). This is proving increasingly successful as a means of reintegrating offenders as law-abiding members of society. Various local initiatives have been developed to provide opportunities for community service: the chief probation officer has commented in her report for 1985-87 that Northern Ireland, despite all its problems, is in some respects better than elsewhere in this respect because of its comparatively low crime rate, its still identifiable small communities, and the preparedness of people in those communities to deal with their own problems of crime.

The probation service provides welfare services for prisoners, prisoners' families and people recently released from prison. In this capacity the officers certainly act not so much as legal officials but as specialized social workers. Whenever life sentence prisoners are taking part in the "working out" scheme during the months before their release on licence, probation officers help to counsel them. In 1986 this scheme was used for 40 prisoners.

Rehabilitation services

In some of its work the Probation Board is obviously supplemented by various voluntary bodies. Indeed the Board has a statutory responsibility to fund some of these voluntary projects. The Extern Organisation and the Northern Ireland Association for the Care and Resettlement of Offenders (NIACRO) are prominent groups in the voluntary sector which find that the services they provide overlap with those of the Probation Board. In 1986 the Save the Children Fund established its LIBRA project in the Belfast area to divert young people away from custody and to assist their personal development. The Probation Board also helps to fund child-minding and family centre facilities at Belfast, Maze and Magilligan prisons; it supports as well the Dismas House project (a hostel for ex-prisoners), the Belfast Rape Crisis Centre and the growing number of victim support schemes throughout the province.

It is worth noting that under the Rehabilitation of Offenders (NI) Order 1978 an individual's sentence (whether or not it involved imprisonment) may in certain circumstances become "spent", which means that from then on that person must for most purposes be treated as someone who has not been convicted of, or even charged with, the offence in question. Such a rehabilitated person can even sue for libel or slander if someone later refers to the fact that he or she has been convicted of the offence, and the failure to disclose a spent conviction is not in law a proper ground for prejudicing a person as regards employment (except in relation to work with people under 18). The period which must elapse before a sentence becomes spent depends on the type and severity of the original sentence. For a prison sentence of up to six months, for instance, the rehabilitation period is seven years, while for sentences of between six and 30 months the period is 10 years. Prison sentences of more than 30 months are excluded altogether from the scheme.

The prison service

This service, though operating within a separate jurisdiction, is run along similar lines to its equivalent in England and Wales. Social and political factors, however, have led to some divergences.

There are at the moment six prison establishments in Northern Ireland: Belfast Prison (Crumlin Road), Maze Prison, formerly Long Kesh (near Lisburn), Magilligan Prison (near Londonderry), the male and female prisons at Maghaberry (near Lisburn) and the Young Offenders Centre for males at Hydebank Wood on the outskirts of South Belfast. The total strength of the prison service including civilian staff was 3,299 in March 1988. The officers are trained at the Prison Services College in Millisle, Co. Down. The service is run by the Northern Ireland Office, one of the Departments of the United Kingdom Government; it issues an annual report on the administration of the prison service by virtue of its obligation under section 5 of the Prison Act (NI) 1953. In 1987-88 the total cost of running the prison service was approximately £99 million. This makes the annual cost per prisoner more than £50,000.

The prison population

Unlike the position in many other countries, the prison population in Northern Ireland is now declining. It reached a peak of almost 3,000 in 1978 but in 1987-88 the average daily population was down to 1,926. About 800 of these were held in Maze Prison, and 500 or so in Belfast. However, the number of *receptions* into prison is still rising: a large number of short custodial sentences are being imposed for minor offences. For instance in 1987 no fewer than 2,018 people were sent to prison for non-payment of fines. This represents 51 per cent of all receptions during that year but on any one day only two per cent of the prison population was made up of these short-term prisoners.

At the end of March 1988 there were 1,938 prisoners. Amongst these were the following categories:

adults	1,721	(89%)
young offenders (aged less than 21 when sentenced)	217	(11%)
untried prisoners (on remand)	242	(12%)
females	32	(2%)
adults serving life sentences	410	(21%)
young offenders imprisoned "at the Secretary of State's pleasure" (see below)	34	(2%)

In June 1988 there were also 92 so-called "special category" prisoners, that is, prisoners accorded a special status (by an administrative arrangement) if convicted before April 1980 of a "political" offence committed prior to February

1976. These prisoners were formerly housed in "compounds" at Maze Prison, while other terrorist prisoners were housed in the H-shaped blocks (Maze Prison, cellular wing). All are now in the H-blocks, but special category prisoners have privileges regarding freedom of association within the prison.

The prison regime

The normal prison regime, although maligned in some quarters, actually compares quite favourably with that in other parts of the United Kingdom, Ireland and western Europe. It is regulated partly by unpublished circulars issued to prison governors by the Northern Ireland Office and partly by the Prison Rules (NI) 1982. The Rules require that prisoners should engage in useful work. Some are employed in servicing the prisons themselves, while others work in prison industries making items such as shoes, clothing and metalwork. At Maze Prison there is a large laundry workshop. As regards education, over half of Northern Ireland's prisoners enrol for courses, ranging from the most basic to Open University level.

The Young Offenders Centre at Hydebank Wood, which opened in 1979, has places for 300 young men, mainly aged 17 to 21, who have been sentenced to less than three years in custody. (The few females in this category are housed at Maghaberry.) The regime is officially described as "brisk", with the inmates gaining privileges by using their time in a positive and constructive way. The Centre offers extensive education, vocational training and physical recreation facilities. Young persons aged 15 or 16 are sometimes held in the Centre when a court has certified them to be unruly or guilty of serious misconduct, even though they may not have been convicted of any crime (see 6.1). Borstal training was abolished in 1980.

There is no parole system comparable to that which operates in England. Instead prisoners can earn up to 50 per cent remission on their sentences, though for prisoners convicted of terrorist offences this is to be reduced to the one-third rule which applies in England. "Lifers" and "SoSPs" (those imprisoned at the Secretary of State's pleasure for committing murder when aged less than 18) have their cases examined, after 10 and eight years respectively, by the Life Sentence Review Board, which makes recommendations to the Secretary of State. The Secretary of State can then decide to release such a prisoner on licence after consulting the Lord Chief Justice as well as, if possible, the judge who originally sentenced the prisoner. Judges sometimes recommend minimum sentences at the time of trial, but these recommendations have no binding force in law. If life or indeterminate sentence prisoners are given a release date, it is usually about a year in advance so that during the pre-release period (usually served at Belfast Prison) the prisoner can take part in a scheme of work and home leaves. Even after release the prisoner remains on licence for the rest of his or her life and can be recalled to prison when the Secretary of State considers this necessary to avoid danger to the public.

Discipline and welfare

Each prison in Northern Ireland has a Board of Visitors, which is appointed by the Secretary of State and must include at least two Justices of the Peace; there were 99 persons serving as Visitors in 1988. The Board has to meet at least once a month, sending copies of its minutes to the Secretary of State, and the prison must be visited by one member of the Board at least once a fortnight. The Board's function is to satisfy itself on behalf of the general public as to the state of the prison premises, the administration of the prison and the treatment of the prisoners. Every Visitor has free access at all times to all parts of the prison. He or she can hear any complaint or request which a prisoner may wish to make, if necessary out of the sight and hearing of prison officers. The Boards draw the attention of the prison governors to particular matters and report regularly to the Secretary of State. For the Young Offenders Centre there is a corresponding Visiting Committee consisting of 16 members.

Discipline in the prisons is primarily the responsibility of the governors, but the most serious punishment a governor can impose is loss of 28 days' remission. Any serious or repeated offence which a governor believes requires a more severe punishment may be referred to the Secretary of State and it is for him to decide how the case should be handled. He may ask officials in the Northern Ireland Office to deal with it or he may delegate the case to the relevant Board of Visitors (not to a governor), which will appoint between two and five of its members to deal with the case; in either event the maximum penalties which can be imposed are loss of up to 180 days' remission and/or confinement in a prison cell for up to 56 days.

At disciplinary hearings before Boards of Visitors prisoners must be allowed to present their own case and to call and cross-examine witnesses. As well they may be granted "assistance by way of representation" (see 3.3). Prison governors also have a discretion to allow legal representation in hearings where they preside. Representation should be allowed where the charge is serious or the penalty grave, where points of law are likely to arise or where a prisoner might be unable to present his or her case properly. Judicial review (see 7.1) is available in respect of disciplinary hearings in a prison, but there are no rights of appeal. In the 12 months up to the end of March 1988, 46 charges of offences against discipline were dealt with by Boards of Visitors or Visiting Committees; legal representation was granted in three of these cases and there were 31 applications for judicial review.

In the 1980s there have been several serious incidents in Northern Ireland's prisons. A hunger strike at Maze Prison, following the long-running "blanket" and "dirty" protests, led to the deaths of 10 prisoners in 1981. The European Commission of Human Rights rejected a case taken by the protesters largely because their conditions were said to be self-inflicted, but the Commission did criticise the inflexibility of the prison authorities. Some of the demands of the prisoners, such as the right to wear their own clothes, were eventually conceded. In 1983 there was a mass escape of 38 prisoners from Maze Prison; this was investigated by Sir James Hennessy, whose report recommended better inspection and self-assessment arrangements. Periodic inspections are conducted by Her Majesty's Inspectorate of Prisons and by the International Committee of the Red Cross. In 1986-87 there were protests at Magilligan Prison over the issue of segregating loyalist and republican prisoners, especially at visiting times. Since 1982 many organisations have expressed concern at the level of strip searching of women prisoners in Northern Ireland; by the end of 1988 there were indications that this practice was being significantly curtailed. There were also signs that the Government was being less inflexible as regards requests from Northern Irish prisoners serving sentences in Great Britain to be transferred back to a jail in Northern Ireland.

Voluntary groups active in the area of prisoners' welfare include the Northern Ireland Association for the Care and Resettlement of Offenders, the Extern Organisation, the Prison Fellowship of Northern Ireland and the Peace People. The Butler Trust has also funded many worthwhile projects.

2

The Branches and Sources of Northern Ireland Law

2.1 The Branches of Law

In Chapter 1 we concentrated on the history of the present-day legal system and described briefly the role of various officials in administering that system. In this chapter we will examine more closely the ways in which the legal system actually creates, applies and develops the law. Our aim here is not to investigate the nature of law or consider what the law ought to be on a certain point; we are taking for granted a conception of law as a set of socially binding rules and principles and are simply inquiring into how those rules and principles come to be fashioned. The bulk of our inquiry will concern the two main sources of law identified in Chapter 1 - Parliament and the courts - but we begin with a short explanation of the ways in which law may be divided into several branches. All of these branches consist of rules derived from each of the main sources of law.

Criminal law and civil law

The commonest way of classifying law is to distinguish between criminal and civil law. Criminal law is that part of the law which prohibits acts deemed to be contrary to public order and the interest of society as a whole. It calls these acts "offences" and prescribes a variety of punishments for any person convicted of committing them. Some offences, such as murder or rape, are extremely serious; others, such as failure to wear a seatbelt, are comparatively minor. But they are all crimes and as such are dealt with by a special set of courts applying special procedures (see Chapter 4).

Most non-lawyers tend to think that criminal law is far and away the chief branch of the law. In fact it is only one relatively small part of it. Students who study for a law degree at a university or polytechnic will spend less than one-tenth of their time on criminal law. Senior judges may spend a quarter of their time on criminal cases, but judicial involvement is not a good way of measuring the law's impact. It has to be remembered that as well as controlling public order and determining how people should be punished for disrupting it, the law must make provision for regulating practically every sphere of human behaviour. It lays down rules for enabling citizens to achieve certain objectives (such as renting a house, buying a car, running a business, making a will, getting married) and it creates principles for the settlement of private disputes - disputes which do not involve breaches of public order. All the law which is not criminal law is sometimes referred to as "civil" law, though, like "common" law, that expression has a variety of meanings depending on the context.

The main feature which distinguishes crimes from civil wrongs lies not in the nature of the behaviour being questioned but in the method by which the behaviour is dealt with by the legal system. A single piece of behaviour can constitute both a crime and a civil wrong (for example, damaging someone's property or stealing something), but the criminal aspects of the incident will be dealt with by criminal courts (where the accused person - the defendant - is "prosecuted", "convicted" or "acquitted", and if convicted, "punished") and the civil aspects by civil courts (where the defendant is "sued", held "liable" or "not liable", and if liable, compelled to pay "damages"). In both criminal and civil appeals the party appealing is termed the appellant; in civil cases the opposing party can then be called the respondent. Under such legislation as the Criminal Justice (Northern Ireland) Order 1980 a criminal court can at times award compensation to the victim of a crime without the need for separate civil proceedings, but this power is rarely used in practice (see 4.6). A civil court, moreover, occasionally awards "punitive" damages and it may issue a "declaration" that certain behaviour *would be* criminal if it were to be carried out. In such cases the distinction between criminal and civil proceedings becomes somewhat blurred.

It should be noted that applications to be compensated by the state for loss suffered as a result of criminal activity are actually civil law claims and are dealt with accordingly (see 5.5). Applications for judicial review (see 7.1) are also civil law matters, even though the review applied for may be in respect of the decision in a criminal case.

Branches of civil law

The names of the various branches of the civil law are mostly self-explanatory. They include land law, family law, contract law and company law. Each of these can in turn be subdivided and some of the subdivisions overlap with other subdivisions or with other main branches; examples are landlord and tenant law, housing law, labour law, partnership law, bankruptcy law, banking law and consumer law. Of the less obviously named branches the law of torts is for the most part concerned with the compensation of people for injuries caused to themselves or damage caused to their property through someone else's recklessness or carelessness; the law's term for such carelessness is "negligence." A subdivison of tort law is the law on libel and slander (or "defamation"). Other torts include trespass, nuisance, false imprisonment and interference with goods.

The expression "property law" is sometimes used to refer to those branches of the civil law which inform us about our rights and duties in relation to the things we own or rent or have some other kind of interest in. As the most important form of property is land - an expression which in law is used to include the buildings erected on land - the term property law is often used to mean the same as land law. Strictly speaking it should also refer to the law concerning property which is not land. There are innumerable forms of such property, ranging from the most tangible - such as cars and antiques - to the most intangible - such as shares in a company, premium bonds, or copyright in a book. To discourage too much property becoming vested in one person, our law has devised methods for splitting up the interests which might be held in a single piece of property: someone who owns a house, for instance, might rent it to someone or give an interest in it to a building society in return for a loan (a mortgage). A specific device which both English and Irish law have developed for splitting up people's interests in property is the "trust". If a fund of money, for instance, is held on trust, the purse-strings are controlled by persons called trustees and the people who actually receive payments out of the fund are called beneficiaries of the trust. It is in the form of trusts that most charities carry on their work.

Public law and private law

Some branches of the civil law, together with the criminal law, are sometimes lumped together to form the category known as "public law" in contrast to "private law". While private law regulates the relations between individuals, public law regulates the relations between individuals and public bodies, including the state. Thus the branch of public law called constitutional law tells us about the way in which we are governed and what our civil liberties are. This is a particularly important branch of Northern Ireland law. Administrative law deals mainly with the power of government ministers and departments and the controls exercised by the courts over administrative tribunals (see 7.1). Some of the principles developed within admininstrative law, such as those concerned with natural justice (*e.g.* each side to a dispute must be given a fair hearing), are beginning to infiltrate into private law subjects such as contract and tort law. Welfare law explains the operation of the welfare state, setting out the conditions which must be satisfied before people will qualify for state benefits. International law can be part of public law or private law: it is public whenever it concerns the relations between states but private whenever it deals with the relations between individuals from different states.

Substantive law and procedural law

All the branches of law so far mentioned can be labelled "substantive" legal subjects because they concern the actual substance or content of the law: they reveal to us our rights, our duties and our privileges. "Procedural" or "adjectival" legal subjects, on the other hand, regulate the methods by which the substance of the law is applied. The law on criminal procedure determines how crimes are to be prosecuted, how the rights of an accused person are to be protected and how punishments are to be enforced. The law on civil procedure similarly lays down the steps which must be taken whenever a civil dispute develops into a civil legal action. Chapters 4 and 5 of this book are mostly concerned with criminal and civil procedure. The law of evidence contains a mass of detailed rules to specify the sort of testimony and documents which can be used in either a civil or a criminal court to support an argument.

All of these procedural subjects are important because if the rules of procedure are not properly complied with it can happen that substantive legal rights are lost. For example, it is a general rule of civil procedure that a legal action claiming compensation for personal injuries must be brought within three years of the injuries coming to light; if the action is not brought within this limitation period, the right to claim compensation is lost (or "time-barred").

2.2 Primary Legislation

All the branches of law described in the previous section have at least one feature in common: the rules which they contain are derived not only from legislation, which is law created by Parliament, but also from judicial precedent, which is law laid down by judges. Practically every legal issue is governed partly by statute law and partly by judge-made law. Two other sources of law are custom and the opinions of deceased eminent scholars, but in practice these are resorted to very infrequently; both legislation and judge-made law take priority over them. On the rare occasions when the law as laid down by Parliament is in conflict with the law as laid down by judges, it is parliamentary law which must prevail. If parliamentary law is itself at odds with earlier parliamentary law, the later in time must prevail.

Legislation consists not just of Acts of Parliament - which are called "statutes" - but also of the myriad number of orders, rules, regulations etc. which are made under the authority of an Act of Parliament. This latter body of laws is called secondary, subordinate or delegated legislation, but to all intents and purposes it is just as binding on the general public as the primary legislation enshrined in statutes. Secondary legislation is considered in more detail in the next section.

There is actually a third type of legislation which ought to be mentioned in passing: legislation created under the Royal Prerogative. This takes the form of Prerogative Orders in Council, whereby the Queen simply assents to proposals put before her by senior Ministers who have been appointed Privy Counsellors (see 1.4). the matters regulated by the Royal Prerogative in this way are limited to particular fields such as the civil service, the armed forces, coinage, and the extent of territorial waters. When in 1984 the Prime Minister wished to ban trade unions at Government Communications Headquarters at Cheltenham, she issued a ruling under a power conferred on her by a Prerogative Order in Council, namely the Civil Service Order 1982. Prerogative Orders with a legislative character are inserted as an Appendix in the annual volumes of

United Kingdom statutory instruments (explained in the next section) but are quite different from Parliamentary Orders in Council, which are made under the authority of an Act of Parliament. Prerogative Orders are not themselves statutory instruments, whereas Parliamentary Orders are. In a sense the Prerogative Orders are subordinate legislation (because Parliament can qualify the power to make them) but not secondary legislation (because Parliament's authority is not required for their creation). They invariably apply throughout the United Kingdom, not just to one part of it (England and Wales, Scotland or Northern Ireland).

The primacy of statute law

In the United Kingdom, unlike some countries such as the Republic of Ireland or the United States of America, it is not possible for the courts to refuse to apply primary legislation on the grounds that it is invalid or in some way unconstitutional. Nor can the courts attempt to alter the wording of such laws. Parliament at Westminster is supreme; whatever it enacts cannot be queried. Only a later Parliament can undo the things which a previous Parliament has done. Constitutional lawyers call this "the doctrine of parliamentary sovereignty". The only qualification which needs to be added to this, as regards the United Kingdom as a whole, is that membership of the Common Market has entailed conceding that whenever United Kingdom domestic law, whether parliamentary or judge-made, runs counter to the law emanating from the European Community, it is the latter which must be given priority. We return to this European Community dimension at the end of this chapter (see 2.6).

As regards Northern Ireland, however, it has to be remembered that the Government of Ireland Act 1920 effectively provided the province with something which the rest of the kingdom still does not possess - a written constitution. The legislative powers of the Belfast Parliament were deliberately restricted by the Act: excepted and reserved matters could be dealt with only by the Parliament at Westminster (see 1.2). If the Belfast Parliament trespassed into these areas, courts in Northern Ireland were entitled to declare the legislation (whether primary or secondary) to be unauthorised. As regards primary Stormont legislation, this almost happened in a case called *Gallagher* v *Lynn* (1937). The Milk and Milk Products Act (NI) 1934 required all sellers of milk in Northern Ireland to have a licence from the Ministry of Agriculture. Mr Gallagher was refused a licence because his dairy farm was situated outside Northern Ireland, even though he sold milk within the province. Upon his conviction for the crime of selling milk without a licence Mr Gallagher, on appeal, tried to argue that the 1934 Act was beyond the power of the Stormont Parliament to make because, by section 4(1) of the Government of Ireland Act 1920, that Parliament could not make laws in respect of trade. The Court of Appeal of Northern Ireland and the House of Lords held that the 1934 Act was not one in respect of trade but one in respect of the peace, order and good government of Northern Ireland and so was valid.

Different types of statutes

Statues are made by being first drafted and then enacted. The precise methods of drafting and enactment differ according to the type of statute in question. For the moment we can identify three types. In the first place there are public general Acts, which are statutes affecting the whole public and with which we are principally concerned here; they are by far the commonest type of primary enactment, with about 60 being created by the Westminster Parliament each year (in 1987 there were 57). Secondly, there are local Acts, which are statutes concerned only with a particular locality. Thirdly, there are private Acts, which are directed purely towards specific individuals or companies. (In 1987 there were 29 local and private Acts.) Between 1921 and 1972, during which time Northern Ireland possessed its own Parliament, Acts of all three types were passed, examples of the second and third types being respectively the Londonderry Corporation Act (Northern Ireland) 1970 and the Allied Irish Banks Act (Northern Ireland) 1971. Private Acts should not be confused with Private Members' Bills, which are proposals for laws introduced and piloted through Parliament by an MP who does well in a ballot at the start of the Parliamentary session; most of these Bills do not eventually get passed into law, but a famous example of one that did is the Abortion Act 1967, introduced by David Steel MP. Another is the Obscene Publicatons Act 1959, introduced by Roy Jenkins MP. Neither Act applies in Northern Ireland and it is nowadays very rare of for a private members' Bill directly affecting Northern Ireland to be passed into law.

Since the imposition of direct rule (see 1.2), the United Kingdom Parliament continues to enact the three types of statute for Northern Ireland, though it·rarely resorts to the second and third type. Even the first type is seldom used specifically for the province: such Acts are normally applied to the whole of the United Kingdom (*e.g.* the Consumer Credit Act 1974). The main way in which legislation confined to Northern Ireland is now enacted is by adopting the Parliamentary Order in Council procedure under the Northern Ireland Act 1974. This is an example of secondary legislation and is therefore described more fully in the following section.

Whenever the Westminster Parliament wishes to enact a law concerning an "excepted" matter (see 1.2), it must embody it in a public general Act, *e.g.* the Northern Ireland (Emergency Provisions) Act 1987. If the subject of the proposed law is a "transferred" matter then such an Act will be employed only if the Government wishes to ensure a full parliamentary debate, *e.g.* the Fair Employment (Northern Ireland) Act 1976. Acts confined in operation to the province will usually have the words "Northern Ireland" either as key words in the title or within brackets before the word "Act." Statutes of the Stormont Parliament 1921-1972 are distinguished from English statutes with similar titles by adding the phrase "Northern Ireland" *after* the word "Act", as in the Legal Aid and Advice Act (Northern Ireland) 1965.

Some statutes are passed merely to *consolidate* previous statutes, that is, not to change the law but simply to bring into one place the various enactments relating to a matter. Examples are the Insolvency Act 1986 and the Income and Corporation Taxes Act 1988. Occasionally statutes are passed in order to *codify* existing statute and judge-made law on a particular topic. These statutes represent a fresh start on the topic and usually change the existing law. An example is the Theft Act (NI) 1969.

The drafting and enacting of statutes

Acts of the United Kingdom Parliament are officially made by "The Queen in Parliament". This means that they must be approved by the House of Commons, the House of Lords and the Monarch. Since 1911, however, the power of the House of Lords to curb the legislative zeal of the House of Commons has been severely restricted. The Monarch, moreover, no longer refuses to assent to an Act of Parliament presented to her. As the House of Commons is usually dominated by Members of Parliament belonging to the political party which has formed the Government, it is in practice the Government which decides what legislation should be passed. The Government's intentions are made clear in the Queen's Speech at the beginning of each Parliamentary session.

The great majority of public general Acts start life as proposals put to the Cabinet, either by a Cabinet committee or by a particular Government department through its representative on the Cabinet. Sometimes the proposals will have been preceded by a Government White Paper on the topic. From the Cabinet the proposals are sent in the form of departmental instructions to the Office of Parliamentary Counsel, whose staff have the task of actually drafting the legislation. A similar office existed in Northern Ireland when there was a Parliament at Stormont; it still exists in the form of the Office of the Legislative Draftsmen, which now confines its attention to drafting Orders in Council issued under the Northern Ireland Act 1974 and helping with the drafting of Northern Ireland statutes to be enacted at Westminster.

Legislative drafting is a specialized skill. The draftsman has to translate the department's policy instructions into unambiguous legal language, being careful not to distort the Government's intentions or leave any gaps. The Act must also be tied in with whatever legislation already exists on the topic. During the legislation's passage through Parliament the draftsman must always be at hand to advise Ministers and prepare any necessary amendments.

Passage through Parliament, or the enactment of the legislation, is usually a long and complicated process. The standard procedure is for a Bill to be introduced into the House of Commons, where it is dealt with in five stages: the first reading stage (a formality), the second reading stage, the committee stage, the report stage and the third reading stage. It is at the committee and report stages that detailed amendments to the Bill are mostly considered. It is then sent to the House of Lords, where similar stages must be gone through, and if any amendments are suggested these must return to the House of Commons to be considered further. In most cases, mainly because of the Government's majority in the House as a whole and in committees, the final form of the law differs little from that put forward at the initial stages. The Bill is then accorded the Royal Assent and immediately becomes an Act. The granting of Royal Assent, however, does not automatically bring the Act into force. This will be so only if the Act contains no other indication as to when or how it is to be brought into force. Often an Act says that it is to come into force only when a "commencement order" has been made (say, by a Government Minister). The Easter Act 1928, which provided for a fixed date for Easter, is an example of an Act where the mechanism for bringing it into force has still not been activated! The Equal Pay Act (NI) 1970 was not brought into force until 1976. There is a constitutional convention to the effect that legislation should not be retrospective in operation, but occasionally this is ignored, as when the Government needs to validate some actions which would otherwise be illegal. An example is the Northern Ireland Act 1972, which declared that as from 1920 the law was different from that laid down by the judges in *R. (Hume)* v *Londonderry Justices* (1972).

The enactment of legislation usually takes months, though really urgent Bills can be dealt with in a day or two. The Northern Ireland Act 1972 obtained its second reading in the Commons and the Royal Assent within the space of four-and-a-half hours.

The form of statutes

Today statutes follow a traditional format, an example of which is given in Appendix 3. The Act set out there, the Fatal Accidents Act (NI) 1959, is an unusually short Act and has since been repealed (see page 49), but it displays most of the standard features. We can note at least nine of these:

(1)   *The chapter number* (18). This is the number given to the Act at the time of its publication as such, simply in order to make its identification easier.

(2)   *The long title.* This provides a brief summary of the Act's purposes and effects; it expands upon the Act's short title, which is simply the Fatal Accidents Act (NI) 1959.

(3)   *The date* (15th December 1959). This is the date on which the Act was finally made, that is, the date on which the Royal Assent was given.

(4)   *The enacting words* ("Be it enacted . . ."). This is a standard formula placed at the beginning of all Northern Ireland statutes simply to indicate which Parliament made the statute. The enacting words for United Kingdom statutes differ accordingly.

(5)   *Sections.* Each Act is divided into sections, which are numbered 1, 2, 3, etc. Sections are in turn divided into subsections, which are numbered (1), (2), (3), etc. Subsections can then be split into paragraphs: (a), (b), (c). The next subdivision, not used in the Fatal Accidents Act (NI) 1959, is called a subparagraph: (i), (ii), (iii), etc. Reference is made to a subparagraph by writing as follows: s.1(3)(b)(ii) (pronounced as "section

one, three, b, two"). When a statute is passing through Parliament it is not called an Act but a Bill, and its provisions are divided into clauses rather than sections, but further subdivisions are still called subsections and paragraphs.

(6) *Marginal notes.* The words in the margins beside each section summarise the effect of the section for ease of reference; strictly speaking they do not constitute part of the law. Whenever other statutes are mentioned in sections a reference is placed in the margin to enable the reader to find it more easily in a library.

(7) *Definition section.* Most statutes contain a section near the end defining more precisely some of the expressions used earlier. The Fatal Accidents Act (NI) 1959 makes do with defining some words in s.2(2); note that an exact definition of "benefit" is provided, whereas only partial explanations of "insurance money" and "pension" are given.

(8) *The short title etc. section.* Every statute ends with a section giving the short title of the Act; when a statute is passed on a topic which has already been legislated for, the Acts can be referred to together, as s. 3(1) of the Fatal Accidents Act (NI) 1959 illustrates. The final section also contains a provision concerning the operation in time of the Act: see s. 3(4) of the 1959 Act; if no specific provision is made for the coming into force of the Act, then it is taken to be in force as soon as the Royal Assent is granted (hence the date after the long title). In United Kingdom statutes the final or penultimate section will normally say whether the statute is to apply in Scotland and in Northern Ireland as well as in England and Wales; some statutes apply in only a part or parts of the United Kingdom, *e.g.* the Marriage (Wales) Act 1986 applies only in Wales and the Congenital Disabilities (Civil Liability) Act 1976 applies throughout the United Kingdom except Scotland.

(9) *Schedules.* Many Acts contain Schedules setting out in tabular form the statutory provisions repealed by the Act. Sometimes a Schedule will also set out the amendments provided for by the Act, but if there are not too many of these they will be catered for in the body of the Act itself, as in s.1(4) of the Fatal Accidents Act (NI) 1959. Occasionally the Schedules contain more substantive provisions, such as guidelines for the application of a particular standard mentioned in the Act. Schedules are not self-enacting: somewhere in the Act there must be a provision stating that the Schedules are to have the force of law: see s.3(3) of the 1959 Act.

An important formal feature of statutes which is not illustrated by the Fatal Accidents Act (NI) 1959 is the division of longer Acts or Schedules into Parts. This is simply a method of ensuring that all the provisions concerned with a particular matter are bunched together in the same place within a statute. To help the reader to find a particular provision some pieces of very long legislation are now published with an index.

The problems of looking for statute law

Even if you can recognize and read a statute when you find one, this will not be much help to you unless you know how to look for it in the first place. The trouble is that most Acts of Parliament are designed to operate prospectively, this is, for the future and not the past. They remain in force even after the Parliament which made them has been dissolved. When new legislation is enacted, insufficient attention is often paid to the statutes which are already in force. It can thus be very difficult to understand the current legal position on a certain matter if there are several statutes, some dating back a long time, purporting to deal with it.

In Northern Ireland the problems are accentuated by the fact that - as we noted in Chapter 1 - since the fourteenth century there have been many Parliaments claiming the power to legislate for the area which is now Northern Ireland. As a result the Northern Ireland "statute book" - the collection of the statutory provisions currently in force in the province - is very large indeed. The collection comprises the work of six separate legislatures:

(1)   the Parliament in Ireland, from 1310 to 1800,

(2)   the Parliament of England, from 1226 to 1707,

(3)   the Parliament of Great Britain, from 1707 to 1800,

(4)   the Parliament of the United Kingdom, from 1800 to the present day.

(5)   the Parliament of Northern Ireland, from 1921 to 1972, and,

(6)   the Northern Ireland Assembly, 1974, the enactments of which are not called Acts but Measures.

Many of the statutes of these Parliaments remain in force, or partly in force, even though they are of virtually no significance in practice: about 50 statutes of the Parliament in Ireland still apply, as do about 70 statutes of the Parliaments of England and Great Britain. In more recent times statutes have included provisions to repeal earlier statutes which are being superseded and indeed sometimes whole Acts are passed purely to rid the statute book of redundant laws - for example, the Repeal of Unnecessary Laws Act (NI) 1954 and the Statute Law Revision (NI) Act 1980. It can still be difficult, though, to determine precisely the current statutory position on a particular topic. The difficulty is compounded when one realises that some statutes passed by Parliament at Westminster have not made it clear whether they are meant to apply in Northern Ireland as well as in the rest of Britain, though the rule is that if the Act is silent on the matter it is presumed to apply throughout the United Kingdom. In 1986 there were 41 United Kingdom statutes (out of 68 passed altogether) which applied wholly or partly in Northern Ireland.

Were it simply a matter of knowing which statutes have been repealed and which are still in force, the problem would be fairly manageable. But we have to remember that statutes can be amended as well as totally repealed. When this occurs (an example is provided by s.1(4) of the Fatal Accidents Act (NI) 1959, reproduced in Appendix 3) the statute is not re-enacted in its new form: you have to read it in its original form and then read what the amending statute provides. Amendments can be introduced by Acts which have very little in common with the original statute, sometimes in the form of a Law Reform (Miscellaneous Provisions) Act or an Administration of Justice Act. They can even be introduced by secondary legislation, described in the next section.

To make the search for the statute law easier, Her Majesty's Stationery Office publishes various auxiliary volumes. The statutes themselves are published and sold singly at the time they are enacted as well as collectively in a bound or loose-leaf volume at the end of each calendar year. These annual volumes have continued to be produced since 1972 even though they now contain not primary legislation but the Orders in Council made under the Northern Ireland Act 1974. Each pre-1972 volume contains tables showing the United Kingdom and Northern Ireland Acts repealed or amended by Northern Ireland Acts during that year, as well as tables showing the Northern Ireland Acts affected by United Kingdom Acts passed during the year and the full list of United Kingdom Acts passed that year which are applicable in Northern Ireland. The annual index to the statutes also lists the amendments made to Acts by secondary legislation.

Every three years (the latest is up to the end of 1984) an index is published to all the statutory provisions currently in force in Northern Ireland, arranged under distinct subject-headings; at roughly the same interval another table is published of all the statute law which affects, or has affected, Northern Ireland, this time arranged in chronological order and with amendments and repeals noted (the latest volume is up to the end of 1986). Both these lists amount to weighty tomes, but they are indispensable because they also include references to statutes passed for the whole of the United Kingdom. They permit you to tell at a glance what primary legislation exists on any matter and whether primary legislation which once existed has been amended or repealed. The position can be so complicated, however, that mistakes and omissions are not rare.

The *Statutes Revised, Northern Ireland* is a 16-volume collection of the public general Acts of the Parliaments of Ireland, England, Great Britain, the United Kingdom and Northern Ireland which have affected Northern Ireland down to 1950, whether or not they deal with matters which were finally placed within the legislative competence of the Parliament of Northern Ireland. The texts are reprinted as amended, with the amending and repealing schedules therefore excluded. During 1982 the Statutory Publications Office of the Department of Finance and Personnel produced in loose-leaf form a nine-volume second edition of the Statutes Revised, which sets out in chronological order the text, also amended, of all the statutes affecting Northern Ireland between 1921 and 1981. Unfortunately this excludes the relevant United Kingdom statutes enacted since 1920, but a four volume series (A-D) appended to the edition reprints the amended texts of all pre-1920 legislation, from whatever parliamentary source, still in force in Northern Ireland. Cumulative supplements to *Statutes Revised* are now published annually to show what changes have occurred during the past year.

All United Kingdom statutes, as well as being published singly and in annual collections, are indexed by the two-volume *Index to the Statutes* published every two years. Two private publishing companies also produce versions of these statutes with comments and annotations: these are the series known as *Halsbury's Statutes* and *Current Law Statutes*. *Statutes in Force* provides the service for England and Wales which *Statutes Revised* provides for Northern Ireland; it comprises dozens of loose-leaf volumes.

Computer-based information retrieval

The advent of computerised information retrieval systems is greatly facilitating the search for primary (as well as secondary) legislation. By keying in the appropriate question, one can discover within seconds the relevant legislation on a particular point. The full text of the up-to-date version of this legislation can be displayed on a screen and printed out if desired. Moves are afoot to include Northern Ireland legislation on databases used in these systems, but at the time of writing the transfer has not yet been achieved. Only legislation passed at Westminster is today accessible. The use of computers is also affecting searches for judge-made law (see below, page 51).

2.3 Secondary Legislation

All pieces of secondary legislation are ultimately the offspring of a parent (or "enabling") Act of Parliament. They are used to lay down the law in more detail than is normally contained in primary legislation, or where it would be too time-consuming to invoke the full Parliamentary process just to make a fairly minor alteration in some existing legislative scheme. The parent Act will give power to a rule-making authority to issue detailed laws on a particular matter. The rule-making authority is usually a Government department but it can also be, for instance, the Privy Council (which makes Orders in Council), a local authority (which makes bye-laws), or a committee of judges and lawyers (which makes Rules of Court; see above, page 14). The exact title of the particular secondary legislation will depend on the wording of the parent Act: it may provide for Orders in Council, orders, rules, regulations, directions, schemes or bye-laws. Nothing turns on the difference in title - all of these varieties are equally binding as laws of the land.

There are various semi-official documents which the lay person often believes have the force of law but which in fact do not. Even though they are sometimes issued pursuant to a power conferred by statute, they can only influence the judges' views on what the law should be. Such publications include the Highway Code, the Codes of Practice on Closed Shops and Picketing (issued for Great Britain by the Department of Employment), the Guide to Effective

Practice in Religious Equality of Opportunity in Employment (issued by the Department of Economic Development), the codes of practice agreed to by various trade associations, the standing orders issued to the prison service by the Northern Ireland Office and the Judges' Rules on the questioning of suspects. The Codes of Practice to be issued under the proposed Police and Criminal Evidence (NI) Order (see 4.3) will replace the Judges' Rules but will still not have the full force of legislation. The Immigration Rules, issued pursuant to the Immigration Act 1971, are another very important example. The Inland Revenue frequently issues policy statements which are treated by the courts as having this semi-legislative status: the statements declare that the Inland Revenue will make extra-statutory concessions, that is, not charge tax on certain specified payments. Statements of practice published by insurance companies, and circulars put out by the Home Office and other Government departments on a wide range of legal matters are also in this category. Judges, Masters and registrars announce what are called "practice directions" in order to provide for better organisation of proceedings within the courts. Just because a matter is catered for in some such semi-official document (which may not even be available to the general public) rather than in a piece of secondary legislation does not mean that it is of little legal significance - it more usually means that strict legal standards are deemed inappropriate for the matter. Consequently, issues as diverse as the level of permissible noise from ice-cream vans and the strip-searching of persons in police custody are dealt with by this kind of document.

Types of secondary legislation

Although all pieces of secondary legislation have the same legal status, they nevertheless differ in form. Quite apart from the variations in their titles, already alluded to, it is helpful to distinguish between three different types of secondary legislation affecting Northern Ireland. The first two are special because they are made in England; only the third type is made within Northern Ireland itself. Because of this difference in the origins of secondary legislation it can often be quite difficult, as in the case of primary legislation, to determine exactly which laws are applicable in the province. However, the difficulty is not as acute as in the case of primary legislation because secondary legislation did not become common until the nineteenth century. We shall look at the three types of secondary legislation separately.

(1) Statutory instruments

In England and Wales most of the secondary legislation is published in the form of consecutively numbered "statutory instruments". Some of these, being made under the authority of an enabling Act which extends beyond England and Wales, are applicable in Northern Ireland. Thus, for example, the Consumer Credit (Quotation) Regulations 1980 apply in Northern Ireland because the enabling Act was a statute in force throughout the United Kingdom, namely the

Consumer Credit Act 1974; but the Packaging and Labelling of Dangerous Substances Regulations 1978 do not apply in Northern Ireland because in this case the enabling Act (the Consumer Protection Act 1961) does not apply outside England, Wales and Scotland.

Furthermore, some Westminster statutes have an effect only within Northern Ireland, so obviously the legislative powers delegated by such Acts can themselves be effective only within Northern Ireland. Their title will contain the words "Northern Ireland" *before* the word "Rule", "Regulation", "Order", etc. An example is the Emergency Provisions (Compensation) (NI) Rules 1982, made under the authority of section 28 of the Northern Ireland (Emergency Provisions) Act 1978 (see 5.5).

In 1987, 458 statutory instruments were made affecting Northern Ireland as well as other parts of the United Kingdom (out of 2,277 made altogether); a further 16 were made affecting only Northern Ireland (excluding the Orders in Council described next). Quite a few of the former category are instruments made to comply with the United Kingdom's obligations as a member of the Common Market; s.2(2) of the European Communities Act 1972 is one of the most important enabling provisions in our law.

(2) Orders in Council

Orders in Council are in fact just one species of the more general category of statutory instruments described above. They are often viewed as the most "dignified" type of secondary legislation because they are formally made by the Queen on the advice of her Privy Counsellors (*i.e.* senior Government Ministers of the day; see 1.4). But in fact they carry no more weight than any other type of delegated legislation and in appropriate cases can be impugned by Parliament or by the courts to just the same extent (see below, pages 47-49).

There are a number of Acts providing for the making of Orders in Council which might apply in Northern Ireland as well as in other parts of the United Kingdom, *e.g.* the Administration of Justice Act 1985. However, the reason for listing Orders in Council here as a separate type of secondary legislation is that there is one enabling Act, the Northern Ireland Act 1974, which in effect substitutes legislation in the form of Orders in Council for the legislation which, had it not been abolished, the Parliament at Stormont would have enacted. More precisely, Orders in Council under the 1974 Act are used to make laws for Northern Ireland on subjects which, being "transferred matters" under the Northern Ireland Constitution Act 1973, would have been legislated for by the Northern Ireland Assembly if it had survived the first few months of 1974. "Reserved" matters under the 1973 Act are also dealt with by Orders in Council. Only "excepted" matters need to be legislated for by an Act of Parliament at Westminster. "Law and order" is a reserved matter but "terrorism" is an excepted matter. It is to be noted that the categories of "transferred", "reserved" and "excepted" matters are not the same under the 1973 Act as they were under the Government of Ireland Act 1920.

Orders in Council made under the Northern Ireland Act 1974 are published and numbered as United Kingdom statutory instruments, a separate number being given to them for publication in annual collections of Northern Ireland Orders in Council. These collections continue the series known as Acts of the Northern Ireland Parliament, so many people would see these Orders as having, to all intents and purposes, the status of primary legislation. This is not strictly the case, because unlike primary legislation they can be challenged by the courts (see below, page 48). Durng the last 10 years there has been an average of 22 of these Orders in Council each year. As we shall see in (3) below, it is not unusual for Orders made under the 1974 Act to subdelegate law-making powers to other authorities, even though the general rule for secondary legislation is that further delegation of powers is not possible. These Orders can also amend or repeal primary legislation, which again is contrary to the normal rule for secondary laws.

It should be noted that not every item of legislation given the title "Order" will in fact be on Order in Council. However, it is rare for a statutory instrument applying only in Northern Ireland to be called an Order unless it is an Order in Council made under the Northern Ireland Act 1974; an example is the District Electoral Areas (NI) Order 1985. The word "Order" is also used for some more ordinary pieces of legislation which fall within the third type described below. These are not statutory instruments at all. An example would be the Statutory Sick Pay Up-Rating Order (NI) 1983, made under the Social Security (NI) Order 1982 (which *was* an Order in Council). See also the example of a statutory rule reproduced in Appendix 3, namely the Lobsters (Prohibition of Introduction) Order (NI) 1982.

(3) Statutory rules

Statutory rules are made by a rule-making authority in Northern Ireland under a power conferred by an Act of the United Kingdom Parliament, by an Act of the Stormont Parliament or by an Order in Council made under the Northern Ireland Act 1974. They are really the Northern Ireland equivalents of the statutory instruments made for the rest of the United Kingdom (see (1) above). Sometimes they differ from the corresponding statutory instruments in title alone, the actual content remaining virtually identical. The title will always contain the words "Northern Ireland" placed in brackets *after* the words "Rules", "Regulations", "Order", etc. A typical illustration of statutory rules would be the Food Hygiene (General) Regulations (NI) 1964, which were made under the Food and Drugs Act (NI) 1958 and are almost identical to the Food Hygiene (General) Regulations 1970 for England and Wales, made under the Food and Drugs Act 1955.

As in the case of Orders, not all laws with the title "Rules" will in fact be what they seem. They may not be statutory rules at all but statutory instruments, *e.g.* the Emergency Provisions (Compensation) (NI) Rules 1982 cited in (1) above. They are recognizable from the position of the words "Northern Ireland" *before* the word "Rules". To repeat, however, the difference in title does not affect the legislation's status.

In 1987 there were 473 statutory rules made for Northern Ireland. They obviously dealt with a huge range of subjects. But some statutory rules are of a recurring variety. One such is the statutory rule known as a "commencement order", which sets a date for the coming into force of provisions in other legislation, *e.g.* the Mental Health (1986 Order) (Commencement No. 2) Order (NI) 1986. Another recurring variety is the statutory rule which sets new financial limits for those originally stated in a parent Act or in a previous statutory rule, *e.g.* the Fisheries (Licence Duties) Bye-laws (NI) 1985.

Like statutes, statutory rules can also be subdivided into public, local and private rules, though here too the distinctions are not very important. The local and private rules usually concern roads or road traffic, one example being the Road Races (Circuit of Ireland Rally) Order (NI) 1986. Bye-laws made by local authorities are another example; they can be made by district councils for, generally speaking, the good rule and government of the whole or any part of the district, provided they are confirmed by a Government department. They can also be made by such bodies as the Fisheries Conservancy Board for Northern Ireland (an example is given in the previous paragraph), Trustees of the Ulster Folk and Transport Museum, Northern Ireland Railways and Harbour Authorities.

The making of secondary legislation

Whatever type of secondary legislation is eventually made, and in whatever form, it is invariably drafted only after a period of considerable consultation with interested parties. Except occasionally, the final drafting is performed by civil servants within the legal branches of the Government department concerned, not by Parliamentary Counsel.

Orders in Council under the Northern Ireland Act 1974 are given special treatment. Proposals for new Orders are first considered by a committee of senior civil servants, the Policy Co-ordinating Committee, and then by a committee of Government Ministers, the Legislative Programme Committee. Instructions are then sent to the Legislative Draftsman's Office. When a draft has been approved by the two above-mentioned committees it is circulated to the public in the form of a "Proposal for a Draft Order in Council" and is accompanied by an Explanatory Document. Usually six weeks are allowed for comments. The Northern Ireland Committee at the House of Commons may be consulted if the area being dealt with is a contentious one. The comments made on the proposal are considered and the draftsman then prepares a final draft for laying before Parliament.

Speaking very generally, the precise method of creation depends on the importance of the secondary legislation in question. Usually the most important - and Orders in Council made under the 1974 Act fall into this category - must be laid in draft form before both Houses of Parliament, and be approved by both Houses, before being presented to the Queen for her formal assent. This process puts the onus on the Government to find time for Parliament to debate and affirm the legislation before it can finally be made; if no debate takes place - the exact period allowed may depend on the wording of the enabling Act - then no further action can be taken. Secondary legislation which is urgent, and for which no time is immediately available for a parliamentary debate, can be made without first being laid before Parliament, but it must cease to have effect if each House does not approve it within a specified period, usually 28 or 40 days. Both of these legislative processes may be termed "affirmative" procedures because the legislation does not have effect, or ceases to have effect, unless it is affirmed.

An alternative is the "negative" procedure, whereby the legislation takes effect, or continues to have effect if already made, unless a "prayer" in either House specifically annuls it within 40 days. This procedure is usually employed for Orders in Council which are almost identical to English legislation already enacted and for which a separate parliamentary debate would be unnecessary. When it is used the draft Order is not preceded by a published proposal but is simply made by the Privy Council and laid before Parliament. Under all of these procedures the legislation must be affirmed or annulled in its entirety; it cannot be amended, though it can be withdrawn and re-laid later in a revised form.

Less important secondary legislation may be required to be laid before Parliament but is not subject to the affirmative or negative procedures. Such legislation cannot be debated, but ministerial questions can be asked about it, and because it must be laid it cannot usually come into force before the date of laying. If it is essential that the statutory instrument comes into force before being laid, the Speaker of the House of Commons and the Lord Chancellor (who is Speaker of the House of Lords) must be notified. The least important secondary legislation need not be laid before Parliament at all, though again questions can be asked about it if an MP happens to have his or her attention drawn to it. The statutory instruments which are afforded this most cursory treatment are mostly local or private in nature. An unfortunate consequence of direct rule in Northern Ireland is that the secondary legislation which in the days of Stormont was subject to the negative resolution procedure is no longer required to be laid before Parliament at all. This is due to the fact that the replacement of Stormont Acts by Westminster Orders in Council required the whole of the legislative machinery for Northern Ireland to be, as it were, "taken down a peg": delegated legislation which was previously subject to the negative procedure at Stormont is now subject to no parliamentary scrutiny whatsoever.

It should be noted, finally, that the making of secondary legislation is not the same as the bringing of it into force. Secondary legislation which is required to be laid before Parliament - even if already made (and not just in draft form) - cannot come into force before it is laid, except very rarely. As well, even if the legislation does not need to be laid, or is laid in draft form and made later, it may still itself provide (and usually does) that it is not to come into force until a certain period has elapsed after it has been made.

Controls on secondary legislation

By Parliament

Secondary legislation is controlled by two bodies: Parliament itself and the courts. Parliament's control comes into play not only at the stage when the parent Act is being enacted - for its delegating provisions can then be debated and amended - but also at the stage when, as is often required, the secondary legislation itself is laid before Parliament to undergo either the affirmative or negative procedure. The time allowed for debates on such procedures on the floor of the House of Commons is one-and-a-half hours. In addition (or more usually instead) they can be discussed for a further two-and-a-half hours by a Standing (or Merits) Committee of the House of Commons and the debate there will obviously be influential on the way MPs vote on resolutions in the House. By convention the House of Lords does not vote down secondary legislation proposed by the Government.

All United Kingdom statutory instruments - but not Orders in Council made under the Northern Ireland Act 1974 - can also be scrutinised from a technical rather than a merit point of view by a Joint Select (or Scrutiny) Committee of the House of Commons and the House of Lords. The Committee consults the rule-making authority concerned if it thinks that the instrument is technically defective, and the attention of the whole House of Commons can then be drawn to the matter.

The specific task of inspecting Northern Ireland secondary legislation to see if it is technically defective is performed by an official called the Examiner for Statutory Rules. The Examiner looks at all the secondary legislation which is required to be laid before Parliament but which is not subject to the affirmative or negative procedures. This means that he examines about half of all the statutory rules which are ultimately made. About 50 sets of rules per year are not required to be laid before Parliament at all. He issues a report every few months (his 30th appeared in November 1988). In it he draws the attention of the Clerk of the Northern Ireland Assembly (a post which was retained even after the 1974 Assembly was dissolved, and which came into prominence again during the 1982-86 Assembly) to those statutory rules with which he is dissatisfied on one or more of a number of grounds.

These grounds include the existence of an unjustifiable delay in publishing or laying the rule, doubts as to whether the rule is *intra vires* (*i.e.* within the powers conferred by the parent Act), and the fact that the parent Act has tried to prevent the courts from challenging the rule. In practice the Examiner also complains if there is a gap of less than the conventional 21 days between the laying of a statutory rule and its coming into force. He ensures as well that the Commons Select Committee on European Legislation scrutinises those Northern Ireland statutory rules which give effect to an EEC obligation. At the end of the day the Examiner finds fault with only a tiny minority of the rules he considers. Whenever he has complained that a rule may not be *intra vires*, the appropriate rule-making authority has either lobbied to have the parent Act extended or has itself repealed the offending provision in the rule.

The Assembly which operated in Northern Ireland from 1982 to 1986 (see 1.2) was consulted about proposals for Orders in Council emanating from Government departments. On a few occasions the views expressed by Assembly Members led to changes being made in the final form of the legislation.

By the courts

Control by the courts over secondary legislation is sometimes described as judicial review. It takes the form of a decision that a piece of secondary legislation of whatever nature is *ultra vires* (*i.e.* beyond the powers conferred by the parent Act). Whether such is the case or not can often be a very controversial legal issue, as is illustrated by the conflicting speeches of the Law Lords in the Northern Ireland case of *McEldowney* v *Forde* (1971). The issue arose there indirectly and not in judicial review proceedings properly so called, but the difficulty of the point was nonetheless great. The question was whether the Minister of Home Affairs for Northern Ireland was acting *ultra vires* the Civil Authorities (Special Powers) Act (NI) 1922 when he added "republican clubs and any like organisation howsoever described" to the list of associations which were unlawful under that Act. The decision turned on whether this action was "for the preservation of the peace and maintenance of order" and by a majority of three to two the Law Lords held that it was.

The scope of the powers conferred by a parent Act was also in issue (again indirectly) in *R. (Hume)* v *Londonderry Justices* (1972). There the High Court decided that the granting of power to an army officer to order an assembly of persons to disperse was beyond the power of the Stormont Parliament (and its delegates) because the Government of Ireland Act 1920 said that the Parliament of Northern Ireland was not to have power to make laws "in respect of the army". In *Dunkley* v *Evans* (1981), on the other hand, it was held, in England, that the West Coast Herring (Prohibition of Fishing) Order 1978, which was made under the Sea Fish (Conservation) Act 1967 and prohibits herring fishing within a defined area, was not totally invalid just because the defined area included an area of the sea adjacent to the coast of Northern Ireland which was expressly excluded from the scope of the 1967 Act; the Order was invalid only as regards that particular area of sea.

These are all instances of secondary legislation being challenged for substantive violation of the parent Act. Procedural violations, such as not consulting the right people before making the statutory rule or including a provision which prevents the courts from pronouncing on the rule's validity, are also grounds for judicial review, but again the exact attitude of the courts to these problems is somewhat unpredictable. In all cases where secondary legislation is held to be *ultra vires* it ceases to have any force in law and can be disobeyed with impunity. In the 1980s there have been several highly publicised cases of ministerial statutory instruments being successfully challenged in the courts (*e.g.* the cases involving opticians' fees and board and lodging allowances for claimants of supplementary benefit).

The form of secondary legislation

Appendix 3 reproduces a typical example of an Order in Council made under the Northern Ireland Act 1974. It is the Fatal Accidents (NI) Order 1977, which repeals all the previous legislation concerning fatal accidents and restates the law with a few amendments.

The following features of a typical Order in Council may be noted:

(1) *Its number.* Each Order made under the Northern Ireland Act 1974 is given both a United Kingdom statutory instrument number (here it is 1251) and a Northern Ireland Order in Council number (18).

(2) *Dates.* The date on which an Order in Council is made is the date on which the Queen assents to her Privy Consellors' recommendations (here, 26th July 1977). The date on which the Order comes into force is provided for in the body of the Order (see art. 1(2)); sometimes it does not come into force until a further statutory commencement rule is made naming an appointed day.

(3) *The enacting words* ("Now, therefore, Her Majesty . . ."). This is another example of a standard formula; the preliminary phrase beginning "Whereas a draft . . ." is called the preamble.

(4) *Articles.* Each Order is divided into articles (not sections), with the further subdivisions being referred to as paragraphs and subparagraphs. The numbering and lettering systems are the same as for statutes, e.g., art 2(3) (b).

(5) *The first articles.* These are devoted to defining the title of the Order, its commencement date, and the meaning of expressions used in it. In statutes, by contrast, these matters are usually dealt with at the end.

(6) *Explanatory note.* This is provided at the very end of all secondary legislation to give a brief indication of the effects of the legislation. It is comparable to the long title of a statute, but, unlike the long title, it forms no part of the actual enactment and should not be used as an aid to interpretation of the rule.

Appendix 3 also reproduces a short, but fairly normal, statutory rule: the Lobsters (Prohibition of Introduction) Order (NI) 1982. There are no special features of this which require highlighting. We can see that its number in the collection of statutory rules for 1982 is 98, and the attached explanatory note is very helpful in placing the rule in context. Note that even though it is a statutory rule it is actually entitled an "Order" (because the Fisheries Act (NI) 1966 says that the Department of Argiculture may do certain things "by order" and hence its provisions should be called articles; if it were entitled "Rules" or "Regulations", the provisions would be referred to as rule 4, regulation 5, etc.

The problems of looking for secondary legislation

As with statutes, secondary legislation is published singly as well as collectively in annual bound volumes. Orders in Council made under the Northern Ireland Act 1974 are published in the series which used to contain the Acts of the Stormont Parliament. Each annual volume, as well as reprinting the Orders themselves, includes tables showing the United Kingdom and Northern Ireland Acts (and previous Orders in Council) which have been repealed, amended or otherwise affected by Orders in Council made during the year. Further tables indicate the United Kingdom Acts passed during the year which apply in Northern Ireland and the effects of these Acts on previous Irish Acts, Northern Ireland Acts and Orders in Council. The consequences for earlier Acts and Orders of the statutory instruments and statutory rules made during the year are also tabulated.

The last volume for each year of the statutory rules for Northern Ireland contains a list of that year's United Kingdom statutory instruments which affect the province (other than Orders in Council made under the 1974 Act) and there is an index categorising the rules on the basis of the authorities which made them. Further tables supply lists of the changes made by the year's statutory rules not just to earlier Acts and Orders (information which is also given in the annual volume of Orders in Council, see above) but also to earlier statutory rules. A large index to all the statutory rules in force, arranged under subject headings, is published every three years - the last goes up to the end of 1985 but this does not give details of the amendments which later statutory rules may have made to earlier ones: the fully amended text can be gleaned only from reading all of the relevant rules together.

2.4 Judge-made Law

The courts are almost as important a source of new law as Parliament. The law which they create is sometimes referred to as case law or common law, as opposed to Parliament's statute law; this is yet another sense in which the expression common law can be used. Generally speaking, new law is created by the courts in two types of situation: where existing statute law has nothing at all to say about the point in issue, and where that which statute law does have to say is unclear. In the latter situation the role of the courts is to interpret the existing legislation; the techniques they adopt in doing so are examined more closely in the following section. For the moment we shall concentrate on situations where the courts make law untrammelled by any existing pronouncement on the matter by Parliament.

Decisions by judges on novel points of law enter the corpus of case law by being reported in one or more of a series of law reports. Only a very small fraction of judicial decisions are reported in this way, and not all of those which do get reported are significant, for they may simply confirm a point which was already fairly well settled. Reported decisions, however, are important because they are available thereafter for lawyers and judges to refer to in future cases in order to back up an argument; what was decided in the past is a good guide for what should be decided in the present (or, as it is sometimes put, "like cases should be decided alike"). The convention once was that the decisions by courts never really created new law at all - the judges were simply "finding" the law in earlier cases and were "declaring" what it was; today, though, there are few lawyers who still adhere to this somewhat fictional view of the judicial function. Whether we like it or not, judges do make law.

With the advent of computer-based information retrieval systems (of which the best known for legal information is LEXIS), the importance of *unreported* cases has grown. Transcripts of these were previously kept in court libraries, which were not very accessible. Lawyers will sometimes search through unreported cases to see if after all they contain a ruling which could be taken as authoritative on a particular point. Unfortunately, no Northern Ireland cases, reported or unreported, are yet included in the databases of information retrieval systems, but there are plans to rectify this situation. In any event the House of Lords has expressed some scepticism about the utility of citing computer-searched unreported cases.

Law reports

In Northern Ireland there are two main series of law reports: the Northern Ireland Law Reports and the Northern Ireland Judgments Bulletin. Both are published under the auspices of the Incorporated Council of Law Reporting for Northern Ireland. The former is the senior series because it was begun in 1925, but all the reports, before they are published, are checked by the judges to make sure that an accurate account has been given of what took place in the case. The Northern Ireland Law Reports appear in four parts per year and contain cases determined in the superior courts in Northern Ireland and on appeal therefrom to the House of Lords. The Judgments Bulletin, sometimes called the Bluebook from the colour of its cover, has been published since 1970, appearing now almost on a monthly basis and simply reproducing the judges' speeches in a case without an editor's summaries of the facts and decisions or details of the barristers''arguments (which are occasionally given in the Northern Ireland Reports). Many cases reported in the Judgments Bulletin are later reported in the Law Reports too. An index to all Northern Ireland cases reported since 1921 has been published and a supplement has brought it up to date to 1975. The Bar Library (see 3.2) has produced more recent updates.

Appendix 3 reproduces a reported case from the Northern Ireland Law Reports: *Campbell* v *Armstrong and Others* (1981). The summary at the start of the case, written by the editor of the series, is called the headnote. There then follows a list of the previously reported cases (and their references) mentioned by the judge in this case, some of which are Northern Ireland cases and some English. If you read the report you will see a typical example of how a judge goes about deciding a dispute on the basis of existing case law and statute law. The case also illustrates the process of statutory interpretation, which is discussed in the next section.

In England there are several main series of law reports. The "official" ones are the Law Reports (divided into four series for Appeal Cases - that is, decisions in the House of Lords and Privy Council - Queen's Bench cases, Chancery cases and Family cases, these last three also containing Court of Appeal decisions in each category) and the Weekly Law Reports. The most commonly used "unofficial" (that is, privately published) series is called the All England Law Reports. The quality newspapers in England publish short reports of important decisions; the most respected of these series is that issued in *The Times*. All law reports are referred to by well established abbreviations, *e.g.* All ER for the All England Law Reports.

In both Northern Ireland and England the decisions of inferior courts (magistrates' courts and county courts) are virtually never reported, because if a truly novel legal point arises in such courts the case will almost inevitably be appealed to a higher court, where the decision will be reported. In practice, of course, by no means every novel point is appealed, often because the litigants cannot afford the time or money involved. This means that many important points never get the full legal airing they deserve and hence, to the general public's amazement, the law on many commonplace problems can be hazy. For some areas of the law special series of law reports have been devised to help publicise lower courts' decisions as well as the decisions of higher courts which would not otherwise qualify for inclusion in one of the major series. In Northern Ireland we have special series of this sort for decisions of the Lands Tribunal, industrial tribunals and social security appeal tribunals (see Chapter 7). Decisions of courts and tribunals which might not otherwise get reported but which may nevertheless be of some legal interest are noted in the Bulletin of Northern Ireland Law, a publication of the Faculty of Law of the Queen's University of Belfast, which attempts to list all developments of legal interest to Northern Ireland on almost a month-by-month basis. In a typical year there would be no more than 100 new cases reported in Northern Ireland. In England there would be as many as 2,500.

The rules of the doctrine of precedent

In the vast majority of court cases the dispute is really about the facts of the case - what was done, by whom, and when - rather than about the law which is applicable to those facts. Do not expect to visit a courtroom and see the lawyers and judges poring over law books. But when law reports do need to be referred to then the doctrine of precedent comes into play. This doctrine (already mentioned in 1.1) which is sometimes referred to by the Latin phrase *stare decisis* (meaning "stand by things that have been decided"), states that a lower court is obliged to follow a higher court's earlier decision in a similar case unless the previous decision can be "distinguished". A higher court can overrule a lower court's decision, but this just means that the higher court is changing the law from that time onwards, not that the losing party in the earlier decision (which may have been taken years previously) can now have that decision reversed.

As the highest court in the Northern Ireland legal system is the House of Lords, the decisions of that court are obviously binding on all the other courts in Northern Ireland. Strictly speaking this is only true of the House's decisions in cases originating in Northern Ireland, but in practice all of its decisions are treated with the greatest respect. It has even been accepted that an English or Scottish House of Lords decision must be followed in preference to a conflicting decision of the Northern Ireland Court of Appeal. Decisions of the Judicial Committee of the Privy Council (see 1.4) are not absolutely binding on courts in either Northern Ireland or England, but their authority is nevertheless persuasive. Within the province itself decisions of the Court of Appeal are binding on the High Court and Crown Court, and their decisions in turn are binding on the county courts. Magistrates' courts, at the very bottom of the hierarchy, are bound by all other courts.

Decisions of courts at equivalent levels

The rules are less clear when a court on one level is confronted with an earlier decision of another court on the same level. For many years the House of Lords adhered to the practice of holding itself bound by its own previous decisions however much it had come to disagree with them. But by 1966 it was apparent that this practice was leading to the law becoming fossilised while the courts waited for Parliament to enact reforming legislation; it also encouraged judicial resort to spurious distinctions and tenuous refinements in order to escape injustices. In that year, accordingly, the Law Lords issued a Practice Statement stating that in future, while they would normally treat former decisions of the House as binding, they would depart from them whenever it appeared right to do so. In the years since, this new power has been sparingly exercised: there are perhaps seven *clear* instances of its use but on more than one occasion the House has refused to overrule an earlier decision even though it thought that it was wrong.

In England there has been considerable controversy in recent years over whether the Court of Appeal in that jurisdiction should be bound by its own previous decisions. The great advocate for its not being bound was Lord Denning, who as Master of the Rolls was in charge of the Court of Appeal's Civil Division from 1962 to 1982. But as often as Lord Denning refused to follow former cases, even one in which he himself had participated, the House of Lords, on appeal, said that he was incorrect to do so. On this stricter view the Court of Appeal can refuse to follow its own earlier decisions in only three situations: (1) where there are in fact two such decisions which conflict, (2) where the earlier Court of Appeal decision is inconsistent with a subsequent House of Lords decision, and (3) where the earlier decision was announced without proper consideration having been given to earlier cases or statutes pointing the other way (in legal language, *per incuriam*). There is also a practice whereby a Court of Appeal consisting of three judges is not bound by decisions taken by a Court of Appeal consisting of only two judges, but, conversely, a court consisting of more than three judges is not taken to have more binding authority. In criminal appeals the Court of Appeal tends to adopt a slightly more flexible attitude to its own previous decisions in cases where the appellant's loss of liberty would be too high a price to pay for case law uniformity. There is also flexibility in cases where a further appeal beyond the Court of Appeal is not possible.

As it operates in a different jurisdiction the Court of Appeal in Northern Ireland is strictly speaking not bound by decisions of the English Court of Appeal. But it still accords these decisions the greatest respect and will follow them unless there are very strong reasons for not doing so. As regards its own earlier decisions, the Court of Appeal in Northern Ireland adopts the same practice as the Court in England. On situations where there is no possibility of a further appeal to the House of Lords - as for nearly all civil cases begun in the province's magistrates' courts or county courts - the Court of Appeal here may disregard its earlier decision if it considers that it is plainly wrong or too vague and that to follow it would be unjust or unfair. There has to be this flexibility, for otherwise the law would stagnate. In the days before the reorganisation of the courts in the 1870s, it was possible for all judges of the Irish Court of Appeal to sit together as a full Court of Appeal in order to review its previous decisions, and the House of Lords would sometimes ask all the High Court judges to advise it on a certain point, but both these practices have long since been abandoned.

In England and Northern Ireland the High Court will abide by its own previous decisions unless persuaded that these are wrong. Each of these High Courts will also be deferential to earlier decisions of its counterpart, especially if in other respects the law on the matter in question is the same in both countries. One can say the same about the attitude of today's Court of Appeal and High Court in Northern Ireland to decisions of the Court of Appeal and High Court in Ireland taken before partition in 1920: they are not technically binding but will be followed unless patently wrong.

In England, the Divisional Courts (see 1.3) adopt the same attitude to their own previous decisions as does the Court of Appeal. Because the Divisional Court in Northern Ireland rarely sits, it is not possible to state what practice it favours.

The ratio of a case

Of course, whether an earlier decision is wrong or not is largely a matter of opinion, which underlines the fact that the doctrine of precedent is not always as limiting a constraint on the inventiveness of judges as might at first be imagined. It must be stressed, moreover, that the doctrine of precedent obliges lower courts to follow higher courts only if the earlier decisions are exactly in point. This makes it essential to deduce from every reported case the precise principle for which it may later be cited as an authority. This nub of the case is called, in Latin, the *ratio decidendi*, that is to say the legal principle on which the case was decided. Whatever is said by the judges which is not directly on the main point is called *obiter dictum*, literally "something said by the way." Only the *ratio* of a case is binding on later judges. The later judge can avoid applying it only if the facts of the case being dealt with can be significantly distinguished from those of the earlier case; lawyers may expend much time and expertise in attempting to find a valid distinction from an earlier case in order to avoid the rigours of the doctrine of binding precedent.

2.5 Statutory Interpretation

However elaborately it is phrased, no rule embodied in primary or secondary legislation can hope to cater for all the circumstances which may arise for consideration. It can be taken for granted that administrators and judges will need to interpret the legislation in order to decide whether or not it applies to a given fact situation. For instance, if Parliament were to pass a law making glue-sniffing a criminal offence and included in the Act a list of the substances which were to be treated as glue for the purpose of this offence, a court of law might still have to decide what exactly amounted to "sniffing". The people who draft legislation obviously try to reduce the uncertainties as much as possible, but the need for judicial interpretation is ultimately inescapable; human foresight and the English language cannot avoid it. Indeed the task of statutory interpretation is one which occupies a great deal of the time of our judges; certainly the majority of reported cases involve a point of interpretation at some juncture. An example from the Northern Ireland Law Reports is the case of *Morton* v *The Air Ministry* (1946), where Black J. had to decide whether the words "local or other public authority", contained in an Act of the Stormont Parliament, referred to Government departments; he held that they did not. Another illustration is provided by the sample case reproduced in Appendix 3.

The doctrine of binding precedent applies to the topic of statutory interpretation as much as to any other in the law. If the Northern Ireland Court of Appeal pronounces on whether inhaling the vapours of glue through one's mouth qualifies as sniffing glue, then all the lower courts in Northern Ireland must construe the same Act in the same way. This is a topic, moreover, where very often a pertinent English decision exists on the point and if the English legislation is identical to the Northern Ireland legislation then the English court's decision will virtually always be followed in this jurisdiction. (There is legislation concerning glue-sniffing in Scotland: the Solvent Abuse (Scotland) Act 1983 talks of "misusing a volatile substance by deliberately inhaling, other than for medical purposes, that substance's vapour". In the rest of the United Kingdom it is the supply of glue which can sometimes be a criminal offence, not the sniffing of it: see the Intoxicating Substances (Supply) Act 1985).

Every piece of legislation within one jurisdiction is unique and the actual interpretation placed on it will rarely be relevant to the interpretation of other legislation even if the very same words are in issue. But there are certain approaches to the whole process of interpretation which can be applied to all sorts of statutes. They range from what really amount to general philosophies concerning judicial activity to what are in practice quite specific presumptions. Over the centuries the law has fluctuated in its adherence to these various approaches, some of which conflict. Controversy still rages today, so one cannot be dogmatic in asserting that a statutory provision must be interpreted with such and such an attitude in mind. All the approaches, it is readily admitted, have exceptions. With these qualifications in mind, we can briefly attempt to state the prevailing views on statutory interpretation in Northern Ireland today.

The rules of interpretation

In the first place the court should try to ascertain the intention of Parliament when it drafted the particular provision. In their efforts to do this, however, the judges are immediately obstructed by the generally accepted rule that reports of proceedings in Parliament (*i.e. Hansard*) cannot be looked at to see what the MPs and peers who voted for the provision thought it meant. In England Lord Denning more than once deviated from this practice but he was criticised by the House of Lords for doing so. The intention of Parliament has to be deduced instead from the long title of the Act, the unambiguous effects of other provisions in the Act, the omissions from the Act, the state of the pre-existing law, official reports preceding the enactment of the legislation, the practical consequences of preferring one interpretation over another, and the conventional maxims of interpretation which it must be assumed the draftsman was aware of when the Act was written (see below). The most important indication of Parliament's intention, though, is the ordinary meaning of the words themselves; if one of the interpretations being contended for is at variance with that ordinary meaning, it is likely that the ordinary meaning will be preferred. To that extent a purely literal approach to interpretation is shunned. A purposive approach - one which asks the question, "What was Parliament really getting at?" - is nowadays preferred.

Left at that, one might conclude, to return to our hypothetical example, that inhaling glue vapours through one's mouth is tantamount to "sniffing" it. Literally, sniffing is a process carried out only through the nose; colloquially, however, glue-sniffing is used to describe a variety of types of solvent abuse and the intention of Parliament would probably be frustrated if inhaling through the mouth was held not to be covered by the Act. But it is at this point that countervailing principles, presumptions and maxims concerning statutory interpretation must be brought into play. One of these is that a statute which creates a criminal offence must be interpreted as narrowly as possible so as to preserve a person's freedom of action. Another is that the express mention of one of a class of things by implication excludes other items of the same class, so that if the Act in one place refers to sniffing through the nose, then inhaling through the mouth should be taken as not covered by the same word. In some instances these principles and presumptions are so well embedded in our law that they cease to be merely arguments to be taken into account by the judge and become instead obligations requiring the judge to decide the case in a certain way; an example is the principle that one cannot take advantage of one's own (independently) illegal act in order to claim a right under a statute - a murderess cannot claim a widow's pension if the person she killed was her husband (*ex turpi causa non oritur actio*).

Some questions of interpretation recur so frequently that Parliament has provided set solutions. These are to be found in the Interpretation Act (NI) 1954 and the Interpretation Act 1978. The former covers the interpretation of Acts of the Northern Ireland Parliament as well as Orders in Council made under the Northern Ireland Act 1974. The latter covers Westminster legislation applying in Northern Ireland. They deal with such problems as the meaning of "month", whether "man" includes "woman" and whether the singular includes the plural. The Law Commission (see 8.9) is still seeking to persuade the Government to adopt more systematic measures for the avoidance of problems · in statutory interpretation.

2.6 European and International Sources

There are many agencies in the world which promote the conclusion of international agreements. When the Government of the United Kingdom signs these agreements, which may be called treaties, conventions or covenants, it does so on behalf of the people of Northern Ireland as well as those of Great Britain. But merely signing the treaty does not render it a part of United Kingdom national law, nor, usually, does it oblige the United Kingdom to comply with the treaty's provisions *vis-à-vis* other states. For the treaty to be made a part of our national law it must be incorporated into that law by statute; sometimes the treaty will then be appended to the statute in a schedule, at other times its provisions will be reworded but with more or less the same effect; it is Parliament's prerogative to depart from the terms of the treaty to whatever extent it wishes. For the treaty to be made a part of the international law binding the United Kingdom it usually has to be ratified by the Government. This normally occurs after it has been signed and laid before Parliament for 21 days (the so-called "Ponsonby" rule).

Examples of domestic statutes incorporating treaties into our national law are the Recognition of Divorces and Legal Separations Act 1971, the Carriage of Passengers by Road Act 1974 and the State Immunity Act 1978. These implemented Conventions which were concluded, respectively, in 1968, 1973 and 1972, each by a different international agency. Occasionally, because of differences between the pre-existing law in Northern Ireland and that in England, separate legislation is required for the province when treaties are incorporated into Northern Ireland law, *e.g.* the Adoption (Hague Convention) Act (NI) 1969. A good example of a treaty which is binding upon the United Kingdom in international law but not as yet in domestic law is the European Convention on Human Rights, discussed below. Another such treaty is the Anglo-Irish Agreement, signed in November 1985 and since ratified by both the British and Irish Parliaments.

The only context in which the sources of Northern Ireland law are to be found outside the United Kingdom altogether - *i.e.* without the Government's participation in its creation at all - is that of public international law, which concerns relations between states. This has some of its sources in international custom and in the decisions of international tribunals such as the International Court of Justice at The Hague in the Netherlands. It is sometimes said that Common Market law is another such context, but strictly speaking this is not so: as will be explained below, Common Market law has effect in Northern Ireland only because a United Kingdom statute says so.

European Community law

When the United Kingdom joined the European Economic Community (the Common Market) as well as the European Coal and Steel Community and the European Atomic Energy Community, the treaties establishing these Communities (including the Treaty of Rome 1957) were incorporated into United Kingdom law by the European Communities Act 1972. According to the most commonly accepted interpretation of this Act the rules of the common law of the three United Kingdom legal systems (England and Wales, Scotland and Northern Ireland), as well as existing and future United Kingdom legislation, have effect subject to European Community law. European Community law thereby became a new source of law in Northern Ireland.

European Community law falls into three categories: (1) the provisions of the various treaties setting up the Communities, which can be said to constitute the primary law of the EC; (2) the Regulations, Directives and Decisions of the Community institutions, that is, the Council of Ministers and the Commission, whose measures can be called the secondary law of the EC; and (3) the rulings and decisions of the Court of Justice of the European communities. At present the European Assembly (or Parliament) does not have any law-making powers.

Some of the legislative acts in the second category (namely, Regulations and most Decisions) are "directly applicable" in member states of the EC, which means that they have the force of law without the need of any further national legislation. Sometimes they are said to be "self-executing". Regulations are binding in their entirety on all member states, while Decisions are binding only on those states, corporations or individuals to whom they are addressed. Because Regulations are of a more abstract nature than Decisions their administrative details often require to be implemented by specific domestic legislation (see 2.3); they nevertheless become operative when the Regulation says so in order that European Community law shall be uniform throughout the EC at any one time, so that if the British Parliament has not passed any implementing legislation it is still possible for people in the United Kingdom to rely directly upon the Regulation. Decisions, on the other hand, are always binding on addressees without the need for any further implementation.

Directives, despite their name, are not directly applicable: they are binding only as to the result to be achieved by them and it is left to each member state to decide upon the means for giving the Directives legal and administrative effect. The Directive may, however, set a time limit for the implementation of its provisions. Thus, by a Directive of July 1985 the United Kingdom had to alter its law on liability for defective products by July 1988, which it did by the Consumer Protection Act 1987 and the Consumer Protection (NI) Order 1987. As mentioned above in 2.3, the European Communities Act 1972 enables subordinate legislation to be made by the relevant Minister or Government department in connection with the performance of obligations and the exercise of rights under the European treaties.

The European Court of Justice

The European Court of Justice, which sits at Luxembourg, is staffed by 13 judges and six advocates-general, all of whom are chosen by the Governments of the 12 member states of the Common Market. The judges are selected from the people who are eligible for appointment to the highest judicial posts in their own countries or who are jurists of recognized competence. They are appointed for six years at a time. Britain's first judge, Lord Mackenzie Stuart, was appointed in 1972 and was reappointed twice. The current British judge is Sir Gordon Slynn. The judges elect their own President, for a three-year term.

Advocates-general are similar to the court advisers used in continental legal systems but unfamiliar to common law countries. One of them is allocated to each case coming before the Court of Justice. In reporting to the judges their task is threefold: to suggest a solution to the case, to tie in that solution with the existing law, and to set out the likely future developments in the law. But the advocates-general do not actually participate in the drafting of the Court's judgments or in the discussions which lead to the Court's decisions. Although their submissions are not binding on the Court, they are reported alongside the Court's judgment (which is usually very terse and provides no detail of any dissenting opinions) and they do provide useful background material explicating the judgment. (Since 1973 the Court's judgments have been published in English in the European Court Reports.)

The Court of Justice has jurisdiction to hear many different types of case involving European Community law, but the most important are probably those concerned with the validity or interpretation of acts of the Community institutions. If such matters arise during the course of a case before any national court or tribunal of a member state they can be referred to the Court of Justice under article 177 of the Treaty of Rome; the opinion of that Court is then handed back to the local court so that it can be applied to the facts of the particular case. Such referrals can take between six and nine months. Examples of referrals are that made by the resident magistrate in Northern Ireland in the case of *Pigs Marketing Board (Northern Ireland)* v *Redmond* (1978) and that made by the President of Industrial Tribunals in *Johnston* v *Chief Constable of the RUC* (1986). Courts and tribunals "of last instance", that is, those against whose decisions there is no further appeal, are *obliged* to refer such matters to the Court of Justice unless the correct interpretation is quite clear; the Northern Ireland Court of Appeal is a court of last instance in several matters and so is affected by this obligation.

The judgments of the European Court of Justice are binding on the national courts and authorities of the 12 Common Market countries - witness the compliance of the British Government with the decision in the *Marshall* case in 1986 concerning the eligibility of women to retirement pensions - although if the national authorities continue to default, the most that the Court can do is to make an unenforceable declaratory judgment against the government in question; it cannot hold national law to be void. In the vast majority of cases, of course, the national authorities do eventually comply with the Court's judgments.

The Court of Justice, in line with the practice followed in the civil law countries which constitute the majority of EC member states, adopts what to British and Irish lawyers seems an unashamedly creative attitude when faced with problems of statutory interpretation. However, judges in the United Kingdom are beginning to imitate their European counterparts when EC legislation requires to be interpreted; through time this is bound to lead to a more purposive approach to the interpretation of national legislation as well. British draftsmen may take a leaf out of the European book and begin to draft legislation in more general terms. The Court of Justice is also much less committed than British courts to the notion of binding precedent in case law (it can refuse to follow its own previous decisions) and this too may gradually persuade British judges to slacken a little their adherence to that notion.

The European Convention on Human Rights

The European Court of Justice should not be confused with the European Court of Human Rights, which sits at Strasbourg in France. The Court of Human Rights has the job of interpreting the European Convention for the Protection of Human Rights and Fundamental Freedoms, which was drawn up by the Council of Europe in 1950. The Council of Europe is an international organisation formed in 1949 and now comprises 23 Western European states; it is distinct from the European Community, being more active on social and cultural fronts than in economics or politics. The United Kingdom was amongst the first to ratify the Convention in 1951, and it entered into force in 1953, but our Government has not yet taken legislative action to incorporate it into domestic law; it is not therefore part of our national law, but it is binding on the United Kingdom internationally. Courts in the United Kingdom do occasionally look to the Convention as an aid to the interpretation of ambiguous domestic statutes.

The states which are parties to the Convention may be proceeded against for an alleged violation of the Convention by other such states or, if they admit this right (as the United Kingdom and Republic of Ireland do), by their own individual citizens. During 1987 there were 860 individual applications registered with the Commission. Complaints are first considered by the European Commission of Human Rights, which decides whether they are "admissible" within the terms of the Convention. They will not be admissible if all avenues for redress in the national courts have not yet been exhausted. If they are admissible, the Commission will carry out an inquiry and seek to bring about a friendly settlement. If no such settlement is possible, the Commission will issue a report on whether there has been a breach of the Convention. It will also decide whether to refer the case to the Court of Human Rights; if it has not done this within three months of issuing its report, the Committee of Ministers of the Council of Europe can look at the case. Normally cases would go to the Court of Human Rights and only the highly political interstate cases stay in the Committee of Ministers.

There are as many Commissioners and judges eligible to sit in the Commission and the Court of Human Rights as there are member states of the Council of Europe; each government nominates one Commissioner and one judge. The Commissioners are full-time officials but the judges are part-timers. A minimum of seven judges sit in any one case, the decision being by majority vote. The decisions are binding on all the states involved in the case, though in practice states wait some time before altering their national law to bring it into line with the Court's pronouncement. The Court may also order a national government to pay compensation to an aggrieved party.

The Convention's effect on Northern Ireland law

The European Court of Human Rights has held against the United Kingdom more frequently than against any other state (in 20 cases altogether). As a result of decisions by the Court of Human Rights the United Kingdom has had to change its laws on (amongst other things) contempt of court, the closed shop, telephone tapping and corporal punishment in schools. Following a partially substantiated complaint by the Irish Government, the instructions to security forces in Northern Ireland with regard to interrogation techniques had to be altered; and following a complaint by an individual, the law on homosexual offences in Northern Ireland was reformed (the *Dudgeon* case). However, a challenge to the legality of the use of plastic bullets in Northern Ireland failed before the European Commission. In November 1988 the Court held in the *Brogan* case that detention for more than four days under the Prevention of Terrorism Act was a breach of Article 5 of the Convention, which requires detainees to be brought promptly before a judge. In Ireland the Government was obliged to introduce a civil legal aid scheme after a woman successfully complained that the Article of the Convention giving her the right of access to courts was being breached because of the prohibitive costs involved in seeking a decree of judicial separation from her husband (the *Airey* case).

Under Article 15 of the European Convention on Human Rights a state may "derogate from" (*i.e.* ignore) certain of its obligations under the Convention "in time of war or other public emergency threatening the life of the nation". Until August 1984 the United Kingdom issued notices of derogation in respect of the Northern Ireland (Emergency Provisions) Act. It seems likely that parts of the Northern Ireland (Emergency Provisions) Act 1987 were enacted in order to bring Northern Ireland law into line with the requirements of the European Convention, although some would argue that there are still discrepancies. In December 1988 the Government announced that in response to the *Brogan* case it was issuing a notice of derogation in respect of the detention provisions in the Prevention of Terrorism Act (see 4.9). Among the rights under the Convention which are non-derogable are the right to life and the right to be free from torture or inhuman or degrading treatment.

The Standing Advisory Commission on Human Rights in Northern Ireland (see 8.6) has recommended that a Bill of Rights based on the European Convention should be enacted for the whole of the United Kingdom. In 1978 the members of a Select Committee of the House of Lords could not agree on whether a Bill of Rights was desirable but were unanimous that, if there were to be a Bill, it should be based on the European Convention. It rejected the proposal, favoured by others, that the European Community should, as a body, become a party to the Convention. An attempt to have the European Convention incorporated directly into British law narrowly failed in the House of Commons in February 1987.

3

Legal Services

3.1 Seeking Legal Help

Identifying a legal problem

When lay people think of law they usually connect it in their minds with such bodies as the police, the courts and judges. Chapters 1 and 2 may have reinforced this impression, but at this point it is necessary to make it clear that the legal system consists of a great deal more than just police work and court cases. In fact only a very small fraction of legal matters ever involve such steps.

Legal problems arise at very many points in our lives but in the overwhelming majority of instances they are easily solved and no further difficulty ensues. They may arise because you want to achieve some objective but you do not know what is the "proper" way of going about it: what forms must be filled in, whose permission must be sought, what fees must be paid, etc.? Examples are making a will, buying a house, borrowing money, or setting up a business. Alternatively, problems may arise during some quite ordinary everyday activity: something goes wrong and you suddenly find yourself having a dispute with another party. For instance, you may buy some article in the shops only to discover when you take it home that it does not work properly; you may be in regular receipt of supplementary benefit but you find that it is not meeting your needs; you may be sacked from your job; you may have an accident while driving your car; or you may be unable to produce a television licence when the Post Office detector van calls at your house. The other party in such disputes may be an individual, a firm or some branch of government.

Before you are able to seek legal help with any of these problems you must be aware that the problem facing you is indeed a legal one. The existence of a legal problem is by no means always as obvious as may be imagined. You may be in breach of legal regulations but not know this; you may be legally entitled to some benefit or award but, again, be ignorant of this right; you may be perfectly aware that you are in dispute with someone, but neither of you may think of it as a legal dispute - you may simply consider it to be an administrative or an organisational wrangle.

But once you begin to think that the law may have something to say about your predicament, you should act quickly. First of all you should tell a friend or a relative about it. As often as not, just talking over the problem with someone can help you to see another way out of it. Your attention may be drawn to some aspect of the situation which now enables you to clear things up. But if this is not so and you feel the need for further advice or assistance, there are many bodies who may be able to help. Before you consult them you should try to gather together all relevant documents relating to your case. If you have already written letters about it, it will help if you have kept copies of these, or at any rate a summary of what they say. A list giving the precise dates of the various stages in the dispute up to this time can also be most useful.

Advice agencies

There are basically two types of bodies which can give you advice on legal matters. We can call them the "private" and the "public" agencies. The private agencies consist of those organisations to which you may belong which either run an advisory service to allow you to cope yourself with particular kinds of problems or are prepared to treat your problem as in effect their own problem and to act on it accordingly.

Examples of these agencies are trade unions, employers' and traders' associations, some clubs, tenants' groups, claimants' groups, and insurance companies. If you are a member of a trade union, for instance, you will often find your union more than willing to take up a grievance relating to your employment in an attempt to remedy it on your behalf. Insurance companies too will often offer to act for you, as in disputes concerning road accidents. If you are a doctor, the Medical Defence Union may pay your legal costs when you are sued for medical negligence. Obviously the schemes which each of these private organisations operates will differ widely in the degree of assistance they provide; some will expect personal and financial commitments from you, others will not. But the mere fact that someone else is interested enough to help you find a way out of your predicament can be great comfort!

The public agencies are those which exist for the benefit of all people in the community whether or not they have joined a scheme. Some are general agencies: they will advise you on practically every problem you bring to them, even if it is just telling you where you can go for more specialist help. Others deal only with particular types of problems. All of them should be ready to help not just on the legal aspects of your problem but also on its other dimensions - its personal, social and financial features. They will also provide their services free of charge, though needless to say they constantly welcome donations so that they can develop their work. For the most part they are staffed by volunteers who may or may not have professional expertise in the field; if they do not, they should certainly be able to advise you on where to contact the professionals. We will examine a few of these public agencies in more detail.

Citizens' Advice Bureaux

Probably the best known agencies accessible to the general public are the

Citizens' Advice Bureaux (CABx). Begun in 1964, there are currently 29 bureaux in Northern Ireland, plus five so-called "extensions"; the addresses of these can be found in the telephone directory. Their opening hours vary. They give advice on a wide variety of topics, the most frequently recurring being housing, consumer affairs and social security.

When you visit a bureau you will be interviewed in private by one of the advisers. A written record of your case will be made so that if some other adviser has to take over the case at a later stage he or she will know at a glance what has already happened. In most cases it does not take more than half-an-hour for the adviser to listen to your story and let you know what action is recommended. Sometimes the advice will be that you yourself should take certain steps; at other times the adviser will be happy to write letters or make contacts on your behalf. It is wonderful what effect an approach by a semi-official person such as an adviser can have on the other party to a dispute: it shows your sincerity and it may be just enough to persuade the other side to see things your way.

If your case is a complex one or involves a lot of money the adviser will probably want you to contact a solicitor. Every CAB in Northern Ireland has a "referral list" which gives the names of practising solicitors in the area who have agreed to receive cases passed on to them by the Bureau; the adviser should be able to tell you a little about some of these solicitors so that you can decide more easily which of them you think would handle your case best. Some of the bureaux actually have solicitors present acting as advisers: they will be there on a rota basis, ready to be consulted about any case which requires their expertise. If it transpires that the case is one which should be dealt with by a solicitor acting in his or her office rather than as an adviser, it is possible for the solicitor in the bureau to take over your case in a professional capacity. This is only allowed, however, if the solicitor has been previously granted a "waiver" by the professional body for solicitors, the Law Society; without this waiver it would be a breach of the rules against touting and advertising which are imposed on all solicitors.

All the CABx in Northern Ireland belong to the Northern Ireland Association of Citizens' Advice Bureaux, which provides the local bureaux with up-to-date information about changes in the law. It also provides training facilities for the advisers. The National Association of Citizens' Advice Bureaux, based in London, publishes many pamphlets dealing with various aspects of the law likely to be encountered by advisers. Although the details of law and procedure are often different in Northern Ireland, most of these pamphlets are very useful here. Your local bureau should be able to tell you if any parts of the pamphlets do not apply.

During the year ending 31st March 1988, CABx throughout the province handled a total of 134,514 enquiries, very close to the figure of the previous year. By far the largest category of enquiry was social security, which accounted for 34 per cent. The service provided is obviously a very essential one. The Royal Commission on Legal Services, which reported in 1979, recommended that the network of bureaux throughout the United Kingdom should be expanded; it thought that salaried lawyers should be seconded where necessary to act as supplementary internal advisers. The Government supported this recommendation in 1983, but it has not proved so willing to provide the required money for an expansion of CAB services.

Other advice centres

A second important type of generalist advice agency are the Local Advice Centres. Like the CABx, these exist to give advice on all sorts of matters, not just those involving legal issues, but points of law which arise very frequently. As their name implies, the Centres are the result of local initiatives and are often funded, in part at least, by the local district council. Not all are open daily, since their staff are volunteer advisers, though recently some have been appointed under the ACE (Action for Community Employment) scheme. A few of the advisers are qualified lawyers, but most are not. The Law Society does not grant a waiver (see above) to solicitors who do voluntary work in an advice centre and so they are not allowed to take over any of the cases privately.

At the moment there are over 90 Local Advice Centres in Northern Ireland, though they may not always call themselves this. During their busiest periods they may handle a total of 2,000 inquiries a month. You can expect the same sort of personal attention and confidentiality as you would find in a Citizens' Advice Bureau, though unfortunately the Centres do not enjoy the relatively comprehensive back-up services which are provided to the bureaux. They receive some information kits and training from the Belfast Law Centre (see below) but not, at least until recently, on a very systematic basis.

Various other advice agencies exist in Northern Ireland, most of them designed to deal with problems which are peculiar to a particular locality or kind of person. There are many community and tenant organisations, and other bodies such as Alcoholics Anonymous, Belfast Housing Aid, Gamblers Anonymous, Gingerbread (for one-parent families), the Society of St. Vincent de Paul, the Samaritans, Shelter and Women's Aid. There are two Consumer Advice Centres - in Belfast and Derry - which deal with the wide range of consumer affairs. For further details of these agencies, apply to the addresses given in Appendix 2, or consult either *The Northern Ireland Index: A Guide to Voluntary Action* (published by the Northern Ireland Council for Voluntary Action; July 1987) or the latest *Legal Aid Solicitors' List,* published annually by the Law Society of Northern Ireland. Both publications should be available in local libraries.

The Belfast Law Centre

One of the disadvantages of the advice agencies so far described is that they are limited in what they can do. They can give advice and write letters; on occasion they will represent a claimant at a tribunal, or at any rate help the claimant to present his or her case there, but they cannot otherwise do the work of practising lawyers. Their big advantage is that they do not charge for their services. To meet the need for an agency which not only does not charge but can operate almost as a firm of private solicitors, offices called Law Centres have been established. The first one to be set up in Britain was in North Kensington in London in 1970. Today there are about 60 throughout the United Kingdom and one in Dublin. The Belfast Community Law Centre began work in 1977. It changed its name to the Belfast Law Centre in 1980.

The Centre in Belfast reaches out to a larger geographical area than any other Law Centre in Britain and fewer than 10 per cent serve comparable populations. It currently employs 13 permanent staff and one part-time worker; some of these are based in premises outside Belfast. Three of the Belfast workers, including the co-ordinator of the Centre, are qualified solicitors. They have been granted "waivers" by the Law Society; this allows the Centre to act in effect as a firm of solicitors, provided that it does not engage in the major areas of work of private practitioners, such as buying and selling houses, dealing with wills, matrimonial disputes and most criminal work. As a result, the bulk of the Law Centre's cases concern social security, housing, debt and employment problems; immigration law is a particular specialism. At the moment about 4,000 queries are handled each year. Approximately 10 per cent of these would be "retained" by the Centre for further attention; the remainder are either dealt with immediately (83 per cent) or passed on to solicitors or other advisory bodies (7 per cent). Although the largest proportion of queries made relate to social security, the largest proportion of those retained, that is, the most troublesome cases, concern housing. It is difficult to be completely objective, but about 70 per cent of all retained cases are eventually settled to the total or partial satisfaction of the Law Centre.

Generally speaking, the Law Centre deals with cases only if they have been referred to it by another advice agency, such as a Citizens' Advice Bureau. There are now more than 50 of these approved referral agencies. They elect the management committee of the Law Centre and must be independent advice groups: no government agency, statutory body or group with a vested interest may become a referral agency. But this "closed-door" principle has not prevented the proportion of queries originating from unapproved referrals rising to about one-half of the total number of queries made, and many are passed on by probation officers or social services agencies. The Centre does not advertise its existence widely, and is not in the telephone directory, but still it receives a flood of inquiries.

The sort of case which the Law Centre will be most happy to deal with is a test case on some new point; if it can obtain a favourable ruling from a court or a tribunal, this will help all the other people who may be encountering the same problem. Its recent forays in this respect include one case on a private landlord's duty to keep rented premises in good repair and another on the Government's duty to make single payment awards under the social security system to particular claimants rather than in the form of a credit slip redeemable at a shop. In concentrating on test cases the Law Centre is coming close to advancing group interests, much in the way that in America "class actions" can be brought on behalf of a large number of people. This is a welcome development, for the legal system of Northern Ireland is otherwise a highly individualised one, that is, each problem has to be dealt with as it affects a particular person. The review body on civil justice (see 5.1) has recently recommended that the Lord Chancellor should institute a study by a law reform agency (see 8.9) of the case for extending the availability of representative or class actions.

Educational role

Since 1985 an especially important part of the Law Centre's work has been the provision of training and information to other groups giving advice, mainly in the area of welfare rights. Six staff are employed full-time on this work. In 1987 the Centre published the results of a survey of existing local advice provision in each of the four health boards ("Advice Service in Northern Ireland"); having identified the areas where there was a need to extend advice provision, the Centre's officers are in the process of filling the gaps. During the year ending March 1987, a total of 109 training courses were held throughout the province, involving no fewer than 1,691 participants; 80 per cent of the training was in the area of social security law. Several new advice groups have been set up in order to benefit from the training courses.

The Law Centre has always set great store by its educative and preventive role in society. It seeks to avoid potential problems becoming real ones as well as to make people more aware of their rights and duties. In some parts of England this active role has brought Law Centres into conflict with local and central government. In 1979 the Royal Commission on Legal Services suggested that Law Centres should transform themselves into Citizens' Law Centres in line with the model proposed in that Report. The Law Centres Federation (the umbrella organisation for existing law centres) disagreed with this suggestion. To date the Government has not forced through a radically new system, but it has been reluctant to continue to fund some centres and one or two have had to close. The effect of reforms to the legal aid schemes being introduced by the Legal Aid Act 1988 will be to make greater demands on Law Centres. It is to be hoped that adequate funding will be provided to cope with this. At present the Belfast Law Centre runs on a budget of more than £200,000 per annum, granted by the Northern Ireland Office and the Department of Health and Social Services.

Every three years the Belfast Law Centre issues a report on its activities. The latest covers 1985-88. It is also the subject of regular reviews, including one in 1987 by the Policy Planning and Research Unit of the Department of Finance and Personnel.

Pressure groups

The distinction between an advice agency and a pressure group is not always a clear-cut one. In some respects it could be said that the Consumer Advice

Centres, for example, are as much one as the other, for they combine their advisory work with some degree of campaigning about consumers' rights. Of the organisations which are primarily pressure groups the most prominent in Northern Ireland on legal matters are now the Committee on the Administration of Justice and the Northern Ireland Association of Socialist Lawyers. Each of these organisations comprises committed volunteers prepared to investigate alleged injustices and to work for improvements in the legal system. The groups carry out research, publish booklets and make submissions to the Government. As a rule they do not hold themselves out as offering legal advice to individuals, but in a few instances they have helped people to present their cases more persuasively to the authorities.

Some groups with headquarters in England have also taken an interest in the Northern Ireland legal system - and not just in the emergency laws which have been introduced to deal with the troubles. Worthy of mention are the Child Poverty Action Group, the Howard League for Penal Reform, JUSTICE, the Legal Action Group, and the National Council for Civil Liberties. They concentrate mostly on welfare and civil liberties issues. Each of them has individual members in Northern Ireland. If you wish to join or be put in touch with local members, write to the offices in England (see the addresses listed in Appendix 2).

3.2 The Legal Professions

Consulting a solicitor

Should your case be one which you want to take to a solicitor - perhaps after having been advised to do so by the advice agencies - you will need to know how to deal with a solicitor and what the implications may be. Finding a solicitor should present no problem. You or your family may have dealt with one in the past and you may want to use the same person again; a friend or somebody at an advice agency may recommend someone to you; as a last resort you can cast your eye down the list of solicitors in the Yellow Pages of the telephone directory and choose one whose office is close to where you live. It is best to call in person or by telephone in order to arrange an appointment. Bear in mind that some solicitors do not handle certain types of case, so you may have to "shop around" a little.

You should not be apprehensive about consulting a solicitor; he or she should be able to let you know quickly what your legal position is on the matter and what you should do next. But always prepare yourself well before arriving at the solicitor's office: rehearse your story with a friend beforehand and bring along all the relevant documents. If you are worried about the costs involved, you can ask if the solicitor will see you under the fixed-fee interview scheme, which provides you with a 30-minute interview for £5.00 (see 3.3). If the solicitor is unwilling to see you under that scheme, you can certainly ask when you make your appointment how much the initial interview will cost. The cost may be covered by the legal advice and assistance scheme described in the next section. At each interview you can ask how much the next proposed step in the case is likely to cost and whether you will be eligible for legal aid, advice or assistance. You may even contact more than one solicitor and compare their estimated charges before you decide which to engage.

The work of a solicitor

Solicitors became a distinct self-governing profession in Ireland with the creation of the Law Society of Ireland in 1830. In 1922 a Royal Charter was granted to solicitors in Northern Ireland to permit the setting up of the Incorporated Law Society of Northern Ireland. Under a statute passed in 1938 (superseded by an Order in Council in 1976, itself to be amended in 1989) the Law Society obtained the power to issue regulations governing the education, the accounts and the professional conduct of solicitors. The current Accounts and Practice Regulations were issued, with the approval of the Lord Chief Justice, in 1985 and 1987 respectively. All solicitors must register with the Law Society every year (though they need not necessarily become members) and an annual practising certificate will be granted only if the Law Society is sure, amongst other things, that the solicitor is properly insured against loss wrongfully caused to clients.

Today, solicitors' offices are found throughout the province; some 400 are listed in the telephone directory. They vary in size from the small one-person office to the large firm which may have several partners and employ several "assistant" solicitors - the latter are fully qualified solicitors who do not have a stake in the ownership of the firm. The firm will also employ secretarial staff and perhaps one or two apprentices; unlike English firms, solicitors in Northern Ireland rarely employ assistants called legal executives. The size of the firm should not affect the quality of the service provided, nor should it greatly influence the charges. Remember that solicitors are in effect professional business people, who need to pay overheads and make a profit. In a sense they are handicapped in this activity because the Law Society does not permit them to advertise or attract business through, for example, price-cutting or sharing offices with non-solicitors. The rules on these matters have recently been relaxed a little in England, but the only foreseeable change in Northern Ireland (which is not of any significance to clients) is that firms of solicitors will soon be allowed to incorporate themselves as limited companies.

The daily work of a solicitor can be very varied. Most of it is office work, though solicitors do have what is called "the right of audience" in magistrates' courts and county courts (and some Crown Court matters), which means that they can speak on behalf of their clients in those courts. Traditionally that is the role of barristers, who still, as we shall see, retain the exclusive right of audience in the higher courts. The largest single category of solicitors' work is conveyancing (the transfer of land and buildings), which occupies about one-third of their time and represents an even greater proportion of their income; the other important categories are matrimonial work, succession work (*i.e.* dealing with the consequences of a death), criminal work and compensation claims. If the firm is large enough it will probably have a litigation department to deal with those cases which may involve court actions; the vast majority of such actions are eventually "settled" (*i.e.* compromised) out of court and it is an essential part of a solicitor's function to try to arrange such a settlement. The time and cost involved in actually bringing matters to court are such that it is a step to be taken only as a very last resort; even during the course of a court hearing the two sides to a dispute may agree to settle it, which then leads to a judgment by consent (see 5.1).

Though varied, much of a solicitor's work is fairly routine. If it does not involve a dispute with another party, it is called non-contentious work, the charges for which are calculated on a different basis from that used for contentious work (see 3.4). All solicitors can now also function as Commissioners for Oaths, and 14 act as notaries public. The former are required as witnesses for certain official documents, though they cannot witness documents prepared by themselves or by their opponents in a case. Notaries public are lawyers who can witness documents for use abroad. As regards two matters solicitors have a virtual monopoly: the drawing up of a conveyance on the sale of land, and the taking out of probate or letters of administration when someone dies; it is a criminal offence, with some minor exceptions, for anyone who is not a solicitor to undertake either of these tasks if payment is demanded for the work. In England the first of these monopolies was removed when the Administration of Justice Act 1985 provided for the licensing of non-solicitor conveyancers, but as yet this freedom of trade has not been extended to Northern Ireland.

Complaints against solicitors

If you wish to complain about a solicitor you should first of all discuss the matter thoroughly with the solicitor involved. You should realise that, because technically they are officers of the Supreme Court, the primary duty of solicitors is not to their clients but to the courts. They certainly must act for you to the best of their ability but this does not allow them to conceal evidence or to ignore established procedures. However, if you are not satisfied with your solicitor's explanation in relation to your complaint you can write to the Law Society about the matter. All complaints are dealt with by the Secretary of the Law Society, and the more serious cases are considered by the Practice Committee. This Committee may either reprimand the solicitor or refer the case to the Disciplinary Committee. The latter is not a part of the Law Society, but it is still comprised solely of solicitors (chosen by the Lord Chief Justice); it has the power, amongst other things, to strike a solicitor off the Solicitors' Roll or to impose a fine of up to £500 (soon to be increased to £3,000). An appeal against a decision of the Disciplinary Committee can be taken by any person affected by it to a judge of the High Court.

There is a proposal to change the Disciplinary Committee into a

Disciplinary Tribunal and include lay representatives on it, but this will probably not be done until 1990. The new legislation will also enable the Law Society and the Tribunal to deal with shoddy professional services which may not amount to misconduct or negligence. The Disciplinary Tribunal, it is envisaged, will be able to order the solicitor to remit all or part of the legal fees charged for the work in question.

The Law Society will consider complaints alleging negligence only if the behaviour would amount to professional misconduct. Other cases of negligence must be processed in the ordinary way through the civil courts (see 5.3 and 5.6) or dealt with under the Solicitors Arbitration Scheme. This was set up in 1988 under the auspices of the Chartered Institution of Arbitrators; the client and the solicitor each pay £46 to allow an independent arbitrator to examine all the documents in the case (there is no hearing as such) and come to a decision. The loser may be ordered to refund the other party's fee for the arbitration and cannot take the matter further (*e.g.* to a court).

Since 1977 Northern Ireland has had an official called the Lay Observer, a non-lawyer whose job it is to report on the nature of complaints being made to the Law Society about the conduct of solicitors and the manner in which the complaints are being dealt with by the Society. The reports are made to the Lord Chief Justice, the Department of Finance and Personnel, and the Council of the Law Society, but unlike the reports of the Lay Observer in England they are not made public. It is understood that about 300 complaints are monitored each year, but it is impossible to say what the ultimate consequences are. Certainly the Lay Observer has no power to punish solicitors or compensate complaining clients. It is possible that the Lay Observer's powers will be increased under the proposed Solicitors (Amendment) (NI) Order 1989.

The work of a barrister

In a small proportion of the cases handled by solicitors it will be necessary for the services of a barrister to be used. Barristers, or "counsel" as they are sometimes called, are experts in advocacy and have the sole right of audience in the higher courts. They began to organise themselves in Ireland as a professional body (the Bar) as long ago as the thirteenth century and in 1541 their headquarters became the King's Inns in Dublin. Following partition, judges and practising barristers in Northern Ireland formed their own Inn of Court of Northern Ireland in 1926. The governing bodies of the profession are the Inn of Court's 19 "benchers", who include the 10 Supreme Court judges, and the Executive Council of the Inn, while the Bar Council, elected by practising barristers, oversees standards and in effect acts as the profession's "trade union".

In contrast with solicitors, who mostly work in firms, barristers are self-employed and are not permitted to form partnerships. In England they share premises known as chambers and are referred to as having tenancies in those chambers. In Northern Ireland (as in Scotland and the Republic of Ireland) the tradition is for all barristers to work out of a Bar Library, which is situated in

Belfast in the Royal Courts of Justice, Chichester Street. That is where solicitors will contact them. There is no need therefore for barristers' clerks, who in England effectively act as business managers in each of the chambers and take a commission on the fees earned. In Northern Ireland the fees are negotiated directly between barrister and solicitor. As it is technically the solicitor who engages the barrister, even though the client may have asked for a particular barrister to be used, the barrister cannot sue the client for fees if they are not paid; by tradition the barrister cannot sue the solicitor either. Barristers who are "briefed" by solicitors must undertake to work on the case unless they do not have the time, or a proper fee is not offered, or they are in some way personally involved in the case; this is known as the "cab-rank principle". There is little specialisation at the Bar in Northern Ireland, so it is rare for a barrister to avoid work on the ground that it is not within his or her usual sphere of practice (therefore requiring too much time to perform properly).

Experienced barristers may apply to the Lord Chief Justice to "take silk", that is, to become a Queen's Counsel (QC). After appointment as a QC a barrister will not generally appear in court without a "junior", as all other barristers are called, and will charge higher fees. The distinction between these senior and junior barristers is sometimes reflected in talk of the Inner and Outer Bars. Most judicial appointments are open only to practising barristers of a certain number of years' standing (see 1.5), so needless to say most of the judges are former QCs. In February 1989 there were 38 QCs and 277 junior barristers in Northern Ireland. The first ever female QC was appointed in that month.

A solicitor will need to consult a barrister whenever an expert's opinion is required as to what the chances are of successfully arguing a particular point in court. The client cannot approach the barrister directly: the latter must be briefed by a solicitor, a rule which is intended to filter out the less difficult cases so that barristers can concentrate on the more important ones. A written opinion by the barrister will often satisfy the client's needs, and even if the case does eventually come to court the client will probably meet the barrister there for the first time: only in a few cases is it deemed necessary for there to be a "conference" with the barrister and solicitor prior to the day of the trial. For cases being heard in the High Court (see 5.6) it is the barrister who drafts the pleadings. Once a barrister is involved in a case he or she will advise the client whether or not to accept an offer of settlement. Otherwise that advice can be given by a solicitor, though sometimes counsel is briefed purely to advise on settlement negotiations.

The work of barristers, it can be seen, is somewhat different from that of solicitors. That the legal systems of England and Northern Ireland should retain this division of labour at all is an anomaly of history. Many other countries whose legal systems are based on the English "common law" system - among them the United States of America and Canada - have long since abandoned the distinction, though it remains in the Republic of Ireland. The main argument for fusing the two professions is that it would reduce costs, but at the moment there are so many vested interests at stake that fusion is an extremely far-off ideal. A tiny step towards fusion was taken by the European Communities

(Services of Lawyers) Order 1978 which, under strict conditions, allows lawyers qualified in other EC member states to provide services in the United Kingdom which could otherwise be provided only by barristers or solicitors. This cross-border legal activity will be facilitated by the creation of the single European market in 1992. Further steps towards fusion may result from the Government's green paper on the legal professions, published in January 1989.

Complaints against barristers

Complaints should be directed to the Complaints Committee of the Bar's Executive Council, which may conduct a hearing on the matter. No lay persons sit on this committee, however, and it does not have power to suspend or disbar a barrister; this can be done only by the benchers, who deal with the serious cases of misconduct. Again, if a client wishes to allege that a barrister has been negligent, he or she will need to begin a civil action. Barristers and solicitors are immune from being sued in respect of their performance as advocates in court (just as judges are immune in respect of their performance as adjudicators), but they can be sued in connection with pre-trial work.

Legal education

There is practically no instruction given in law to school-children in Northern Ireland. The province's Schools Examinations Council does not have a syllabus in law at either GCSE or 'A' Level. Any examinable courses which are followed will therefore usually be organised from England and will deal with English law. There is one university law faculty at the Queen's University of Belfast and a School of Legal and Administrative Studies at the University of Ulster at Jordanstown. Both institutions offer a variety of degree, certificate and diploma courses, some taken through study at evening classes. Other colleges of further education provide lower-level instruction in law.

The way to become a solicitor or barrister in Northern Ireland is to complete successfully the vocational course organised by the Institute of Professional Legal Studies at Queen's University. A person can apply for this course if he or she has a law degree (of at least second class honours for intending barristers) or, having another kind of degree, has completed a Certificate in Academic Legal Studies at Queen's (two years full-time or three years part-time). All applicants, however, must also sit an admissions test specifically designed to assess their aptitude for practising law, and some candidates will be interviewed. In 1988 there were 90 places on the Institute's course, of which approximately 20 were for prospective barristers and the remainder for trainee solicitors. Department of Education bursaries are available for all but 20 of the 90 places, the rest being fee-paying. Every year there are many more applicants than there are places.

For intending solicitors the Institute course is now a component part of a two-year "apprenticeship". The first four months are spent in a solicitor's office, the student having found a so-called "master" before gaining admission to the

Institute. The next year consists of lectures and vocational exercises at the Institute, at the end of which the student sits examinations for a Certificate in Professional Legal Studies. The service in a solicitor's office is then continued for a further eight months. This qualifies the student for a restricted practising certificate, which means that for two years he or she cannot practise on his or her own account or in partnership, but only as an assistant solicitor in a firm or under a solicitor in a public body or government service. "Apprentice" solicitors are the equivalent of what are termed "articled clerks" in England. A further prerequisite for a full practising certificate is attendance at Continuing Legal Education seminars.

For intending barristers the Institute course runs for nine months, from October to June. They then obtain their Certificate in Professional Legal Studies and are "called to the Bar" in the following September. For a further 12 months they must serve a "pupillage", acting as "pupils" to experienced "masters" (barristers of at least eight years' standing at the Bar). During the first three months of this year they accompany their master to court and learn how things are done in practice; during the next three months they can take cases by themselves in the motions court (see 1.3), but only after the first half of the year can they accept other types of fee-earning work. It may be some months before they actually begin to receive an income from the briefs they have handled for solicitors.

In exceptional cases the arrangements just described for admission to the legal professions may be altered. This is particularly so for applicants who have already worked as a law clerk in a solicitor's office for seven years, for university lecturers in law and for persons who are professionally qualified in other jurisdictions.

The troubles in Northern Ireland have coincided with a dramatic increase in the numbers wishing to practise law: in 1965 there were 500 solicitors and about 60 barristers, but by mid-1988 there were over 1,000 solicitors and nearly 300 barristers. There is one barrister in Northern Ireland for every 5,500 residents; in England and Wales the ratio is 1:9,000 and in Scotland it is 1:25,000. The number of would-be students remains high today, despite the sizeable expenses which must be incurred and the low incomes received during the lengthy training periods. Unfortunately, unlike the situation in England, there is no longer an increasing workload to absorb all the fresh recruits. The problem is a constant headache for the Council of Legal Education for Northern Ireland which, as the governing body of the Institute of Professional Legal Studies, has the responsibility for deciding policies and setting standards concerning admission to the Institute.

Lawyers not in private practice

Not everyone who obtains a law degree or qualifies as a solicitor or barrister will actually want to try to practise law. Many will find employment in other positions where they can use their legal knowledge in less direct ways. Government departments (including the Northern Ireland Court Service), district councils, the Housing Executive, public companies, watchdog bodies and teaching institutions all engage such persons in various capacities. On account of the smallness of the province, however, there is obviously not the variety of opportunities that there would be in Great Britain. Few qualified solicitors who are so employed will want, or be permitted, to continue to hold a practising certificate, but barristers, being otherwise self-employed, are usually a little freer in this respect. One disincentive, perhaps, is the requirement laid down by both the Law Society and the Bar Council that their members must at all times be covered by a professional indemnity insurance policy, the premium on which can be very costly. Occasionally an employer will pay this on the employed lawyer's behalf.

The future of the professions

In January 1989 the Government published three green papers relating to the work of the legal professions in England and Wales; similar proposals are to be made for Northern Ireland. The main professional division is unlikely to remain that between barristers and solicitors but instead to become one between lawyers who are certified advocates and those who are not. Advocates will be allowed to contract directly with clients, while all lawyers will be permitted to practise in firms offering other business services. Lawyers will be able to issue advertisements, and it will become lawful to supply legal services on a "no win, no fee" basis. The office of the Lay Observer is to be replaced by a Legal Services Ombudsman similar to existing commercial ombudsmen (see 8.1). On the whole the Government's proposals have been welcomed except by the Bar. It remains to be seen to what extent they will be implemented.

3.3 Legal Aid, Advice and Assistance

There are three quite separate state schemes - the first of which has a variant which really constitutes a fourth scheme - for the provision of financial assistance in legal matters. By and large these schemes operate regardless of the nature of the legal problem involved, but a few special problems are not covered, such as libel and slander actions or queries about the law outside Northern Ireland. Some matters are catered for by separate specially designed schemes, like the assistance which the Equal Opportunities Commission is empowered to give in some cases of alleged sex discrimination (see 8.5). Individuals may also receive financial assistance from purely private sources; your employer or trade union may help you, or a club to which you belong (*e.g.* the Automobile Association). It is also possible to take out an insurance policy against the incurring of legal expenses, though these vary, of course, in the degree of protection they provide. If you have rights to such private help but resort instead to the state schemes, the state schemes may be able to seek an indemnity (*i.e.* reimbursement) from the sources of private help; this applies mainly to insurance policies.

Probably the most widely used of the non-state schemes is the fixed-fee interview scheme, which certain solicitors operate. Under this the client can receive half-an-hour's interview with a solicitor for a flat fee of £5 (which includes VAT). This contrasts with the £15 or £20 which would normally be charged for such a period. Anyone can qualify for this assistance, though it is at the discretion of the solicitors participating in the scheme whether or not they will see a particular person under it. The names of the solicitors who may be prepared to give a fixed-fee interview are indicated in the *Legal Aid Solicitors' List*, which is available from the Legal Aid Department of the Law Society of Northern Ireland, and from Citizens' Advice Bureaux, public libraries, etc. The scheme can even be used as a means of discovering whether you would be likely to qualify for help under one of the state schemes.

The three state schemes provide for legal advice and assistance, legal aid for civil court proceedings, and legal aid for criminal court proceedings. It is not possible to enjoy assistance under the first scheme at the same time as you are receiving aid under one of the other two schemes, but it can happen that aid under both the second and third schemes is given to a person who is involved in civil as well as criminal proceedings arising out of the one incident. We will now examine each of these schemes separately. They operate on the basis of the Legal Aid, Advice and Assistance (Northern Ireland) Order 1981 and numerous complex regulations made thereunder or under previous legislation. New consolidated regulations are expected to be made in 1989. These will probably reflect changes introduced into English law by the Legal Aid Act 1988. When the Law Society takes a decision on a legal aid matter it is not possible to appeal against that decision to the courts. It is possible, though, to take judicial review proceedings (see 7.1), and at times the judges give guidance on the schemes in the course of their judgments.

The legal advice and assistance scheme

When this scheme was started in Northern Ireland in 1974 it was confined to the giving of oral advice. It was extended to written advice in 1978 and was sometimes referred to as "the £25 scheme", as that was the limit on the value of the assistance which could be granted under it. In 1980 this limit was raised to £40 and in 1983 to £50, but the Legal Aid Advisory Committee (see below, page 85) has recommended a further increase to £75. The scheme is now popularly referred to as "the green form scheme", after the colour of the appropriate application form. The form is reproduced (in black and white!) in Appendix 4.

The decision whether to grant legal advice and assistance is made by a solicitor. When you go for your initial interview, whether this is under the fixed-fee system or not, you can ask the solicitor to calculate whether you qualify under the legal advice and assistance scheme. Solicitors can even accept applications from persons residing outside Northern Ireland, but they cannot grant assistance in any matter which has already attracted assistance unless they first obtain the permission of the Law Society.

Eligibility

The eligibility test applied by the solicitor is a purely financial one: the "merits" of your legal position are irrelevant. The stipulated financial limits are revised every year. As from April 1988 you will not qualify if you have what is termed "disposable capital" of more than £850. This is an absolute disqualification, regardless of how low your weekly income is. "Disposable capital" basically means the savings you have in a bank, post office, building society or premium bonds, or any "valuables" such as a car or jewellery; the value of capital assets such as a privately owned house, household furniture or personal clothing is ignored because these items are considered to be "indisposable." If your disposable capital is less than £850 you will qualify for advice and assistance if you are in receipt of income support or family credit, or if you have a "disposable income" of less than £122 per week. "Disposable income" basically means your take-home pay minus your regular living expenses (for rent, rates, hire-purchase payments and other necessary outgoings).

Your solicitor will help you to work out your disposable capital and disposable income. The value of the subject matter of the problem (*e.g.* a car whose ownership is in dispute) must be ignored for this purpose. Normally the capital and weekly income of your husband or wife must be included in the calculations. If you have dependants - a spouse, child, or other relative - the maximum disposable capital for financial eligibility is increased (by £200 for the first dependant, £120 for the second, and £60 for others). Allowances are made as well in the assessment of disposable income: £30.95 for a spouse, £13.45 for a child under 11, etc. The solicitor will also be able to tell you whether you will be required to make a contribution to the advice and assistance granted to you and, if so, how much. You will have to contribute if your disposable income exceeds £58 per week, the size of the contribution depending on your exact income. It will vary between £5 and £67, being always approximately £55 less than your disposal weekly income. The solicitor will usually agree to the payment of these contributions by instalments, if necessary.

A solicitor is entitled to give you £50 worth of advice and assistance under the green form scheme, which represents about one-and-a-half hour's work and excludes an allowance for VAT. If the work needed to be done will cost more than £50 the solicitor can apply to the Law Society for an extension on the upper value of the work he or she can do. The Law Society will grant the extension if it is satisfied that it is reasonable for the advice and assistance to be given and that the estimated amount of the costs to be incurred in giving it is fair and reasonable. It is obviously only in these cases of extended assistance that your contribution to the costs can be more than £50.

Assistance by way of representation (ABWOR)

The solicitor can do all kinds of legal work under the legal advice and assistance scheme, including the preparation of applications for civil or criminal legal aid certificates (see below). So he or she may write letters for you, draft documents (such as a will), negotiate with someone, take statements, get an opinion from a barrister, or prepare a case to help you appear before a tribunal. Before 1980 the solicitor could not personally represent an assisted person in court or before a tribunal. Now, however, such representation is possible in a limited range of situations:

(a)   Whenever a solicitor successfully applies for the approval of the Law Society to represent a client in certain civil proceedings in a magistrates' court (domestic cases, debt or land cases and some welfare cases); the Law Society will grant its approval only if it is shown that there are reasonable grounds for taking, defending, or being a party to the proceedings and that the application is not unreasonable in the particular circumstances of the case; this "merits" test distinguishes this variant of the legal advice and assistance scheme from situations not involving representative work.

(b)   If a person appearing before a magistrates' court or a county court is unrepresented, a solicitor who is within the precincts of the court may be asked, or may apply, to represent that person; this enables "duty solicitor" schemes to be set up, whereby a solicitor happening to be on duty may be called in to help unrepresented persons. Such a scheme has operated in Belfast's magistrates' court since 1982. A similar scheme has been running in Craigavon since 1986, but is now on a "call out" basis only, not "in court" as well.

(c)   Proceedings before the Mental Health Review Tribunal (see 7.4), provided the application is reasonable, and disciplinary hearings before the Boards of Visitors at prisons (see 1.6).

Representation under the legal advice and assistance scheme - or indeed under the legal aid schemes to be described shortly - is still not possible in any other kind of tribunal except the Lands Tribunal. The Legal Aid Advisory Committee has argued for the extension of the representation scheme to industrial tribunals, but the Government has not yet acceded to this. However, a solicitor can still give you advice and assistance (short of representation) on a case which is due to come before any sort of tribunal.

In cases of ABWOR the disposable capital limit for eligibility is the same as for legal aid in civil proceedings (£3,000; see below). But the rule still applies that only £50 worth of assistance is obtainable unless the Law Society grants an extension.

How the legal costs are recouped

The difference between the value of the work done for a client under the advice and assistance scheme and the amount of contributions which the client may have to pay is recoverable by the solicitor out of (in order of priority): (a) the costs which the other side agrees, or is ordered by the court, to pay to the assisted person; (b) the property which is recovered or preserved for the assisted person in the case, unless it is exempted property such as a house or maintenance payments; (c) the Legal Aid Fund, which is an account established and administered by the Law Society. The debt owed to the solicitor constitutes a "charge" on these three funds, but the charge may not be enforced against (b) if, on the application of the solicitor, the Law Society so authorises. The solicitor can make this application whenever he or she thinks that enforcing the so-called "clawback" provision would cause grave hardship or distress to the client or would be unreasonably difficult because of the nature of the property.

In short, under the green form scheme if you win your case you will normally end up paying little or nothing towards the overall costs involved: any contributions you have already paid will be recouped by the award of costs made in your favour by the judge; if you lose, the cost to you should normally not exceed the amount of the contribution payable under the scheme. If a person who is assisted by representation is ordered by the court to pay the costs of the proceedings, he or she does not have to pay more than what the court thinks is reasonable having regard to all the circumstances. The other side may recover the balance of the costs from the Legal Aid Fund.

The Law Society's Legal Aid Committee has issued guidelines (*not* rigid rates) for the assessment of costs for work done under the green form scheme. At present these suggest an award of £34.50 an hour for preparation of the case and attendances at hearings. For waiting and travelling time lawyers can expect to receive £19.50 an hour and for advocacy (under the ABWOR scheme) £43 an hour. Letters and phone calls are normally remunerated at the rate of £2.65 each.

In 1986-87 the Law Society approved the payment of legal fees in 32,867 cases where oral or written advice was provided by solicitors. This represents a 6 per cent increase on the number of claims paid in 1985-86. Almost half the cases involved criminal matters. In addition, 4,197 claims were refused on financial and other grounds. During the same year there were 8,732 applications by solicitors for authority to exceed the £50 limit; only 303 of these were refused. Contributions were paid in 630 cases, the amount received totalling just £6,782. Also in 1986-87 there were 10,644 applications for authority to proceed by way of representation; 10,493 were granted, all but 60 of these cases involving family law matters. £13,384 was taken in as contributions. Approximately £1.75 million was paid to solicitors out of the Legal Aid Fund for work done under the green form and ABWOR schemes in 1986-87.

Legal aid for civil proceedings

Legal aid for court proceedings in civil cases was not introduced in Northern Ireland until 1965, 16 years after its introduction in England and Wales. The civil aid schemes remain very similar in both jurisdictions.

If you are honestly contemplating civil court proceedings, whether as plaintiff or defendant, you should contact a solicitor. He or she can help you to fill in the relevant legal aid forms, but the decision whether to grant civil legal aid in any particular case is taken not by the solicitor but by officials of the Law

Society, to which the forms will be sent. Persons living outside Northern Ireland can apply for legal aid for civil proceedings which are to take place within Northern Ireland, but persons living outside the province who want aid for proceedings elsewhere - whether England, Scotland, the Republic of Ireland, or further afield - must apply to the authorities in those countries.

The "merits" test

An important difference between the civil legal aid scheme and the legal advice and assistance scheme (apart from ABWOR) is that for the former there is not only a financial eligibility test to be satisfied but also a "merits" test. As regards the financial limits, you will be eligible for civil legal aid from April 1988 if your disposable capital is not more than £5,000 and your disposable income does not exceed £5,765 per annum. As the capital limit is quite high, more people qualify under this scheme than under the legal advice and assistance scheme. If your disposable capital is more than £5,000 you may still be granted aid if you cannot afford to proceed without legal aid because the costs of the case are likely to be too great, but the £5,765 limit on disposable income is absolute. Your disposable capital and income are calculated in similar ways to those described for legal advice and assistance, except that the calculation is performed by the Legal Aid Assessment Office of the Department of Health and Social Services. In calculating disposable capital no allowances are made for dependants, but allowances are made in calculating disposable income: they are the same as for legal advice and assistance claims, though converted from weekly into annual amounts.

Once you have shown that you are within the financial limits, the Law Society's Legal Aid Department must still be persuaded that you have reasonable grounds for being a party to the proceedings and that it is not unreasonable for you to receive legal aid in the particular circumstances of the case. So if the action is a trivial one, or if the cost to the Legal Aid Fund would be disproportionate to the advantage you might gain from the litigation, legal aid may be refused even if you are financially eligible. This is the same "merits" test as needs to be satisfied in applications for representation under the legal advice and assistance scheme, and indeed civil legal aid may be refused if representation under that scheme would be more appropriate. As it can take several weeks for both the financial and merits tests to be considered, there is a procedure for applying for an "emergency certificate", which can be granted at once provided you promise to pay whatever contributions are later assessed. If a civil or emergency certificate is refused on the ground that the merits test has not been satisfied, you may appeal to a committee of the Law Society but not to a court.

Financial contributions

Contributions towards the cost of civil legal aid have to be made by applicants whose disposable capital is between £3,000 and £5,000 or whose disposable income is between £2,400 and £5,765. Any part of the excess capital can be requested as a contribution, but only one quarter of the excess income can be requested. The contributions can be required to be paid in one sum or in instalments. Further contributions do not usually have to be made if another application is made in respect of an appeal in the case to a higher court.

Coverage under the scheme

If the Law Society considers that you have fulfilled both the financial and merits tests, it will grant you a civil aid certificate. This will cover legal services by a solicitor or barrister both before and during a court hearing. You are entitled to choose any solicitor (and, if needed, any barrister) to act in your case: you do not have to stick to the one who forwarded your application for legal aid to the Law Society or to the one from whom you may have already received legal advice and assistance. Practically every type of hearing is within the civil aid scheme, with the exceptions of tribunals (other than the Lands Tribunal), arbitrations (which include proceedings in a small claims court) and coroners' courts. In Northern Ireland "care" proceedings regarding children and bail applications for scheduled criminal offences (see 4.1) are classified as civil matters for this purpose, as in fact are all appeals in the Court of Appeal on a case stated by a magistrates' court (even in what is otherwise undoubtedly a criminal case). The cost of taking proceedings in the Enforcement of Judgments Office (see 3.4 and 5.7) or of referring an issue to the European Court of Justice (see 2.6) is also covered by the scheme. People who take cases under the European Convention on Human Rights can benefit from a special legal aid scheme administered in Strasbourg (see 2.6). Particular types of case are excluded in all courts, such as libel and slander claims, admitted debts, and claims relating to elections.

While the case is progressing, your solicitor will be in regular contact with the Law Society. Before certain steps can be taken, such as the engagement of a barrister in a magistrates' court or a Queen's Counsel in a county court or High Court case, the permission of the Law Society must be sought. But there is no £50 limit on the value of the legal work that can be done for you as there is under the advice and assistance scheme.

How the legal costs are recouped

The solicitor will be paid for the work, as will any barrister involved in the case, out of the Law Society's Legal Aid Fund. In proceedings at or above High Court level the work will generally be paid for at 95 per cent of the normal rate for work not legally aided. In county court proceedings the full rate will be paid if the costs are "taxed" (see 3.4); if the costs are not taxed, and in all magistrates' court proceedings, the sums paid will be in accordance with scales of renumeration laid down in regulations. At the moment these allow for maximum payments of, for instance, £700 (plus outlays) to a solicitor in a county court case and a basic £36.75 (plus £12.60 per day, and outlays) to a solicitor in a magistrates' court case. In exceptional cases a judge can order that these scales should not apply.

Once the case is over, any sums recovered by the assisted person by virtue of a court order (or agreement) for costs must be paid to the Legal Aid Fund. If these exceed the sums paid out of that Fund on the assisted person's behalf the excess is retained by the Fund; if they are less, the balance is recouped from the assisted person's contributions, the amount unused, if any, being returned. If even the contributions are not enough to satisfy the debt owed to the Legal Aid Fund, a "charge" may be imposed on any property recovered or preserved by the proceedings. This charge is similar to the solicitor's charge in connection with legal advice and assistance mentioned above, but unlike that charge it cannot be waived. The Law Society can, however, take its time over enforcing it and may accept an alternative charge on substitute property; certain forms of property, such as maintenance payments, are in any event exempt from the charge. If an assisted person happens to be insured against the legal expenses incurred, the insurance money received must be paid to the Legal Aid Fund. If the Fund is still owed money after all this, the loss must be borne out of the public purse.

If an unassisted party wins a case against an assisted party the court may order the former's costs to be paid out of the Legal Aid Fund, provided that this is just and equitable in all the circumstances and that (except in appeals) the unassisted party would otherwise suffer severe financial hardship.

During the year ending 31st March 1987 there were 19,517 applications for civil legal aid. This is an 11 per cent increase on the previous year's figure, with most of the rise occurring in county court applications. Civil aid certificates issued totalled 13,108 of which 2,579 were emergency certificates. Only 95 certificates were issued for magistrates' courts, largely because solicitors preferred to use the ABWOR scheme. In four out of every five cases no financial contributions were required from the aided person, with only £223,000 being contributed altogether. The cases where damages were being claimed netted a total of £19 million and in approximately 200 cases deductions were made from the damages awarded because of the Legal Aid Fund's statutory charge.

Legal aid for criminal proceedings

Criminal legal aid has been available in one form or another for decades. The two distinguishing features of the present scheme are that the decision whether or not to grant aid is taken by the court itself (not by a solicitor or by the Law Society) and that, if it is granted, the aid is free; unlike the scheme in England, no contributions are required from the aided person. However, if it transpires that the oral or written statement of means provided to the court by the applicant for legal aid is incorrect, the court may then take action to recover some or all of the costs from the applicant.

The scheme allows for a criminal aid certificate to be granted to persons who have been charged with a criminal offence (see 4.5) or who have been brought before a criminal court on a summons (see 4.3). It operates in the juvenile courts too, where parents or guardians can apply for aid on behalf of children or young persons. People who bring private prosecutions, however, cannot rely on the scheme, except when after winning their case the other side appeals against the decision. The introduction of ABWOR (see above, page 78) has provided an attractive alternative to criminal legal aid in some situations.

Applications are best made through a solicitor and preferably before the case is due to be heard in court. They can be made by letter addressed to the clerk of the petty sessions for the relevant district; if unsuccessful at that stage a later application can be made at the hearing itself. In practice in Northern Ireland most applications are made orally at the hearing. The applicant will usually be asked to fill in a form (reproduced in Appendix 4) stating his or her means, although there is no rigid financial eligibility test as there is for legal advice and assistance or civil legal aid. Having received an application the court may ask the Department of Health and Social Services to inquire into the applicant's means and report back to the court; in that event the case will obviously be a little delayed. For aid to be granted it must simply appear to the court that the applicant's means are insufficient to obtain legal help in preparing and conducting a defence. In appeals from the Crown Court to the Court of Appeal (or, further, to the House of Lords) legal aid is obtainable under provisions in the Criminal Appeal (NI) Act 1980.

Conditions of aid

As a "merits" test it must also appear to the court that it is desirable in the interests of justice that the applicant should have free legal aid. The sorts of factors which the court will take into account in applying this merits test (the so-called "Widgery" criteria) are the gravity of the criminal charge, the ability of the applicant to present his or her own case, and the nature of the defence. If a court has any doubts whether the applicant qualifies for aid these must be resolved in favour of granting it, even when the applicant intends to plead guilty to the criminal charges. In cases where the charge is murder, or in situations where a court intends to sentence the defendant to imprisonment, detention in a young offenders centre or a period in a training school, criminal legal aid *must* be offered.

The aid comes in the form of a criminal aid certificate. A solicitor and, where necessary, a barrister are assigned to the case by the court after it has taken into account any representations which the applicant may want to make on this matter. In a Crown Court trial the judge may request a solicitor or barrister to undertake the defence of a person who has not been granted a criminal aid certificate, in which event the case proceeds as if a certificate had in fact been granted.

The costs payable to the lawyers are assessed by a Criminal Taxation Committee consisting of one barrister and two solicitors, who are drawn from the Criminal Costs Assessment Panel (consisting of eight barristers and eight solicitors). The Panel is appointed by the Lord Chancellor. There are no scale costs (though some are soon to be introduced); the Taxation Committee simply takes into account all relevant circumstances including the complexity and duration of the case and the experience of the lawyer involved. In a magistrates' court a solicitor or barrister can be awarded such amount not exceeding £75 as the court thinks just. Some Crown Court cases which have lasted a long time or involved numerous defendants (*e.g.* supergrass trials) have proved very lucrative to lawyers concerned in them.

During the year ending 31st March 1987 the courts granted 27,685 criminal aid certificates, of which 82 per cent were for magistrates' courts. About one-third related to theft offences. Only 726 applications were turned down. A total of £4.7 million was paid out to lawyers for fees and outlays.

The administration of the state schemes

Since April 1982 Ministerial responsibility for legal aid, advice and assistance has rested with the Lord Chancellor rather than the Secretary of State for Northern Ireland. It is the Law Society of Northern Ireland, however, which administers the schemes on a day-to-day basis. It carries out most of its functions through an annually appointed Legal Aid Committee, which consists of six to nine solicitors nominated by the Law Society, two barristers nominated by the Bar Council, and one barrister or solicitor nominated by the Lord Chancellor. There is also what is termed a Certifying Committee, whose main task is to consider applications for civil legal aid which have been turned down by the legal officers in the Legal Aid Department; if it does not want to grant the aid, the application can then be considered by the Legal Aid Committee.

The Law Society makes an annual report to the Lord Chancellor on the operation of the legal advice and assistance scheme and on the civil and criminal legal aid schemes; the Lord Chancellor in turn lays this report before Parliament. An advisory committee exists to advise the Lord Chancellor on such questions relating to these schemes as may be referred to it and to comment on the Law Society's annual report. At the moment the Legal Aid Advisory Committee comprises 10 persons under the chairmanship of a county court judge (Judge Porter). The report of the Legal Aid Advisory Committee is bound and published together with the Law Society's reports.

3.4 Lawyers' Fees

The cost of employing a professional lawyer can be very high. In cases of genuine hardship some form of legal aid may be available, as the previous section has explained, but the truth remains that our legal system is still a long way from ensuring free or subsidised legal help in all situations. If you do not qualify for legal aid or legal advice and assistance, or if your case is one for which the £5 fixed-fee interview is inadequate, the choice is stark: you must either try to conduct your legal affairs in person or else engage a solicitor and run the risk of incurring significant expenditure.

Generally speaking it is inadvisable for a person who is untrained in the law to attempt to conduct his or her own legal affairs, or even to help a friend to do so. Rather drastic errors may be made, with the result that much greater expense is eventually incurred than it was originally hoped could be saved. In addition, in many situations it is actually a criminal offence for untrained persons to do legal work on other people's behalf if they ask payment for it. Some committed individuals do get as far as handling the conveyance of their house or conducting their own legal cases in court, but unless you have lots of free time and spare cash you could well find this to be so inconvenient as to be counterproductive. "Litigants in person", as such individuals are called if cases come to court, are few and far between.

The alternative of engaging a solicitor will not, however, always be unattractive! In particular, if the legal matter is one which involves a dispute with another person, rather than one (like drafting a will) which purely affects yourself, you may well stand a chance of getting back from the other person most of what you have to pay to your solicitor - provided you win the dispute. As regards the solicitor's charges, the basic principle, as you would expect, is that the more work a solicitor does, the more he or she will require you to pay. The cost of a first visit should not be very high (perhaps £5 or £10), and if the solicitor has to take any further action on your behalf you can ask to be kept informed about how much the work is going to cost. The bill, when it is finally received, should itemise all the work carried out and the corresponding charge. It will be made up differently depending on whether the work done was contentious or non-contentious, though there are no hard-and-fast rules as to when work becomes contentious.

Non-contentious work

Generally speaking, a solicitor's non-contentious work consists of all jobs done excluding those which concern proceedings in court. This may be work of a more or less routine nature - like conveying a house or drafting a will - or work concerning a dispute which is settled before a date is fixed for a court appearance. The solicitor's bill in such non-contentious cases will be made up as follows:

(1)   a charge for disbursements, or outlays, such as the stamp duty on the value of a house or the fee for obtaining probate of a will,

(2)   a professional fee, and

(3)   VAT, at 15 per cent, on those items liable to it (which include the professional fee).

The size of the professional fee will depend on such factors as the time involved in handling the affair, the complexity of the affair, and the value of the property concerned. It is not unusual for a solicitor to charge at a rate of about £40 per hour for time spent on a case. In some matters, though not often, the fee is determined in accordance with guidelines laid down either by the Law

Society, which is the governing body of the solicitors' profession, or by a local solicitors' association: the Belfast Solicitors' Association, for example has guideline prices for the conveying of houses. The typical charge for the conveyance of a house priced at £25,000 will be in the region of £350 (which is somewhat more than in England); the charge for administering a deceased person's estate could be greater, perhaps around 2 per cent of the estate's total value. Without going into the details of each case, which will vary greatly, it is impossible to be more precise in indicating likely charges. Remember that help with the costs involved may be available under the legal advice and assistance scheme described in the previous section.

Challenging a solicitor's bill

If a client is dissatisfied with a bill provided by a solicitor for non-contentious work, two things can be done. He or she can require the solicitor to obtain what is called a Remuneration Certificate from the Law Society. This will state the charge which would be a fair and reasonable one for the work done in the case and the client will have to pay that amount. Alternatively, or in addition, the client can apply to have the costs officially assessed (or "taxed") by an official of the Supreme Court called the Taxing Master (see 1.5).

A Remuneration Certificate has to be sought within one month from the date when the solicitor informed the client of the right to apply for one (as the solicitor is bound to do). It comes free of charge, but experience shows that only about one in every five applications will result in a reduction of the bill.

An application to the Taxing Master must be made within three months of delivery of the bill to the client. This time limit can be extended, which will usually be necessary if the client has first taken time to ask for a Remuneration Certificate, but the absolute limit is six months. The fee for applying to the Taxing Master, in the case of bills relating to non-contentious work, is a flat £10. There are only a handful of such applications each year.

Contentious work

A solicitor's contentious work consists of all the business which eventually leads to appearances in court. If judicial proceedings are begun, *e.g.* by the issuing of a writ or a summons, but are settled before the date fixed for the trial, all the work done up to then is usually classified as non-contentious. In considering how much a client will have to pay for contentious work it is essential to distinguish between criminal proceedings and civil proceedings. In both it is also essential to bear in mind the implications of the legal aid scheme.

Criminal proceedings

If your find yourself defending a prosecution for a criminal offence you will need to consider whether to apply for a criminal legal aid certificate (see 3.3). If a certificate is granted the costs are eventually met in the way described in the previous section. If you do not succeed in obtaining a criminal aid certificate it is not possible to appeal against a refusal to grant one, except during the course of an appeal in the case itself, and you must yourself pay for the services of any solicitor or barrister engaged by you. You can, of course, conduct your own defence, but in serious cases this is not at all wise. You can also have a friend in court to help you with your case (such people are called "McKenzie men" after the name of the case where their appearance was first approved), but he or she is not permitted to speak on your behalf. If you lose the case, however, it is very rare for an order to be made compelling you to contribute towards the prosecution's costs as well as paying your own. On the other hand, if you win the case and are acquitted it is also very rare in Northern Ireland for the prosecution to be ordered to pay your costs. It is only when the prosecution, or the defence, has been outrageously unsubstantiated that the costs will be ordered "to follow the event."

If an order as to costs is made by a magistrates' court, the precise amount of costs will be calculated by the court in accordance with the Magistrates' Courts (Costs in Criminal Cases) Rules NI 1988, which allow for up to £75 per lawyer per day. The recipient of the award will also be reimbursed the court fees which have had to be paid during the proceedings, these too being fixed by regulations. If an order as to costs is made by the Crown Court or, in appeals, by a county court or the Court of Appeal, the precise amount in the absence of agreement between the parties will usually be assessed by the Taxing Master, who is obliged by statute to allow such sums as are reasonably sufficient to compensate the party for the expenses properly incurred. An allowance is usually also made for the compensation of witnesses who, if they are professional people, can be allowed a professional fee in addition to out-of-pocket expenses. The costs actually awarded to a party may not be in line with those charged by the solicitor or barrister; the client is then left to bear the difference, though, as explained earlier, he or she can always apply to the Taxing Master for a reduction in the solicitor's bill.

Civil proceedings

A person involved in civil proceedings, whether as plaintiff or defendant, should also consider whether to apply for a civil legal aid certificate (see 3.3). The costs, whether borne by the litigants themselves or by the Legal Aid Fund, are calculated differently accordingly to the forum in which the proceedings are brought.

(1) Proceedings in a magistrates' court

The amounts which can be in issue in civil cases in magistrates' courts are small. The fees for issuing a summons and for the various pieces of work which a solicitor or barrister might do are laid down in regulations. Parties are usually left to bear their own costs even if they win the case, but in a "domestic" case (see 5.2) it is more normal for the court to award costs against the loser of the case. In a typical case these might amount to £100.

(2) Proceedings in a small claims court

From August 1988 the maximum sum which can be claimed in these so-called "arbitration" proceedings, which take place before a circuit registrar, is £500 (see 5.4). The application fee for a claim for less than £75 is £5; for a claim between £75 and £500 the fee is £12. The other party (the "respondent") does not pay any fee for defending the case, only if he or she makes a counterclaim. Here again each side will usually be left to bear his or her own costs, including the cost of providing witnesses and (unless arranged by the circuit registrar) expert reports; only the application fee itself will be recoverable by the winner from the loser. If a plaintiff makes a claim in a county court for a fixed amount of money less than £500 and the defendant insists upon fighting it in a small claims court but loses, the circuit registrar may award to the plaintiff such costs as he or she would have received if the case had been heard in the county court.

(3) Proceedings in a county court (County Court Rules, Order 55)

Up to £5,000 can be claimed in most civil cases in a county court. However, for claims concerning matrimonial property or compensation for criminal injuries and criminal damage to property there is no financial limit (see 5.3 and 5.5). The fees for commencing the proceedings (i.e. issuing and serving a "civil bill") and summoning witnesses and the costs for the work done by solicitors and barristers are laid down in regulations (see the County Court Fees Order (NI) 1988). The amount payable (except in the case of a witness summons) depends on the amount of money or the value of the property being claimed. For example, the cost of issuing a civil bill for a claim amounting to £400 is £42, and a further fee of £5 will be exacted for serving this document on the other party. A solicitor's costs for work done in a case where £600 is claimed will be £227 or £238, and the barrister's costs will be £66. The reason why two figures are given for the solicitor's costs is that a slightly lower sum is payable if the solicitor was acting for a defendant rather than a plaintiff.

It is important to note that in a county court case the loser will have to pay the winner's costs unless the judge orders otherwise, but even this may not be enough to reimburse the winner completely for the outlay: the bill received from his or her own solicitor will include an amount for the time and responsibility involved, which will not be wholly reflected in the fixed scale laid down in the regulations. In such instances the winner must bear the balance of the expense; this could be a significant fraction of the total expense, especially if what was claimed in the case was much more than he or she actually succeeded in winning.

To encourage settlements out of court the scales of costs in county court cases are greatly reduced if a defendant agrees to satisfy a claim within 14 days of the service of the plaintiff's civil bill or if he or she fails to defend the action. A defendant can also safeguard the position on costs by "paying into court" so much of the plaintiff's claim as the defendant is prepared to admit liability for. If the plaintiff does not accept this payment but then does not succeed in getting a higher award from the court, he or she will have to pay virtually all the costs, both his or her own as well as the defendant's.

A plaintiff's costs in the county court may also be reduced if the amount recovered is less than £1000. In that event the case should have been brought before a circuit registrar and not a county court judge, so only half the scale cost for the amount of the successful claim is allowed. If the recovery is less than £500 then, whether the case was heard by a county court judge or by a circuit registrar sitting in a county court, no costs at all will be allowed; the matter should have been dealt with by arbitration in a small claims court. Only in cases of misconduct by one party or in proceedings for a fixed amount of money may costs up to the county court scale be awarded.

(4) Proceedings in the High Court (Supreme Court Rules, Order 62)

Any amount of money can be claimed in High Court proceedings. The court fees are again set out in regulations but lawyers' costs are not specified to the same extent as in county court proceedings. Naturally both fees and costs are higher than in county courts. Senior counsel (*i.e.* QCs) are more likely to be involved; their charges are high, and the junior counsel who assist them usually get one-half to two-thirds of the fee paid to "the silk". If a plaintiff recovers less than £5,000 in the High Court proceedings he or she will be restricted to costs on the county court scale.

The decision as to which side is to bear the costs in High Court proceedings is in the complete discretion of the judge, but in the vast majority of cases the loser will be ordered to pay most, if not all, of the winner's costs. (An exception is made to this in Northern Ireland in cases where a husband successfully petitions for divorce against his wife.) Once the judge has ordered who is to pay the costs, the actual amounts to be paid will be agreed between the parties or, in the absence of any agreement, assessed by the Taxing Master. The Master will allow costs only for work which was essential or proper; any "extra" work must be paid for by the party requiring it to be done. This is termed the assessment of costs on a "party and party" basis. (If the winner of a case is legally aided, the costs will be taxed on what is called a "common fund" basis, according to which he or she will recover a reasonable amount for all expenses reasonably incurred.) A litigant in person in the High Court - someone who is unrepresented by a lawyer - can be allowed up to two-thirds of what the costs would have been if he or she had engaged a solicitor.

(5) Proceedings in a tribunal

Tribunals (see Chapter 7) do not normally have the power to order one side to pay the other side's costs. As legal aid is not available for tribunal proceedings (except in the Lands Tribunal, and for representation under the advice and assistance scheme in the Mental Health Review Tribunal) the parties usually end up paying their own costs. In some situations, however, the tribunal can make payments to cover travel expenses and loss of earnings. Exceptionally (for example, if the respondent's arguments are considered frivolous or vexatious) a tribunal may order the respondent to pay the applicant's costs. This occurred in *Johnston* v *Chief Constable of the RUC* (1988), the case where female police reservists complained successfully of sexual discrimination.

(6) Enforcement of judgment proceedings

As is explained in 5.7, the cost of enforcing a judgment, if the losing side refuses at first to comply with it, can be quite substantial in relation to the size of the judgment itself. The fees payable to the Enforcement of Judgments Office may be high, and to these must be added the solicitor's fee for acting on the winner's behalf. If the losing side can afford to pay the judgment debt, the enforcement costs are added to it; otherwise the enforcement costs must be written off by the "winning" side as another bad debt.

Challenging costs for contentious work

After any contentious proceedings a party may apply to the Taxing Master for his or her solicitor's bill to be officially examined, provided the application is made within 12 months of the bill's delivery. (In non-contentious cases, as we have seen, the time limit is usually just three months.) A party who is ordered to pay the other side's costs may, rather than agree them, insist on those being taxed too, this time within six months of the court order.

The Taxing Master will arrange a date for a hearing to take place. He will then assess the costs at what he takes to be a reasonable amount in the light of all the relevant circumstances, referring of course to any appropriate regulations on the matter. A party, whether solicitor or client, who is dissatisfied with the Taxing Master's assessment may ask for a second review by the Master and for yet a further review by a judge. The costs of the taxing process are usually borne by the party paying the bill being taxed.

4

Proceedings in Criminal Courts

4.1 The Types of Criminal Offence

The criminal law of Northern Ireland, like that of England, rests on two fundamental principles. The first is that any kind of behaviour is criminal only if it is *expressly* prohibited by the criminal law. The second is that no-one can be convicted of a crime unless the behaviour in question was prohibited *at the time it occurred*. In recognition of these principles most of our criminal law has been embodied in statutes. Only a few offences - the most prominent of which is murder - are still regulated by judge-made law, though of course the judges are responsible for interpreting the criminal law statutes whenever their provisions are ambiguous or unclear. It is occasionally a difficult legal question to decide if all the required elements of a crime are present in any particular case, but in most cases the issue is simply whether the prosecution has proved sufficient facts to establish the defendant's guilt.

With rare statutory exceptions, no accused person can be convicted of crime unless the prosecution has proved his guilt "beyond reasonable doubt": since the accused person must be presumed innocent until proved guilty, he must be acquitted if the Court is not sure that he is guilty. There are rare occasions when, once the prosecution has proved certain basic facts, the burden of proving that he is not guilty rests on the accused. In such cases, however, it is usually enough for him to prove this on a balance of probabilities. This is a lower degree of proof than beyond reasonable doubt and it really means that the accused must prove that what he is saying is more likely true than not. Examples of this occur when the accused claims to have an impaired mental responsibility or to be insane (Criminal Justice Act (NI) 1966), or when he has been charged with possession of certain types of prohibited goods. This is the same standard of proof as is required in all civil cases.

The law recognises that not all crimes are equally serious by providing two different forms of procedure and trial. Less serious offences are dealt with by a summary trial in a magistrates' court (sometimes called a court of petty sessions or court of summary jurisdiction), and they involve no jury. More serious offences are tried on indictment in the Crown Court by a judge and jury (though there is also a preliminary step which takes place in a magistrates' court). However, during the present emergency in Northern Ireland some offences are tried on indictment without a jury; these trials take place in the so-called Diplock courts - it was a Committee chaired by Lord Diplock which in 1972 recommended a trial by judge alone in such cases. Some offences must always be tried summarily and some always on indictment; others (called hybrid offences) may be tried either way. In addition, while some offences must always be tried in Diplock courts, others may at times be tried either in Diplock courts or under the normal procedures. We will now examine all of these categories of offence in a little more detail. The differences between the procedures adopted in summary trials and in trials on indictment are explained more fully in 4.6 to 4.8; some special features of the emergency laws and Diplock courts are described in 4.9. A diagram summarising the criminal court system can be found at the end of 4.8.

Offences which must be tried summarily

These are relatively minor offences which have to be tried in a magistrates' court by a resident magistrate (an RM) sitting without a jury (see 1.5 and 4.6). They have all been made triable in this way by a statute, not by the common law, and for most of them proceedings must be begun within six months of the offence. All the offences in this category are considered to be not serious enough to merit the extra time and expense required for a trial on indictment.A common example is careless driving, which is an offence under article 153 of the Road Traffic (NI) Order 1981.

Even some offences under the emergency laws have to be tried summarily, such as refusal to answer a soldier's questions concerning a recent explosion, which is an offence under section 18 of the Northern Ireland (Emergency Provisions) Act 1978.

Offences which must be tried on indictment

These are serious offences which have to be tried in the Crown Court by a judge and jury, though like all cases heard in the Crown Court they are originally dealt with at committal proceedings in a magistrates' court. There is usually no time limit on the commencement of proceedings. Murder, manslaughter, rape and robbery are all offences in this category. There are considered to be no circumstances which would justify trying such offences in full at the level of a magistrates' court.

Offences which may be tried summarily or on indictment

For three kinds of crime there is a choice of proceedings. (The position in Northern Ireland differs from that in England, where significant changes were introduced by the Criminal Law Act 1977.)

(1)   A handful of offences which are normally tried summarily can be tried on indictment if two conditions are satisfied. First, the offence must be one

for which a person, if convicted, can be sent to prison for more than six months. Second, the defendant himself must ask to be tried on indictment. An example of this type of hybrid offence is the improper importation of goods, which is a crime under section 45 of the Customs and Excise Act 1952.

(2)   Some offences which are normally tried on indictment can be tried summarily if the resident magistrate who first hears the case at the committal stage (see 4.7) considers that it is not a serious one and if the prosecution and defendant have no objections. The RM can take the initiative to try the case summarily at any stage of the proceedings, but he or she must first give the defendant 24 hours' written notice (or procure a waiver of this requirement). Examples of such offences are theft, indecent assault and assault occasioning actual bodily harm.

(3)   In many cases the statute which creates a crime expressly states that it can be tried summarily or on indictment. It is then up to the prosecution, bearing in mind the seriousness of the particular case, to decide which form of trial to use. An example of this kind of offence is reckless driving, a crime under article 139 of the Road Traffic (NI) Order 1981.

Scheduled offences under the emergency laws

These are the offences which are listed in Schedule 4 to the Northern Ireland (Emergency Provisions) Act 1978. They are the ones most commonly committed by terrorists in Northern Ireland for which the United Kingdom Parliament has accordingly considered it necessary to establish emergency procedures. The distinction between scheduled and non-scheduled offences overlies that between summary and indictable offences; that is to say, not all of the scheduled offences will be tried on indictment. None of them is in the category of offences which must be tried summarily, but many of them, such as membership of a proscribed organisation or threats to destroy property, are in the category of hybrid offences and so will be tried summarily if the conditions outlined in (3) above are fulfilled. But the procedures for dealing with the summary trial of scheduled offences do not differ to any great extent from the ordinary procedures in magistrates' courts. The main differences are that the Director of Public Prosecutions must consent to the prosecution, there are special arrangements for holding young persons in custody (whether on remand or after a finding of guilt), and after the trial of a scheduled offence a resident magistrate must give a reasoned judgment, not just a decision, if convicting the accused person. Trials on indictment of scheduled offences, on the other hand, are much more extraordinary (see 4.9).

To complicate matters further, some of the offences listed in Schedule 4 to the 1978 Act may be "de-scheduled" by the Attorney-General certifying in a particular case that the offence is not to be treated as a scheduled offence. Amongst these offences are murder, manslaughter, assault occasioning actual bodily harm, assisting prisoners to escape, arson, kidnapping, intimidation and bomb hoaxes. They should be de-scheduled if no element of terrorism was involved in their commission, but if the Attorney-General refuses to de-schedule it is not possible to appeal against that decision to a higher authority. A few of the offences which cannot be de-scheduled are, however, to be treated as scheduled only in particular circumstances: robbery, for example, is a scheduled offence only where it is charged that an explosive, firearm, imitation firearm or weapon of offence was used in its commission. The offences which under all circumstances must be dealt with as scheduled offences include rioting, causing grievous bodily harm by explosives and withholding information about acts of terrorism. In 1987 the Attorney-General issued 479 "de-scheduling" certificates and refused 369 applications; 713 persons were tried for indictable scheduled offences.

4.2 The Level of Crime in Northern Ireland

Statistics on offences committed in Northern Ireland are made available through the annual reports of the Chief Constable of the Royal Ulster Constabulary. The Northern Ireland Court Service also distributes a booklet called *Judicial Statistics* which deals mainly with the level of court business (criminal and civil) each year. The Northern Ireland Office publishes an annual *Commentary on Northern Ireland Crime Statistics*, where trends are identified and comparisons drawn. Also worth consulting is the *Law and Order* chapter of the *Northern Ireland Annual Abstract of Statistics*, published by the Policy Planning and Research Unit of the Government's Department of Finance and Personnel. At all stages it is necessary to bear in mind the distinctions between indictable and summary offences and between adult and juvenile defendants.

Table 5 reproduces parts of Tables 2.1 and 3.2 in the *Commentary on Northern Ireland Crime Statistics* for 1987 and Table 1 of the Chief Constable's 1987 Annual Report. It indicates the recorded number of various types of indictable offences during each of the last four years. Attempting, conspiring, inciting, aiding, abetting, causing or permitting an offence is generally included under the heading of the offence itself. We must remember that recorded crime is not the same as actual crime: for various reasons many offences never come to the notice of the police. Alongside the number of recorded crimes in Table 5 is the percentage which were "cleared" by the police. This means that they are offences for which a person has been charged, summonsed or cautioned, or which a court has taken into consideration when sentencing someone for other crimes, or which cannot be proceeded with because, although there is enough evidence of someone's guilt, the person is too young to be prosecuted (or is dead).

Crime	1984		1985		1986		1987	
	Number recorded	*% cleared*	*Number recorded*	*% cleared*	*Number recorded*	*% cleared*	*Number recorded*	*% cleared*
Violence against the person	3389	57	3458	58	4205	57	4198	71
Murder	63	74	59	80	85	46	100	51
Attempted murder	180	44	225	32	173	24	282	20
All sexual offences	496	67	653	77	834	79	817	91
Rape	75	62	75	71	107	78	80	87
All burglary	22364	25	20275	25	19973	26	17294	30
Burglary in a dwelling	9016	19	8171	19	8545	20	7844	27
All robbery and hijacking	2009	26	1740	23	2204	19	2504	19
Armed robbery	800	30	674	27	839	16	969	20
All theft	28746	28	29490	34	30189	38	30136	43
Theft of cars	6370	15	6815	26	7441	34	7873	39
Shoplifting	3912	76	4796	80	5081	84	5077	91
Fraud and forgery	3117	67	3697	73	4209	70	4150	79
All criminal damage	4419	22	3194	27	4055	31	2592	43
Arson	1412	13	1172	16	1371	23	871	30
Explosive offences	125	27	92	39	79	39	74	32
Offences under the Emergency Provisions Act	237	61	99	101*	89	95	86	101*
Firearms offences	233	79	166	75	167	68	203	81
All indictable offences	66784	31	64520	35	68255	37	63860	43

* Includes offences recorded in previous years

Table 5. Recorded crime and clear-up rate, 1984-1987

Table 6 (which is drawn from Table 6.1 in the *Commentary on Northern Ireland Crime Statistics 1987*) compares the rate of commission in 1987 of a variety of offences per 100,000 of the population in Northern Ireland,' the Republic of Ireland and England and Wales. "Homicide" refers to murder, manslaughter and infanticide. The overall crime rate in Northern Ireland in 1987 was 3,849 per 100,000 of the population, and falling. It was higher in 40 of the 42 police force areas of England and Wales. The figures for France and Germany are higher still.

	Northern Ireland	Republic of Ireland	England and Wales
Homicide	7	1	1
Rape	6	2	5
Robbery	159	43	65
Aggravated assault	148	41	274
Burglary	1098	856	1798
Theft	1413	1116	3320
Car theft	500	75	778

Table 6. Crime rates per 100,000 persons

It can be seen from these two tables that approximately 70 per cent of all recorded crime in Northern Ireland is either burglary or theft, though the rate of commission of these is significantly less than in England and Wales. The clear-up rate for burglary is amongst the lowest for any crime, whilst that for shoplifting is amongst the highest. Across the board in Northern Ireland the clear-up rate has been rising since 1982, though it is still not as high as it was in 1969. When the Northern Ireland crime rate is compared with that of police force areas in England with a comparable population (*e.g.* Merseyside), it is clear that Northern Ireland has a lower crime rate than any of them, except for certain offences such as homicide, sexual offences and robbery.

Table 7 (compiled from figures in chapter 4 of the 1987 *Commentary on Crime Statistics*, which do not always tally with those in Parts C and E of the 1987 *Judicial Statistics*) provides details of the proceedings taken in the criminal courts in Northern Ireland between 1983 and 1987. Alongside the number of people in each category is the percentage of those who were found guilty. It can be seen that the conviction rate is very high. The overwhelming majority of defendants in criminal cases are male and most defendants plead guilty. In 1986 about 40 per cent of persons convicted in magistrates' courts had previous convictions; the figure for defendants in the Crown Court was closer to 50 per cent.

Crime	1984 Number proceeded against	% found guilty	1985 Number proceeded against	% found guilty	1986 Number proceeded against	% found guilty	1987 Number proceeded against	% found guilty
Magistrates' courts			Adults (aged 17 or over)					
Indictable offences	6041	94	6403	92	8214	92	8662	91
Non-motoring summary offences	8135	91	8940	89	6556	88	6940	848
Summary motoring offences	26292	96	28176	96	26921	96	29197	96
Commited to Crown Court	934	-	1739	-	1389	-	1314	-
Crown Court								
Scheduled offences	497	91	666	89	576	95	704	95
Non-scheduled offences	1078	91	1269	90	1205	93	1174	94
Magistrates' courts			Juveniles (aged 10 to 16)					
Indictable offences	991	93	869	95	1157	93	1024	92
Non-motoing summary offences	445	88	453	86	371	84	305	86
Summary motoring offences	265	94	220	97	155	92	139	92
Committed to Crown Court	57	-	83	-	76	-	23	-
Crown Court								
Scheduled offences	10	100	32	100	20	100	9	100
Non-scheduled offences	43	98	64	95	58	97	36	89

Table 7. Criminal proceedings in Northern Ireland 1984-87

"Terrorist" crime

Table 8 gives a picture of the level of "terrorist" crime in Northern Ireland since 1969. The figures are from the annual reports of the Chief Constable of the RUC. A total of 2,711 people had died by the end of 1988. The worst years were 1971-76.

Year	Police	Deaths Army	Civilians	Shootings	Explosions/ defusings	Finds Firearms	Explosives (tons)
1969	1	0	12	73	10	14	0.1
1970	2	0	23	213	170	324	0.3
1971	11	48	115	1756	1515	716	1.2
1972	17	129	321	10628	1853	1259	18.5
1973	13	66	171	5018	1520	1313	17.2
1974	15	35	166	3206	1113	1236	11.7
1975	11	20	216	1803	635	820	4.9
1976	23	29	245	1908	1192	736	9.7
1977	14	29	69	1081	535	563	1.7
1978	10	21	50	755	633	393	0.9
1979	14	48	51	728	564	300	0.9
1980	9	17	50	642	400	203	0.8
1981	21	23	57	1142	529	357	3.4
1982	12	28	57	547	332	288	2.3
1983	18	15	44	424	367	166	1.7
1984	9	19	36	334	248	187	3.8
1985	23	6	25	237	215	173	3.3
1986	12	12	37	392	254	174	2.4
1987	16	11	66	674	384	206	5.8
1988	6	33	54	537	253	489	47
Totals	257	589	1865	32098	12702	9917	95.1

Table 8. Terrorist crime in Northern Ireland 1969-1988

4.3 Summonses and Arrests

Criminal proceedings are begun in one of three ways: by the issue of a summons, by the issue of a warrant of arrest, or by an arrest without a warrant. A sizeable proportion of persons appearing in court do so after having been originally arrested but then released and later summonsed. The two processes, however, are quite distinct.

Summonses

If the police (or anyone else for that matter) believe that a person is guilty of a summary offence, or a not very serious indictable offence, they can give the details in a "complaint" to a Justice of the Peace or to a clerk of petty sessions. If the JP or clerk of petty sessions is satisfied that there is sufficient evidence to suspect the person he or she will issue a summons giving details of the alleged offence and ordering that person to appear at a magistrates' court on a particular date to answer the complaint. If the offence allegedly committed is a summary one, a summons should not be issued more than six months after the date of its commission; if the offence is indictable, a summons can be issued at any time. The forms used as summonses are reproduced in Appendix 4.

The summons will usually be served by the police on the defendant (as the person being summonsed is called) a reasonable time before the case is to be heard in court. The summons will tell the defendant the nature of the complaint being made against him, but will not set out the evidence on which the police intend to rely. It is usually the only document which the defendant receives, besides perhaps a statement of his previous convictions and a copy of any written statements which the prosecutions intends to use at the trial. The defendant must prepare his defence before appearing in court, though of course he may consult a solicitor and obtain legal representation. The cost of advice or representation may be allowed to him under the schemes described in 3.3.

Arrests

In more serious cases, or where a magistrate is satisfied that a person suspected of a summary offence cannot for some reason be served with a summons, the police may arrest a person, that is, take him into custody. An arrest can lawfully be made in two different ways: either with or without a warrant.

Arrests under warrant

Like a summons a warrant of arrest can be issued by a JP (but not a clerk of petty sessions) provided he or she is satisfied that there is reasonable evidence to suspect a named person of a serious offence. The complaint to the JP must, however, be in writing and substantiated on oath. The warrant is an order by the JP to the police to arrest the person named in the warrant and to take him before a court to answer the charges which may be brought against him.

Arrests without a warrant

The law on this matter is about to be reformed. At the time of writing a proposed Police and Criminal Evidence (NI) Order is circulating in draft form. It is intended to bring the law in Northern Ireland largely into line with that in England under the Police and Criminal Evidence Act 1984.

Under the present, ordinary (that is, non-emergency) law, as enshrined in the Criminal Law Act (NI) 1967, the police in Northern Ireland may arrest a person without a warrant if they have reasonable grounds for believing that that person has committed, is committing or is about to commit a "arrestable" offence (that is, an offence for which, if convicted, the person could be sent to prison for five years or more).In addition quite a few statutes give the police a power to arrest without a warrant persons reasonably suspected of less serious offences. The powers of private citizens to arrest are in two respects more limited than those of the police: (i) only if an arrestable offence *has in fact been committed* can they arrest someone who is reasonably suspected of being guilty of the offence; (ii) they have no power to arrest someone who is reasonably suspected of *being about to commit* an arrestable offence.

At the moment there are two main safeguards for persons who are arrested without a warrant: in the first place, they must be told at the time of arrest why they are being arrested; secondly, after arrest they must be released from custody within 24 hours or be brought before a magistrates' court to answer charges as soon as practicable thereafter and at any rate not later than 48 hours after the arrest.

The Police and Criminal Evidence (NI) Order will make significant changes in the law. It retains the concept of an arrestable offence but includes within the definition some specific statutory offences for which a person, if convicted, could *not* be sent to prison for five years or more (*e g* some offences under the Official Secrets Acts). The law on citizens' arrests is not otherwise affected. Under the proposed Order a constable may also arrest without a warrant for a non-arrestable offence if it appears to him or her that service of a summons is impracticable or inappropriate because, for instance, the name of the person to be arrested cannot be readily ascertained by the constable. As under the existing law, persons arrested must be told immediately why they are being arrested.

The Order proposes that arrested persons should, if it appears that it may be necessary to keep them in police detention for more that six hours, be taken only to a "designated" police station where "custody officers" will be responsible for them. As under the current law, detention without charge will normally be permissible for a maximum of 24 hours. If the person is to be detained for up to 36 hours the authority of a superintendent has to be obtained and the offence in question must be a "serious" one: the Order defines "serious" in terms of the loss or harm caused by the offence and lists some offences as always being in this category (*e.g.* rape or kidnapping). Detention beyond 36 hours is permissible only on the authority of a magistrates' court; it can be extended by that court up to 72 hours, and then again to 96 hours, but that is the absolute maximum.

Arrest and questioning

We cannot here go into all the complexities of the law on arrest and questioning, but the following general points should be noted. In several respects the provisions of the emergency laws are different (see 4.9).

(1) No person is under a legal obligation to accompany a police officer to a police station unless that person has been formally arrested (with or without a warrant). People who are simply "helping the police with their inquiries" are present at the police station of their own free will and must be allowed to leave if they want to. This is confirmed by the proposed new Police and Criminal Evidence (NI) Order.

(2) No more force than is reasonable may be used to effect an arrest. The use of excessive force will make the arrest unlawful.

(3) Although ordinary citizens can arrest people under certain circumstances, they can detain people only if a breach of the peace would otherwise be likely. The arrested persons should be taken to a police station as soon as possible, otherwise the arresting citizen may be committing the civil wrong of false imprisonment.

(4) The general rule is that no-one is legally obliged to volunteer information or to answer questions put by the police (or army). But by virtue of the Criminal Evidence (NI) Order 1988 this right to silence has been qualified in that prosecutors, judges and juries are now permitted to draw inferences about guilt from an accused's silence in the face of questioning. The inference alone cannot be enough to convict the accused, but it can corroborate other evidence implicating the accused in the alleged offence. It shoud also be noted that under road traffic legislation there is a duty to report certain accidents and under section 18 of the Northern Ireland (Emergency Provisions) Act 1978 there is a duty to answer certain police or army questions (see 4.9).

(5) Until December 1988 the questioning of persons by the police in Northern Ireland was regulated by the so-called Judges' Rules dating from 1976. As mentioned in 2.3, these did not have the full force of law, but they were meant to be adhered to in practice. Answers to questions asked in contravention of the Rules were still admissible as evidence in a court, subject to the judge's discretion to exclude them. As a consequence of the making of the Criminal Evidence (NI) Order 1988, which altered the law on a suspect's right to silence, the judges rescinded the 1976 Rules and to replace them the Secretary of State for Northern Ireland issued written guidance to the RUC Chief Constable. This guidance requires the police

to caution a person being questioned in the following terms: "You do not have to say anything unless you wish to do so but I must warn you that if you fail to mention any fact which you rely on in your defence in court, your failure to take this opportunity to mention it may be treated in court as supporting any relevant evidence against you. If you do wish to say anything, what you say may be given in evidence."

Under the proposed Police and Criminal Evidence (NI) Order, Codes of Practice on questioning and other matters will be issued, and there is to be non-statutory guidance on the exercise of emergency questioning powers. But again, although breaches of these directives will render a police officer liable to disciplinary proceedings, they will not of themselves render the officer liable to criminal or civil proceedings and evidence obtained as a result will not automatically be declared inadmissible as evidence in a court.

(6)   Under the present law the only detained persons who have a statutory right of access to a solicitor are those detained under the emergency laws (see 4.9). The new Police and Criminal Evidence (NI) Order will extend this right, albeit qualified, to all detained persons. There will be a similar extension of the right (conferred in England as long ago as 1977) to have another person informed that an arrest has taken place.

(7)   The new Order requires the Secretary of State to issue a Code of Practice governing the tape-recording of interviews. When tape-recording becomes standard practice this should help to eliminate disputes over whether a detained person was physically or verbally abused while being questioned.

(8)   Under the existing law, persons may not be fingerprinted without their consent unless an order is first obtained from a magistrates' court. Under the proposed new Order fingerprints can be taken without the person's consent if he or she has been arrested and if a police officer of at least the rank of superintendent gives written authorisation for them to be taken.

(9)   At the moment the police have the power to search anyone who is in detention, but they cannot take any body samples without the person's consent - to do so would be an assault. The new Order regulates in detail the searching of detained persons and goes on to distinguish between intimate and non-intimate body searches. Intimate searches are physical examinations of body orifices. They can be carried out without consent only if there are grounds for believing that the person may have a concealed weapon or drug.

(10)   The new Order also distinguishes between the taking of intimate and non-intimate samples. The former can be taken only with the person's consent; they include blood and urine samples. Non-intimate samples, such as hairs from the head or footprints, do not require the person's consent. In Northern Ireland, but not in England, saliva and mouth swabs

are to be classified as non-intimate samples. Special rules will continue to apply to persons suspected of road traffic offences.

(11)   If a person makes a statement confessing to a crime, this is admissible as evidence in a court only if, under the present law, the prosecution prove that it was made voluntarily. This means that it must not have been made out of fear of prejudice or hope of advantage or in oppressive circumstances. The Police and Criminal Evidence (NI) Order will change this so that the prosecution must prove that the confession was not obtained by oppression or in consequence of anything said or done which was likely to render it unreliable.

(12)   A person who has been arrested unlawfully, or unlawfully treated while in detention, can bring a civil action for compensation against the police (see Chapter 5). The police (or indeed army) will be guilty of the civil wrongs (or "torts") of false imprisonment or assault. But the wrongful police behaviour is not of itself a defence to a criminal charge: the person arrested can still be found guilty of an offence.

4.4. Bail and Remand

Usually a person arrested under warrant is held in custody pending appearance in court, but when issuing the warrant the Justice of the Peace may authorise the police to release the accused on bail once they have arrested him. This means releasing him in exchange for a promise to return to the police station, or to attend at a magistrates' court, on a certain day. This promise, or the money which may have to be forfeited if the promise is broken, is called a recognisance. Persons arrested with or without a warrant may also be released on police bail. This is available when the police officer in charge of the station to which the arrested person is brought is satisfied that the offence charged is not of a serious nature and that the arrested person's release would not tend to defeat the ends of justice or cause injury or damage to any person.

When a person who has been charged (see 4.5) eventually appears in a magistrates' court, the prosecution or the defence may still not have fully prepared its case and the resident magistrate will then be asked to postpone, or "adjourn", the hearing. In such circumstances the RM also has to decide whether to release the accused from custody or to remand him, and, if the latter, whether to remand him in custody or on bail. In practice the views of the police are highly influential on this point. The factors which are meant to be taken into account include the character of the accused, the nature of the alleged offence, and the strength of the evidence against the accused. Having considered such factors the court should grant bail if it is satisfied that the accused will not fail to turn up again at court, will not commit another offence, and will not try to obstruct the course of justice by, for example, putting pressure on witnesses. (The law in England, under the Bail Act 1976, is slightly different; see also 4.9.)

Remands in custody

Remands in custody cannot normally be for more than eight clear days, but they can be for 28 days in a case where the accused and the prosecution agree to this, or where the accused is already serving a prison sentence or is detained in a young offenders centre. Before the end of each period of remand the defendant must again be brought before a court; he or she can then reapply for bail, but this will usually be refused unless there has been a significant change of circumstances.

When a magistrate refuses bail it is possible that the defendant can exercise a common law right to apply to a judge of the High Court for bail, but again there is great reluctance to overturn a magistrate's previous refusal. If the magistrate has awarded bail but at such a sum or on such conditions as to make it impossible for the defendant to accept release on such terms, the defendant can apply to the High Court to have the sum or conditions altered. In such circumstances he or she can also apply for a writ of *habeas corpus,* which is a declaration that the continued detention of the accused is unlawful. *Habeas corpus* may nowadays also be available if access to a solicitor is denied or if a suspect is maltreated while detained. All applications to the High Court for bail or *habeas corpus* are considered to be civil, not criminal, proceedings. A person who has already been convicted can apply for bail to the court which is hearing an appeal in the case.

4.5 Charge and Prosecution

The right to silence

When a person is arrested he is normally taken to a police station and questioned. Many people also volunteer to accompany the police to a police station in order to answer their questions. Failure to answer police questions cannot of itself amount to the offence of obstructing the police in the execution of their duties; and until recently all citizens had a right of silence in the face of police questioning. This meant that, if later tried, no adverse inference could be drawn from their refusal to answer questions. But now, by virtue of the Criminal Evidence (NI) Order 1988, the refusal to answer questions or even the failure to answer particular facts when charged, *can* be taken as amounting to evidence which corroborates other evidence implicating the accused in an offence. This applies to all accused persons, not just those in "terrorist" cases. A similar law is soon to be introduced for England and Wales.

As soon as the police have evidence reasonably to suspect that the person has committed an offence they must caution him by saying: "You are not obliged to say anything unless you wish to do so, but what you say may be put into writing and given in evidence". Questioning can then continue, though the accused still has the right to silence in the highly qualified sense just mentioned.

Being charged

When the police officer in charge of the police station believes that there is enough evidence to show that the suspected person committed an offence he should either prefer a charge against that person or tell him that he may be prosecuted for that offence (*e.g.* by the issue of a summons). At that time the accused should again be cautioned. Only in exceptional cases should the police then put to the accused further questions relating to the offence and even when such questions are put (for example, to clear up an ambiguity in a previous statement) the accused must once again be told of his "right" to remain silent.

Even a person who has not already been arrested can in this way be charged, or informed that he may be prosecuted, though if the police want to detain him in custody they should formally arrest him immediately before charging or informing him.

If the police decide not to charge or prosecute a suspect he can instead be formally cautioned by a senior police officer and will not then have to appear in court. Such a caution will usually only be administered if the suspect has admitted his guilt of an offence and if the police believe that the person's own interests as well as those of society can just as well be served by a formal caution as by forcing an appearance in court. If the police decide not to charge or formally caution the suspect, he should be released.

Being prosecuted

Once a person has been charged or summonsed for an offence the process of prosecution has begun. If at any stage it becomes clear that it is not going to be possible to prove the accused's guilt beyond reasonable doubt the charge should be dropped or ordered by a court to be withdrawn.

In Northern Ireland the Royal Ulster Constabulary act as the prosecuting authority for many minor criminal offences. Their own officers will do all the paperwork and present the case in court. But the prosecution of major criminal offences and certain types of less serious cases is the responsibility of the Office of the Director of Public Prosecutions. This is an office created in 1972 as a further safeguard against unjustified prosecutions and to relieve the RUC of some of their workload. As explained in 1.5, the main function of the DPP is to consider any information brought to his notice with a view to initiating or continuing any criminal proceedings.

In all but minor cases then, when the police have completed their investigations into an offence, during which time the accused may have been remanded in custody or on bail (see 4.4) or may not have been charged at all, they will pass the investigation file to the DPP's Office. It will be considered by a member of that Office under the supervision of an Assistant Director, and a decision will be taken as to the offences, if any, for which the accused should be prosecuted. The Office itself cannot carry out more investigations into the case but it can ask the police to do so.

If the Director's Office decides that no prosecution is justified a direction is issued to the RUC that no evidence should be offered against the accused and the charges must then be dropped. If the Office decides that a prosecution is justified it will direct which charges are to be pressed (usually these will be similar to those which may already have been preferred by the police) and (if a choice is available - see 4.1) whether the trial is to be summary or on indictment. If a trial on indictment is directed, the committal proceedings (see 4.7) will be arranged and conducted on the prosecution's side almost entirely by the DPP's Office. If the accused person is then committed for trial to the Crown Court the committal papers (including all the evidence submitted at the committal proceedings) and the police investigation files are sent by the DPP's Office to Crown Counsel. It is this barrister who will draw up the required form of indictment (see 4.8) and act as the chief representative of the prosecution in the trial on indictment. In less serious cases a junior barrister alone will be employed; in more serious cases he or she will be led by senior counsel.

In theory there is not meant to be any bargaining between the prosecution and the defence as to which offences, if any, the accused should plead guilty to. In practice it is acknowledged that such plea bargaining does occur (as it does quite openly in America), but the rule is maintained that a judge is not allowed to tell the accused, or a lawyer acting for the accused, that a plea of guilty will ensure a lighter sentence than conviction following a plea of not guilty. It is common knowledge, though, that a guilty plea will often lead to a sentence discount.

Private prosecutions

In addition to "public" prosecutions by the police and the DPP's Office, it is possible to bring a "private" prosecution. Any individual can pursue a private prosecution - but legal aid is not available for the process - and it is believed that to date only one case has ever reached the Crown Court in Northern Ireland. In recent cases in Great Britain there have been private prosecutions for manslaughter and rape.

The DPP has the power to take over or abort a private prosecution if he thinks fit to do so at any stage of the proceedings, and any prosecution, whether public or private, can be brought to an end by the Attorney-General entering what is called a *nolle prosequi* ("unwilling to proceed"). This has the effect of preventing further consideration of the charge against the accused in that particular trial. It does not operate as a formal acquittal, so in theory the accused could be prosecuted later for the same offence.

It must be remembered, of course, that whoever is called the prosecutor, the actual representations in court will in the vast majority of cases be made by solicitors or barristers engaged by the prosecutor. Many official bodies and private companies employ staff to detect and investigate offences; when they think that they have sufficient evidence against a suspect they pass the case to the police or the DPP's Office. This happens, for instance, in cases of shoplifting, where large stores employ detectives but suspected culprits are dealt with by the RUC. Other common examples are the so-called "Departmental" prosecutions, though in England many of these are prosecuted entirely by employees of the Departments concerned. Examples commonly occurring in Northern Ireland are prosecutions instigated by the Department of Health and Social Services (for non-payment of national insurance contributions or making false claims for social security benefits), the Department of the Environment (for failure to license motor vehicles), the Department of Economic Development (for breaches of the Trade Descriptions Act), the Inland Revenue (for non-payment of taxes), HM Customs and Excise (for failure to make VAT returns), the National TV Licence Records Office (for non-payment of TV licence fees) and Northern Ireland Electricity (for redirection of electricity).

4.6 Summary Trial in a Magistrates' Court

Usually the official name for a magistrates' court is a court of petty sessions, that is, a court of summary jurisdiction which sits at regular specified times and is presided over by a resident magistrate (see 1.5). But a magistrates' court may also be constituted by a resident magistrate or JP sitting "out of petty sessions". Magistrates' courts deal with criminal cases in two different ways: they try persons accused of summary offences or indictable offences being dealt with summarily (see 4.1) and they undertake an initial examination of the case against persons accused of offences being tried on indictment. This latter sort of hearing is called "committal proceedings" because its object is to decide whether the defendant should be "committed" for trial on indictment in the Crown Court; it is discussed in the next section. In the present section we concentrate on summary trials.

The vast majority of all criminal offences dealt with in Northern Ireland (as in England and Wales) are tried summarily in magistrates' courts (see Table 7 on page 98 for details). Well over half of all the charges tried summarily are motoring offences. Even where the defendant has a choice between summary trial and trial on indictment (see 4.1), approximately three out of every four cases are dealt with summarily. Some 20-25 per cent of the charges dealt with by magistrates' courts each year are for indictable offences being tried summarily. Summary trial is quicker, less expensive and subject to less publicity - advantages which usually outweigh the fact that in a summary trial there is no jury and the defendant has no prior knowledge of the strength of the evidence against him. Furthermore, if the defendant pleads guilty or is convicted, the sentence which the RM can impose is likely to be much less severe than the sentence which could be imposed by a judge in the Crown Court. If the case is one which is being tried summarily but which might have been tried on indictment, the RM can send the accused to the Crown Court for sentencing if he does not think that his own powers are sufficient in this regard, but this is a very rare occurrence.

Pleading

A criminal trial in a magistrates' court begins with the clerk of the court (the clerk of petty sessions) explaining to the defendant (if he is present) the details of the offence for which he has been summonsed or charged. If the offence is one for which the defendant can choose to be tried by a jury in the Crown Court he must be there in person to indicate his choice to the magistrate. Similarily, if the case is one which the prosecution can claim to have tried by jury this claim must be made immediately. If the summary trial is to go ahead, the clerk of petty sessions will then ask the defendant if he wishes to plead guilty or not guilty.

If the defendant has been summonsed for an offence which must be tried summarily - but in no other situation - he can plead guilty by post. He can then be tried without having to appear in court, and unless a custodial sentence is to be imposed he can even be sentenced in his absence. A plea of not guilty cannot, technically, be accepted through the post, but if no plea of guilty is received it will be assumed that the accused is not admitting the offence. If the accused does not turn up in court on the day in question, a warrant can be issued for his arrest or he can be tried in his absence.

Procedure in a summary trial

If the defendant chooses to plead guilty, the prosecutor will outline the facts of the case to the resident magistrate and hand to him a list of the defendant's previous convictions, if any. After listening to defence arguments for leniency - "a plea in mitigation" - the magistrate will pronounce sentence.

If the defendant chooses to plead not guilty, the prosecutor will outline the facts and then call his witnesses to give their evidence. The defendant or his lawyer can cross-examine any of the prosecution witnesses. At the end of the prosecution case the defendant can apply for a direction, that is, submit that he ought to be acquitted because the prosecution has failed to produce any evidence to establish an essential element of the offence or because the evidence adduced is so weak that no reasonable jury (if one had been involved) would convict the accused. If the RM grants the direction, that is the end of the case and the defendant is free to go. He is not, however, formally acquitted, and so may be prosecuted later for the same offence. If the application is rejected, the defence can either rest its case on that point or go on to call its own witnesses including, usually, the defendant himself. The defendant also has the right to make an unsworn statement from the dock, a right taken away from defendants in England in 1983 and proposed to be abolished in Northern Ireland by the Police and Criminal Evidence (NI) Order. By virtue of the Criminal Evidence (NI) Order 1988 an accused person must indicate at the start of his defence that he intends to give evidence or, if he does not do this, he must be told that he will be called upon to give evidence in his own defence. If he then refuses to testify or without good cause refuses to answer any question, the court or jury may use this as corroborative evidence against the accused.

The prosecution can cross-examine all the defence witnesses (except a defendant who makes an unsworn statement) but if it wants to introduce any new evidence to contradict anything proved or said on behalf of the defence it must first ask the magistrate's permission to do so. With the consent of the other side either party to the proceedings can also submit written statements made by any person; if necessary, the maker of the statement can be called to give oral evidence to supplement what is related in the written statement. When all the evidence has been given, the defence may make a final address to the magistrate outlining its arguments.

Criminal proceedings (whether in magistrates' courts, the Crown Court or appeal courts) are "adversarial" in nature. Each side is engaged in a battle against the other with the magistrate or judge acting as a neutral umpire. In continental Europe a much more investigative function is given to the judge.

The magistrate's decision and sentencing powers

The RM may give his decision on the spot or take a few hours or days to make up his mind. If he decides that the defendant is guilty he considers the defendant's previous convictions, if any, and listens to a plea in mitigation by the defence before passing sentence. The defendant may also ask for other offences he concedes he committed to be "taken into consideration" (TIC's). To await reports, or to see how the defendant behaves in the meantime, the RM can defer sentence for up to six months. Generally speaking the most serious punishment which a magistrate has power to impose is a fine of £2,000 or six months in prison, or both, though if the offence is an indictable one being tried summarily (see 4.1) the maximum prison sentence is 12 months, and this may extend to 18 months if consecutive terms of imprisonment are imposed for more than one indictable offence. Prison sentences may be suspended for between one and three years (only two years in England), which means that they may be "activated" only if the convicted person commits another imprisonable offence within that period. In 1986, 1,216 adults were sentenced to immediate imprisonment by magistrates' courts. Periods spent on remand in custody are counted as part of a sentence imposed later.

The commonest punishment in magistrates' courts is a fine. In 1986 it was imposed in 33 per cent of the cases where indictable offences were tried summarily, in 64 per cent of the non-motoring summary cases and in 76 per cent of the summary motoring cases. Since 1984 there have been five scales for fines, the limits of these being set by secondary legislation from time to time. At the moment the limits are £100 for Scale 1, £200 for Scale 2, £400 for Scale 3, £1,000 for Scale 4 and £2,000 for Scale 5. Community service orders are also becoming popular with magistrates: about 500 are issued each year.

Under the Criminal Justice (NI) Order 1980 magistrates have the power, rarely exercised, to make compensation and restitution orders against a convicted person. These require a person to pay compensation for any personal injury, loss or damage resulting from any offence for which the court has convicted him or from any other offence which the court took into consideration when sentencing him. The maximum which can be ordered to be paid in respect of any one offence is £2,000, and losses arising out of a road accident, except where the vehicle has been stolen, are excluded from the scheme. Sums paid are deducted from any award of damages later obtained by the victim of the crime in civil proceedings. Under the Theft Act (NI) 1969 any property which has been stolen, or its proceeds, can be ordered to be restored by the defendant to the victim of the theft and under the 1980 Order property used for the purposes of crime can be ordered to be forfeited.

Compensation, restitution and forfeiture orders, as well as fines, are all enforceable in the same way, namely by issuing a warrant of distress or a warrant of commitment to prison. Distress is the process whereby property belonging to the defendant is seized and sold in order to pay the sums owing. Imprisonment is a last resort, but one which is quite often needed; the duration of the imprisonment will depend on the amount of the sums owing (*e.g.*, not more than 30 days for an amount exceeding £100 but not exceeding £400).

Two further types of "sentence" which a magistrate might impose are those for the conditional discharge or absolute discharge of the convicted person. The former is like a probation order: the convicted person is released without punishment but may be sentenced at a later date if he breaks the conditions of his discharge. An absolute discharge means no punishment at all: it is not an acquittal, however, so technically the defendant still stands convicted of the offence.

It is worth noting at this point that if a person serves time in prison, after having been convicted of an offence, and it is later proved that he or she did not in fact commit the alleged offence, there may then be the possibility of claiming compensation from the state. The Criminal Justice Act 1988 sets up a limited statutory scheme for the whole of the United Kingdom. It will apply whenever a convicted person is pardoned or the conviction is quashed after an appeal beyond the normal time limit for appealing. A specially appointed assessor will decide how much compensation should be paid.

For a magistrate's sentencing powers in cases involving juveniles, see 6.1.

Appeals by the defendant

When a criminal case is tried summarily and the defendant is convicted, as the vast majority of them are, the defendant has the right to appeal within 14 days. He must give notice of appeal to the prosecution and a copy of the notice to the clerk of petty sessions of the court where he was convicted. (Appeals are not the same as applications for judicial review, for which see 7.1.)

The defendant may wish to appeal against his conviction, his sentence, or both - though obviously he cannot appeal against his conviction if he pleaded guilty at the trial. If he pleaded not guilty at the trial and wishes to appeal against his conviction, or if (whether or not he pleaded guilty) he wishes to appeal against his sentence, he has a choice of two procedures: he can appeal to a county court, or by way of case stated to the Court of Appeal.

Appeals to a county court

An appeal to a county court will be heard by the county court judge who sits for the area in which the magistrates' court itself sits. If it is against conviction the appeal takes the form of a complete rehearing of the case: witnesses are called again and all the written statements are reconsidered. The facts, in other words, have to be re-established. The county court judge (sitting without a jury) can reverse the conviction or confirm it - even on grounds different from those given by the magistrate. In these proceedings he can also increase or decrease the accused's sentence, even though this was not specifically appealed against. If the appeal to the county court is only against sentence, all that is required is a review of the accused's previous convictions, if any, and a reconsideration of his plea in mitigation. In 1987 the county courts disposed of 3,781 appeals from magistrates' courts in criminal cases; 80 percent of these were against sentence only.

Appeals to the Court of Appeal

An appeal by way of case stated to the Court of Appeal can be used only where there is a disputed point of law. If it is the facts which are disputed, the defendant must appeal to a county court. Points of law can be raised in appeals to a county court as well as in appeals by way of case stated to the Court of Appeal, but the latter procedure *must* be used if only a point of law is involved. If we apply this distinction between points of law and points of fact to appeals against sentences, we should understand that a complaint that the resident magistrate had, for example, no power to order disqualification from driving for the offence which the accused has committed would be an appeal on a point of law, whereas a complaint that the RM disqualified the accused for too long a period would be an appeal on a point of fact.

Under the procedure by way of case stated, the resident magistrate is asked by the side appealing (the appellant) to pose a question to the Court of Appeal for its opinion on what the law is on a particular point. The Court of Appeal answers the question and on the basis of that answer affirms, reverses or varies the decision appealed from. It may also consider any points of law not considered in the court below or give directions on what the law is and remit the case to the lower court for a further hearing. But it may not increase the defendant's sentence, least of all in cases where the appeal was only against conviction. All that the Court of Appeal can do to increase a sentence is decide to discount a period spent in custody pending the appeal.

Appeals by the prosecution

All the appeal procedures so far considered have been concerned with appeals by the defendant. The prosecution has fewer rights of appeal. If the defendant is acquitted by a magistrates' court, or if a conviction is reversed by the county court, the prosecution cannot appeal against those decisions on the ground that the facts were wrongly found by the resident magistrate or the county court judge. The only avenue open to the prosecution is to appeal directly to the Court of Appeal on a point of law by way of case stated. Even then' the appeal can only be against an acquittal, not against too lenient a sentence.

Further appeals

If the accused has appealed to a county court the main way in which the case can be taken further is by either side stating a case from that court to the Court of Appeal. But if the county court acquits a defendant in an appeal, the prosecution may get the original conviction restored if it has grounds for judicial review proceedings (see 7.1).

All decisions of the Court of Appeal are in turn appealable to the House of Lords, the highest court in the land. Before this can happen, however, the permission (or "leave") of the Court of Appeal or the House of Lords must be granted, and this leave will not be obtained unless two conditions are satisfied: the Court of Appeal must certify that a point of law of general public importance is involved, and it must appear to the Court of Appeal or the House of Lords that the point is one which ought to be considered by the latter. All appeals to the House of Lords are therefore on points of law only. Understandably, it is very rare for a case which has been tried summarily in the province's magistrates' courts to travel as far as the House of Lords, but two examples are *McEldowney* v *Forde* (1971) (see 2.3), and *Seay* v *Eastwood* (1976).

4.7 Committal Proceedings in a Magistrates' Court

The other type of criminal case which a magistrates' court deals with is committal proceedings. These are held for persons charged with indictable offences which are not triable summarily or which, although triable summarily, the defendant or prosecution has elected to have tried on indictment. The purpose of committal proceedings is to decide if there is a *prima facie* case (*i.e.* a case "on the face of it") for the accused to answer. A finding that there is simply means that the defendant is then committed for trial to the Crown Court: it does not imply any presumption that the accused is guilty.

Committal proceedings take the form of either a preliminary investigation (a PI), where witnesses attend and give their evidence by word of mouth on oath in court, or a preliminary enquiry (a PE), where copies of witnesses' written statements are simply presented to the court and, if either side so requests, read out aloud. When evidence is given by word of mouth on oath it is written down in court and is then called a deposition. Witnesses are then "bound over" to attend and give evidence if required at the main trial. In all cases the defendant can opt for either form of proceeding, though in practice he rarely objects to a preliminary enquiry. Occasionally there can be a mixture of both types of committal proceedings - a preliminary enquiry where the defendant nevertheless insists that the evidence of certain witnesses be taken down by way of deposition.

In the committal proceedings the prosecution does not have to reveal all its evidence and the accused will usually reserve his defence by saving nothing at all, but he may try to assess the strength of the case against him by cross-examining some of the witnesses for the prosecution. The only situation in which a defendant is obliged to disclose any part of his defence in advance of the main trial is where he intends to rely on an alibi, that is, a defence that he was somewhere else at the time the offence was committed: if the defendant is committed for trial, the particulars of such a defence must be given to the prosecution within seven days of the end of the committal proceedings, provided the prosecution has told the defendant of the need for this period of notice.

Discharging the accused

If the resident magistrate considers that there is not enough evidence to require the accused to answer the charge against him, he will not commit the accused for trial. This is called "discharging" the accused, or "refusing an information". The defendant is then free to go, though because he has not been formally acquitted he may be charged again with the same offence at a later date. The prosecution cannot appeal against a discharge but they can apply to a judge of the Court of Appeal, High Court or Crown Court for permission to present an indictment notwithstanding the absence of any committal by a magistrate's court.

This is known as a "voluntary" indictment, and is very rare in Northern Ireland. It has been used in cases where no committal proceedings at all have taken place (because, for example, the chief prosecution witness was an alleged accomplice and the prosecution wished to protect him before the main trial), but it may also be used where there have been committal proceedings and the magistrate has discharged the defendant. In either case, it is then a matter for the judge to decide whether or not there is a *prima facie* case against the defendant and, if so, to give leave for the presentation of a "voluntary" indictment to an appropriate Crown Court.

Reviews of committals

If a resident magistrate does commit the accused for trial the accused or his barrister can, before arraignment in the Crown Court (see 4.8), apply to the trial judge to have the committal reviewed or the proposed venue changed. Under this procedure, if the judge is satisfied that the evidence does not disclose a sufficient case to justify trying the accused for an indictable offence, he can order an entry of "No Bill" in the Crown Court book, thereby discharging the accused without requiring any further answer from him. From the accused's point of view this is not as good as a formal acquittal because he can still be indicted again in the future on the same facts or evidence. The same applies if the accused successfully brings judicial review proceedings on account of some irregularity at the committal hearing. If the review application is unsuccessful the trial will proceed.

4.8 Trial on Indictment in the Crown Court

Trial on indictment involves two distinct court stages. There must, first, be committal proceedings in a magistrates' court or leave given for the presentation of a voluntary indictment (see 4.7). There is then the main trial in the Crown Court, which is the stage described in this section.

When a person has been committed by a magistrates' court for trial, it is the responsibility of the Office of the Director of Public Prosecutions (see 1.5 and 4.5) to prepare a formal document known as the form of indictment, sometimes referred to inaccurately as the bill of indictment. This contains details of the specific charge or charges against the accused arising out of the committal proceedings (see Appendix 4). Each offence charged in the indictment is known as a "count", and each count must contain a statement of the offence and particulars indicating the person indicted, the person (if any) injured, and the necessary ingredients of the offence. A copy of the indictment must be given to the defendant to let him know precisely for what offences he is being tried. The case is then ready to proceed to trial at the sitting of the Crown Court determined by the magistrate who committed the accused. The trial should take place no sooner than eight days and no later than 14 weeks (eight weeks in England) after the date of the accused's committal. During 1987 the average delay between committal and trial was eight weeks (but 10 weeks in Diplock cases; see 4.9)

The Crown Court

The Crown Court was created as a branch of the Supreme Court of Judicature of Northern Ireland in April 1979. It sits at eight different places in the province and often there are several sittings occurring at the same time. The court can be presided over by the Lord Chief Justice, a judge of the Court of Appeal, a High Court judge or a county court judge, but the Lord Chancellor has directed that some offences (*e.g.* murder) must be tried by at least a judge of the High Court. In 1987 the Crown Court disposed of 1,227 cases, which involved 2,070 defendants; 1,468 defendants pleaded guilty to all charges against them. Only 8 per cent of defendants were acquitted of all charges.

In all cases there will be a jury of 12 persons, except when the offence being dealt with is a scheduled offence, which is tried by a judge sitting alone (see 4.9). The trial of non-scheduled offences takes place at the sitting of the Crown Court determined by the magistrate who committed the accused, though this venue can be altered by a ruling of the Crown Court itself. Usually, non-scheduled offences are tried at the Crown Court acting for the county court division in which the offence is alleged to have been committed, but a different venue can be arranged on account of special circumstances such as the convenience of witnesses, security reasons, or the need to speed up the proceedings.

Arraignment

Proceedings in a Crown Court commence with the "arraignment" of the accused, that is, with the court clerk reading the indictment to the accused and asking him how he pleads on each count. If the accused pleads guilty to all counts there will be no need for a jury to be sworn: the prosecution will outline the facts and the judge will pass sentence after considering the accused's previous convictions, if any, and any plea in mitigation by his barrister. If the accused pleads not guilty to any count, and if the offence is not a scheduled offence, a jury must be sworn from the panel already summoned to the Court for that day. Technically the trial begins only with the swearing of the jury.

Juries

Jurors for particulars courts are selected from local "Area Jurors Lists" by the Juries Officer (until 1982, by the under-sheriff) of the appropriate county court division. These lists are drawn up annually from registers prepared by the Chief Electoral Officer for Northern Ireland. Every registered elector aged between 18 and 70 is qualified for inclusion, though certain individuals (persons currently or recently imprisoned) are disqualified and others (by reason of their jobs, for example, lawyers, ministers of religion, doctors, nurses and chemists) are exempt. The Juries Officer selects a jury to serve not just for one particular trial but for all the hearings in a particular court or place over a prescribed period of time. To keep the size of a jury panel manageable the judge of any court may divide the selected jurors into two or more sections and may excuse from attendance jurors whose names appear in any one or more of those sections.

People called for jury service are paid allowances, but these may not fully compensate them for expenses incurred. From November 1987 the financial loss allowance is £27.40 per day (if more than four hours are taken up), the daily subsistence allowance is £2.85 (for periods between five hours and 10 hours), and the allowance for travelling by car to and from the court is 15.6p per mile.

When the members of a jury panel are being "empanelled", or sworn in to serve a particular trial, a defendant can, without giving reasons, object to any 12 of them. This is called the right to a peremptory challenge and those members must then stand down. Such challenges were abolished in England and Wales by the Criminal Justice Act 1988. After that the defendant can challenge would-be jurors only if he gives reasons, and the jurors will have to stand down only if the judge considers the reason to be satisfactory. The prosecution has no right of peremptory challenge but can require any would-be juror to "stand by", that is, to wait on one side until the rest of the jury group has been gone through to see if a full jury can be sworn. If by then a full jury has not been sworn the prosecution can prevent a would-be juror from serving only if it provides the judge with good reasons why this should be so. Even if the defence or the prosecution do not object to a particular juror, the judge himself may excuse jurors who have already participated in a trial of an exceptionally exacting nature and a juror may always apply to be excused on the grounds of hardship or ill-health. In England and Wales the Attorney-General has laid down guidelines for what amounts to acceptable "jury-vetting" by either side in particularly sensitive trials. In Northern Ireland, juries would tend not to be involved in such trials anyway.

Procedure in a trial on indictment

Once a jury has been empanelled for the case in hand - and it must be stressed that no jury will be sworn in trials on indictment of scheduled offences (see 4.9) - it is the duty of the prosecution to prove beyond a reasonable doubt that the defendant committed the offence. Only in exceptional cases is there any burden on the defendant to prove his own innocence (*e.g.* when he claims to be unfit to plead, or to be of impaired mental responsibility, he must prove these matters "on the balance of probabilities"). Examination, cross-examination and re-examination of witnesses take place as in a magistrates' court, but will usually be conducted in more detail and with the utmost attention to the law's rules of evidence. All witnesses may remain in court during the hearing of evidence, unless a special application to exclude some of them is granted by the judge. This differs from the position in England, where witnesses remain outside the courtroom during the taking of evidence. Proving the accused's guilt beyond a reasonable doubt means that the jury has to believe that the evidence produced shows that the accused committed the offence and that it leaves no real doubt about that.

Trials within a trial

If at any stage of the trial either side wishes to produce evidence which may not, according to the strict rules of evidence, be admissible, the judge will ask the jury to withdraw while he himself hears the evidence and decides whether or not it is admissible. Technically it is for the defendant to decide whether the jury should be present or not, but in practice the judge controls this. This is an example of a *voir dire* hearing, or a trial within a trial. If the judge decides that the evidence is admissible the jury will be recalled and the trial will proceed with the evidence being presented. If the judge decides that the evidence is not admissible the jury will be recalled and the trial will proceed with no mention being made of the inadmissible evidence. In this way the jury is protected from hearing evidence which for one reason or another the law considers to be improper. Hearsay evidence, for instance, is generally inadmissible because it tends to be unreliable. Another commonly recurring example of questionable evidence is a confession extracted by dubious methods. In trials of non-scheduled offences such a confession is inadmissible if made involuntarily, that is, through oppression or through fear of prejudice or hope of advantage exercised or held out by a person in authority. The test in England is slightly different after the coming into force of the Police and Criminal Evidence Act 1984, and the equivalent Order will alter the law in Northern Ireland too (see 4.3).

The verdict in trials on indictment

After all the evidence in a Crown Court trial has been presented, the lawyers representing prosecution and defence make final speeches summarising their case. The judge must sum up the whole case for the jury by drawing its attention to the rival versions of the relevant facts and directing it on the relevant law to be applied to those facts. In long trials the judge's summing-up may last for days.

The jury's verdict should be unanimous, but since 1971, if it has been deliberating for at least two hours and cannot come to a unanimous decision, the jury can reach a majority verdict by 11 to 1 or 10 to 2 (but not by 9 to 3 or some smaller majority). If the jury finds it impossible even to arrive at a majority verdict the judge may discharge that jury and order a new trial before a different jury. If the jury's verdict is "not guilty" the accused must be acquitted and he cannot be held in custody or tried again in connection with the offence charged. He is said to have the defence of "autrefois acquit" and to be protected by the principle which forbids a person being subjected to "double jeopardy". If the verdict is "guilty", the judge will pass sentence. Before passing sentence, the judge will consider the defendant's previous convictions, if any, and may be addressed by the defence on points of mitigation as well as being assisted by reports from probation officers, welfare officers, doctors, etc.

Sentencing in the Crown Court

The sentencing powers of the Crown Court embrace all of those exercisable by resident magistrates (see 4.6) but include as well other powers conferred by the common law and statute. The commonest sentence is immediate imprisonment, which, if we include detention in a young offenders' centre (see 6.1), was imposed in 49 per cent of the cases in 1987. In a further 30 per cent of cases a suspended prison or detention sentence was given.

At the moment a suspended sentence must not exceed two years and the period of suspension must be between one and three years; the sentence *may* be activated if the offender commits another imprisonable offence during the period of suspension. Crown Court judges in Northern Ireland (and the equivalent judges in the Republic of Ireland) also exercise a self-professed power to impose what are known as "recorded" sentences, a form of punishment not known in England. It allows a prison term of *any* length to be suspended for *any* period and it is activated automatically if there is *any* breach of the suspension. The proposed Treatment of Offenders (NI) Order 1988, however, abolishes the power to impose recorded sentences and alters the power to suspend sentences so as to allow sentences of up to seven years' imprisonment to be suspended for periods ranging from one to five years.

The precise sentence which a convicted person will receive will depend on a number of factors. Some of these relate to the nature of what the accused actually did - whether he was particularly brutal, malicious or dishonest, whether he acted with premeditation, whether he co-operated with police enquiries, etc; - while others relate to the kind of person he is - whether he has an otherwise unblemished record, whether he is genuinely remorseful, whether he is easily influenced by others, whether he is mentally unstable, etc. Each crime is subject to a maximum possible sentence, but not to any minimum. A judge will know from his experience what is the normal "tariff" for a certain kind of offence and in all cases he will adjust this in the light of the factors referred to above. An important influence might be the wish to deter others from perpetrating similar crimes.

There are many offences for which the maximum punishment by statute is life imprisonment, but the only offences for which that sentence *must* be imposed are murder and torture. The death penalty was to all intents and purposes abolished in Northern Ireland in 1973 (the last execution having taken place in 1964), though, as in England, hanging still exists for one or two obscure offences (including high treason). When judges impose life sentences they are at liberty to state that in their view the accused should serve at least a certain number of years in gaol before being released. This recommendation will be respected by the Secretary of State (who has the responsibility for the continued detention of prisoners) but is not binding on him. "Lifers", as such prisoners are called, are in any event subject to a special review system which may lead to their release after, say, 12 or 15 years. Their release can then only be "on licence": they are liable to be recalled to prison at any time.

People who are under 17 when they commit a serious crime cannot be sentenced to life imprisonment. Instead they must be detained "at the Secretary of State's pleasure". This means that, like lifers, they do not have a definite release date; but unlike lifers they do not benefit from a formalised review system for assessing their suitability for release. There are about 30 so-called SoSP's in Northern Ireland at the time of writing.

In 1987 only 2 per cent of all Crown Court defendants were fined, 5 per cent were given probation orders and 8 per cent community service orders.

Appeals by the defendant

When a criminal case is tried on indictment the accused person can appeal against conviction on a point of law alone without obtaining the permission of any court. If he wishes to appeal against the conviction on a question of fact alone, or on a question of mixed law and fact, he needs the permission, or "leave", of either the Crown Court judge or the Court of Appeal. As a general principle appellate courts are very reluctant to interfere with the findings of fact made by a lower court, though it can often be a nice question whether a disputed point is indeed one of pure fact, or of mixed law and fact, rather than one of pure law. If a convicted person wishes to appeal only against sentence he needs the leave of the Court of Appeal.

There is also a power vested in the Secretary of State for Northern Ireland (under section 14 of the Criminal Appeal (NI) Act 1980) to refer a conviction or a decision of not guilty on the ground of insanity to the Court of Appeal either as a proper appeal or for the Court's opinion on a point of law. There is no case stated procedure (see 4.6) for trials on indictment, nor is the judicial review procedure (see 7.1) available, because it lies only in respect of proceedings in tribunals or "inferior" courts (*i.e.* magistrates' courts and county courts).

Appeals by the prosecution

As far as the prosecution is concerned there is no right of appeal against the acquittal of a defendant who has been tried on indictment. All that can be done is for the Attorney-General (under section 15 of the Criminal Appeal (NI) Act 1980) to refer a point of law to the Court of Appeal for its opinion. This is only a reference and not an appeal as such. Even if the Court of Appeal considers that the trial judge made an error of law which resulted in an undeserved acquittal, the acquittal still stands; once a person has been formally acquitted he cannot be tried again for the same offence. The Court of Appeal's opinion will guide the prosecution in the trials of other defendants in the future.

The Criminal Justice Act 1988 has also conferred on the Attorney-General (whether in Northern Ireland or England) the power to refer a case to the Court of Appeal if he believes that the sentence imposed by the Crown Court was too lenient. This new provision was provoked by highly publicised cases in England where violent sex offenders were given comparatively light sentences by the trial judge.

The powers of the Court of Appeal

Pending the determination of an appeal the Court of Appeal can permit the defendant to be released on bail, though this rarely occurs. When it has heard the defendant's appeal against conviction the Court of Appeal can take one of five courses of action. It may:

(1)   straightforwardly dismiss the appeal;

(2)   dismiss the appeal by "exercising the proviso" (to section 2 (1) of the Criminal Appeal (NI) Act 1980), that is, acknowledging an error at the trial but deciding that no miscarriage of justice has occurred because a reasonable jury would still, despite the error, inevitably have convicted;

(3)   allow the appeal but substitute a verdict of guilty of another offence;

(4)   allow the appeal but order a retrial because, for example, new evidence has come to light since the first trial or (a ground for retrial not existing in England) because there has been a wrong decision on a question of law or a material irregularity in the course of the trial;

(5)   allow the appeal and acquit the defendant.

If it adopts any of the first three courses the Court of Appeal may also (even on its own initiative) reduce, increase or vary the appellant's sentence. It can do likewise in any appeals against sentence. In England the Court of Appeal cannot increase sentences.

In 1987, 286 appeals were lodged with the Court of Appeal - 165 of these were in ordinary cases; 121 in "Diplock" cases (see 4.9). More than three-quarters of the appeals lodged were against sentence only. The success rate in ordinary cases was 22 per cent; in Diplock cases it was 17 per cent.

Further appeals

Decisions of the Court of Appeal relating to trials on indictment can be further appealed *by either the prosecution or the defence* to the House of Lords. But, as with appeals after summary trials, the leave of either the Court of Appeal or the House of Lords is first required, and this is granted only if the Court of Appeal certifies that a point of law of general public importance is involved and if the Court of Appeal or the House of Lords thinks that the point is one which ought to be considered by the House. There are on average only one or two such appeals each year. A "reference" under section 15 of the 1980 Act (see above) can also be further referred by the Court of Appeal to the House of Lords, but the decision of that House can still not reverse the original acquittal.

The appeal system for criminal proceedings is represented diagrammatically in Table 9.

4.9 Special Features of the Emergency Laws

As mentioned in 4.1, the United Kingdom Parliament (and, when it existed, Stormont) have enacted emergency laws for Northern Ireland to help deal with "the troubles". Some of these are civil law statutes (*e.g.* the Payments for Debt (Emergency Provisions) Act (NI) 1971) but most are criminal. The most important are now the Northern Ireland (Emergency Provisions) Acts 1978 and 1987, successors to the Civil Authorities (Special Powers) Acts (NI) 1922-33. Some comparable provisions are to be found in the Prevention of Terrorism (Temporary Provisions) Act 1984, a statute applying throughout the United Kingdom and due to be replaced by updated legislation in 1989. As well as these "temporary" laws some permanent measures have been taken, such as those in the Protection of the Person and Property Act (NI) 1969 and what is now the Public Order (NI) Order 1987.

The 1978 Act confirms the existence of scheduled offences and the no-jury Diplock courts, but as well it contains special powers and procedures for nearly every stage in the ordinary criminal process whenever a scheduled offence is being dealt with. A few of these special rules apply even when a scheduled offence is being tried summarily (see above, page 94), but clearly it is in relation to trials on indictment that the emergency procedures have their greatest impact. We can identify nine relevant points.

Table 9. The appeal system for criminal cases.

(1) As regards powers of arrest, under section 12 of the Prevention of Terrorism (Temporary Provisions) Act 1984, (which will become section 14 of the 1989 Act) the police may arrest without a warrant any person whom they reasonably suspect to be guilty of certain specified offences or of being concerned in the commission, preparation or instigation of acts of terrorism. Terrorism is defined as the use of violence for political ends. In addition, section 14 of the Northern Ireland (Emergency Provisions) Act 1978 allows any soldier on duty to arrest without a warrant any person whom he reasonably suspects of committing, having committed or being about to commit *any* offence. The police, arguably, remain under the common law duty to give a reason for an arrest at the time it is effected, but by section 14 the army do not. In 1987, 492 persons were arrested under the arrest powers in the 1978 Act; only 47 of these were later charged. In the first nine months of 1988, 433 people were detained under the Prevention of Terrorism Act in Northern Ireland and only 78 of these were later charged.

(2) As regards powers of detention, persons arrested by the police under section 12 of the 1984 Act may be detained for up to 48 hours and the Secretary of State may extend this by a further period not exceeding five days. A person arrested by the army under section 14 of the 1978 Act may be detained for up to four hours, but may then be passed to the police for detention under section 12. These powers of detention are obviously designed to enable the security forces to place arrested persons under sustained questioning, but there is still no legal obligation on such persons to answer any questions, and (on one view at least) the ordinary law on cautioning and charging must still apply. There is an obligation under section 18 of the 1978 Act to answer questions about your identity, your movements and what you know concerning any explosion or any incident endangering life, but this arises only after you have been stopped in the street by the police or army. As many as 84 per cent of those arrested under the 1984 Act are detained beyond the initial 48 hour period.

(3) Persons arrested under section 12 of the 1984 Act may be forcibly photographed and fingerprinted by the police.

(4) For scheduled offences tried on indictment the law on bail has been altered by section 2 of the 1978 Act so as to permit only a judge of the High Court or the Court of Appeal, or the judge at the trial itself, to grant bail. Resident magistrates have no power to grant bail in these cases.

(5) In committal proceedings for scheduled offences the prosecution is entitled to insist on a preliminary enquiry rather than a preliminary investigation (see 4.7), unless the court is of the opinion that in the interests of justice a preliminary investigation should be conducted into the offence.

(6) Trials on indictment of scheduled offences take place before a single

judge sitting without a jury. It is felt that the risk of perverse verdicts, either through bias or intimidation of jurors, is too great to allow continued use of jury trials. One implication of this is that when scheduled offences are involved, trials within a trial (see above, page 103) are not very different from the main trial: the judge who decides the *voir dire* issues will usually be the one who goes on to decide the issue of fact at the main trial. If he has held certain evidence to be inadmissible during the *voir dire* he is meant to put that evidence out of his mind when deciding the main issues; sometimes, because he realises how difficult this will be, he directs the main trial to be continued before a different judge. In 1987 over 35 per cent of all the defendants dealt with in Crown Court trials were tried in the absence of a jury. 713 persons were tried for indictable scheduled offences and 680 were convicted.

(7)   One of the commonest reasons for holding a trial within a trial is to assess the admissibility of a confession. The test for admissibility in non-scheduled cases (set out above on page 104) has been significantly altered for scheduled cases: the confession is inadmissible only if made by a defendant who was subjected to torture, violence, threats of violence, or inhuman or degrading treatment inflicted in order to induce him to make the confession, though as always the confession may still be excluded from the evidence at the judge's discretion even if this test is not satisfied.

(8)   In trials on indictment of non-scheduled offences the burden of proving the defendant's guilt is on the prosecution. In some trials on indictment of scheduled offences this principle appears to be qualified in at least two respects. In the first place, whereas under the ordinary law the burden of proving that a confession was made voluntarily clearly rests on the prosecution and requires proof beyond a reasonable doubt, under section 8 of the 1978 Act the accused must first adduce *prima facie* evidence that the statement was obtained after he was subjected to degrading treatment (or worse) and the prosecution must then satisfy the court that the confession was not obtained. In the second place, section 9 of the 1978 Act appears to place the burden of proving their innocence on persons found to be in possession of explosive substances or firearms. In actual fact, however, the judges in Northern Ireland have mostly interpreted these provisions in section 8 and 9 in a way which equates them with the ordinary law.

(9)   All persons convicted of a scheduled offence tried on indictment in Northern Ireland can appeal against conviction to the Court of Appeal on any ground and without any leave. This is largely because there is no jury in the case, an absent safeguard which the automatic right of appeal is intended in part to replace. Because the judge, unlike a jury, is obliged to give reasons for his decisions, it should be easier for a defendant to establish grounds for appeal. In 1987, 145 appeals in scheduled cases were disposed of; however, only two persons had their *convictions* quashed.

It is worth noting that, perhaps surprisingly, there are no special laws dealing with the use of force by security forces in Northern Ireland or with the status of prisoners. There are of course special laws governing discrimination; these are referred to in Chapter 8. The Emergency Provisions Acts and the Prevention of Terrorism Act are the subject of annual reviews (currently conducted by Viscount Colville); the reports are considered by Parliament before it decides whether to renew the Acts for a further year.

5

Proceedings in Civil Courts

5.1 The Nature of Civil Proceedings

Civil proceedings have to be distinguished from criminal proceedings. The best way to understand the difference is to consider the legal action that may be taken after a road accident, where one person's careless driving damages another person's car. The careless driver may receive a summons from the police, which means that criminal proceedings are being taken in a magistrates' court with the object of punishing the driver if he or she is found guilty of the crime of careless driving (see 4.6). But this will not help the other person to pay for the repairs to the car. Even if the careless driver is fined by the magistrates' court, the money paid will go to the state and not to the other car-owner. Unless the careless driver or an insurance company pay up voluntarily, the other car-owner must commence civil proceedings against the careless driver in a county court or in the High Court (depending on the amount involved), claiming damages to cover the cost of repairing the car. The same distinction is apparent whenever some property is stolen. The owner of the property may well sue the culprit for the recovery of the property or its value, but the state - in the shape of the police or the Director of Public Prosecutions - may also prosecute the defendant for the crime of theft.

It can be seen, therefore, that one incident can give rise to both civil and criminal proceedings, but the person initiating the proceedings and the object of those proceedings are different, and the courts hearing the cases are also different (though the judges may be the same). Criminal courts do have some powers to award civil law remedies in the course of criminal proceedings, but these powers are limited and are not frequently exercised (see 4.6). Furthermore, the right to claim compensation from the state for losses suffered through violent criminal action is a civil right and must be processed through the civil courts; it is described in more detail in 5.5 below.

Settlements

Once criminal proceedings have begun they must go to court unless the charges are dropped; even if the defendant pleads guilty, the court must impose the appropriate sentence. But in civil proceedings (with some rare exceptions, most notably divorces) the plaintiff and the defendant can at any time - even after the court has started to hear the case, or when the case has reached an appellate court - decide between themselves that they want to settle, or compromise, the case by agreement; once they so decide, the civil proceedings are usually terminated. The vast majority of civil actions are in fact settled before they ever see the inside of a courtroom. Once court proceedings have actually started, the court must be officially notified of any settlement (so that "judgment by consent" can be decreed) and it must grant its approval before an action involving a person under 18 can be settled. The question of who is to bear the costs of a settled action is usually made part and parcel of the settlement agreement, but failing this the court can order the costs to be "taxed" (see 3.4).

If the case is not settled there are three types of court for civil proceedings, depending largely on the amount of money or value of property at stake. They are magistrates' courts, county courts and the High Court. These will be examined in turn, together with the procedures for appealing to higher courts. We shall then consider how judgments in civil cases are enforced.

The civil justice review

In June 1988 a review body set up by the Lord Chancellor issued a report on how to improve the machinery of civil justice in England and Wales. As well as recommending a shift in workload from the High Court to the county courts, the report deals in detail with specific types of case such as those involving personal injuries, small claims, debt, housing or commercial matters. There is a proposal that every court should have a "link officer" with the specific job of liaising with advice agencies regularly present at the court. Such agencies should qualify for funding from the new Legal Aid Board (established under the Legal Aid Act 1988). In the review body's opinion the feasibility of allowing a contingency fee system, like that in America, where lawyers get paid by results, should also be re-examined. Other recommendations are mentioned in passing later in this chapter, for although the report is confined to England and Wales, it is very likely that the changes it brings about will in due course also be made in the civil justice system of Northern Ireland.

5.2 Civil Proceedings in a Magistrates' Court

The powers and jurisdiction of a magistrates' court in relation to civil proceedings are much less important than its criminal law powers (see 4.6). Resident magistrates spend only about 15 per cent of their time in court on civil work. But in both spheres it is a local court, mainly dealing with comparatively unimportant matters arising within the petty sessions district where the court sits. At the moment there are 25 magistrates' courts in the province, which are listed in Table 2 on page 8. They sit at intervals varying from every day (in Belfast) to once a month. As implied in 4.6, the jurisdiction of these courts is called summary because the procedure used in them is simple, informal and speedy; in civil matters there is none of the elaborate procedure normally found in High Court cases or to a lesser extent in county court cases. When the case comes to court it is determined by a resident magistrate sitting without a jury. The litigants are usually represented by solicitors rather than barristers, though witnesses are examined and cross-examined in the same way as in a higher court. Because there is often not a great deal at stake in the case, compared with proceedings in a higher court, the proceedings do not usually take much time and most decisions are announced straightaway.

The main types of civil cases which a magistrates' court can deal with are domestic cases, claims to recover small debts, claims to deprive someone of the occupation of land, and applications for licences. Of the 52,782 applications in civil cases considered during 1987 about one fifth related to domestic matters, while over 64 per cent concerned small debts or ejectment. A few words must be said about each type of case. For further details see the Magistrates' Courts (NI) Order 1981 and the Magistrates' Courts Rules (NI) 1984.

Domestic cases

Domestic cases are those involving family matters. Many legal remedies (but not decrees of divorce or nullity) are now available in a magistrates' court to a husband or wife whose marriage is not working out very happily. Even cohabitees can sometimes obtain relief. Under the Domestic Proceedings (NI) Order 1980, a resident magistrate may grant any of the following orders:

(1) A financial provision order

If things are going badly between husband and wife it is obviously very important that proper financial provision is made for both spouses and any children. In many instances the court may have to compel these arrangements to be carried out. If the spouses have agreed in writing between themselves that one of them should pay an amount of money to the other, or to a child of the family, the court can confirm this agreement and order the payments to be made. Similarly, if the parties are living apart by agreement and one of them has been paying money to the other or to a child of the family for at least three months, these voluntary payments can be ordered by the court to be continued. Finally, if a person contests his duty to pay anything at all to his spouse the latter can apply for a financial provision order to compel such payment. This last course of action is possible, however, only if certain grounds are first satisfied: these are (i) that the spouse has failed to provide reasonable maintenance for the applicant or a child of the family, (ii) that he has committed adultery, (iii) that he has deserted the applicant, or (iv) that he has behaved in such a way that the applicant cannot reasonably be expected to live with him. In all of these situations the financial provision which an RM can order to be made may take the form of a regular weekly or monthly sum, or one single lump sum not exceeding £500.

(2) A personal protection order

This may be granted if the RM is satisfied (i) that one party has used, or threatened to use, violence against the other or a child of the family, and (ii) that an order is necessary for the protection of that other party or child. This order restrains the violent party from "molesting" the other party or child, which means not only that he must not use or threaten violence but that he must not cause trouble to them or pester, vex, annoy or inconvenience them. If the order is disobeyed, a police officer can arrest the guilty party without a warrant.

(3) An exclusion order

This can be granted on its own or in conjunction with a personal protection order. It is available on the same grounds as a personal protection order but its terms will prohibit a party from entering the matrimonial home or other specified premises, or some area in which the matrimonial home or those specified premises are situated. It can remain in force for up to six months or for extended periods of up to six months. If it is disobeyed, the guilty spouse can be arrested.

(4) Orders concerning children

As well as being able to make a financial provision order to ensure that children are reasonably maintained, a magistrates' court can decide who should have the custody of children or access to them, or whether a child should be placed under the supervision or committed to the care of the Department of Health and Social Services. All of these powers concerning children can only be exercised, however, if the court is already considering financial provision arrangements between the spouses; they cannot be exercised in isolation from those arrangements. They really exist because the 1980 Order compels the court, when considering financial provision arrangements, to regard the welfare of any children of the family as the first and paramount consideration.

It should be noted that magistrates also have the power to make affiliation orders, which compel a man to pay for the upkeep of illegitimate children he has fathered. Magistrates do not, however, have jurisdiction to grant adoption orders: for those the applicant has to go to a county court.

The party who wants any of these domestic remedies in a magistrates' court (the complainant) can begin the civil proceedings by stating the facts (in a "complaint") to a JP or clerk of petty sessions and asking for a summons to be issued ordering the other spouse to come before a magistrates' court on a certain day. As in criminal cases this summons is then served on the defendant, who must appear at the time and place stated in the summons. This is all that is required, though of course it will usually be wise to seek proper legal advice before making the complaint to the JP or clerk. The complaint must be made within a year of the action complained about. Domestic cases are heard at different times from other cases and in camera, that is, with the general public excluded.

Small debts

Claims to recover small debts are a second common type of civil case in a magistrates' court. Generally speaking, the debt in question must be for a fixed amount and less than £100. If you are in arrears with your rent, for example, you are liable to be proceeded against in this way. If the claim is for the balance of an account - say you still owe £120 on a bill for £240 - you can be proceeded against in this way provided the total bill is for no more than £250. Larger sums are also recoverable, but only if a statute so provides (as does the Rent (NI) Order 1978 in the case of rent). Proceedings for debt recovery are initiated not by way of complaint or summons but by way of a process, which is a form filled in and served by the creditor or the creditor's solicitor. It can be issued at any time within six years of the debt falling due. The jurisdiction of magistrates' courts to deal with cases of debt overlaps with that of small claims courts, which are really a branch of the county courts (see 5.4).

Land cases

Claims to deprive someone of the occupation of land are in this context known as ejectment proceedings. They can be brought by landlords to get rid of tenants who are no longer entitled to stay on the premises. But unless a statute provides otherwise, a magistrates' court has jurisdiction in such matters only when premises have been let at a rent which is less than £110 per annum. Most commercial and residential tenancies would therefore not be affected by this procedure were it not for the fact that the Housing (NI) Order 1981 confers special recovery rights upon housing associations and the Northern Ireland Housing Executive. In these matters proceedings are begun by a process, just as in claims to recover small debts. In 1987 there were altogether 34,274 applications for small debt recovery and ejectment in the province's magistrates' courts.

Licences and appeals

Magistrates also have the important functions of renewing licences authorising the sale of intoxicating liquor, certifying that premises are suitable for the conduct of the business of bookmaking, judging whether an applicant for a bookmaker's licence is of suitable character, granting bingo-hall, gamekeepers' and general dealers' licences, and granting or renewing registered club certificates. They deal too with appeals against certain decisions taken, for example, by education authorities. Thus if an Education and Library Board refuses to issue a licence to someone under 16 to allow participation in public performances on the stage, an appeal can be heard by a magistrate. The document which is used to bring any of these applications to a magistrate's court is itself called a notice rather than a complaint or a process. In 1987, 3,771 applications for licences were dealt with.

Appeals from a magistrates' court

If either side is dissatisfied with the civil decision of a court of summary jurisdiction it may appeal against that decision in one of two ways: by way of ordinary appeal (in the form of a complete rehearing of issues of both fact and law) to a county court, or by way of case stated (on a point of law only) to the Court of Appeal. If the first course is taken, there is then a further right of appeal for either side - by way of case stated only - to the Court of Appeal. The procedure by way of case stated and the composition of the Court of Appeal are described in more detail in 4.6 and 1.5 respectively. (For the different procedure known as judicial review see 7.1.) In 1987 there were 14 cases stated to the Court of Appeal by resident magistrates.

In these appeals the decision of the Court of Appeal is to all intents and purposes final. The only occasion when a civil case begun in the province's magistrates' courts (or indeed county courts) can be taken to the House of Lords is when it involves a question as to the validity of a piece of legislation passed by the Northern Ireland Parliament.

5.3 Civil Proceedings in a County Court

With the establishment of the Crown Court in 1979 (see 4.8) the county court has become almost exclusively a civil court. County courts, however, still hear appeals from criminal cases tried summarily in magistrates' courts, and judges who sit as county court judges also frequently sit as Crown Court judges (see 4.6 and 1.5).

The civil work of the county courts is much more varied than that of the magistrates' courts, but it is still subject to restrictions as regards both type and size of claim. We will first of all list the main types of case dealt with in a county court and then look at a few typical procedures. Further details are to be found in the County Courts (NI) Order 1980 and the County Court Rules (NI) 1981. The report of the English civil justice review body (1988) recommends that the upper financial limits on county court jurisdiction should be removed and that only exceptionally should a case involving less than £25,000 be heard in the High Court. It is unlikely that such a drastic change will be made in Northern Ireland within the next two or three years.

At the moment the main types of case, or "action", heard in the county courts in Northern Ireland are the following:

(1)   actions in tort, or for breach of contract, where the amount claimed is less than £5000 (£1,000 in libel or slander claims); an action in tort is what lawyers call a claim for compensation, or "damages", for personal injury or damage to property caused by the defendant - the kind of legal action taken by the victims of assaults, thefts or accidents at work or on the roads;

(2)   actions for the recovery of land or involving disputed claims to the ownership of land where, generally speaking, the land does not have an annual rateable value of more than £500 (this covers, for example, disputes between landlords and tenants or between neighbours);

(3)   Chancery work, such as the management of funds held in trust, the enforcement of mortgages, the ending of partnerships, and the supervision of contracts for the sale of land, provided that in all these cases the sum of money or value of property involved is less than £15,000 or the annual rateable value of any land involved is less than £500 (in the county courts, Chancery work is always referred to as Equity business; see 1.3);

(4)   disputes as to the validity of a will and as to who is to act as executor under a will, or administrator of the estate of someone who dies without making a will, provided that in such cases the estate does not exceed £15,000 in value after payments of all taxes, etc.; this heading includes disputes as to "legacies" in wills, where the legacy claimed is less than £5,000;

(5)   undefended petitions for divorce, and certain applications for a share in matrimonial property (regardless of the value of the property);

(6)   applications to adopt children;

(7)   equality of opportunity and sex discrimination cases brought under the Equal Pay Act (NI) 1970, the Fair Employment (NI) Act 1976 and the Sex Discrimination (NI) Order 1976, though cases alleging sex discrimination in employment practices are dealt with by industrial tribunals (see 7.3.);

(8)   applications brought under the Consumer Credit Act 1974, *e.g.* to reopen a credit agreement on the ground that it is extortionate;

(9)   applications for licences to sell intoxicating liquor (applications to renew or to transfer licences, or for club licences, are made to a magistrates' court);

(10) actions to recover rates under the Rates (NI) Order 1977 and applications to determine the proper rent for a protected tenancy under the Rent (NI) Order 1978;

(11) appeals against decisions of the Secretary of State for Northern Ireland on applications for compensation for criminal injuries and criminal damage (note that these are civil claims even though they arise out of the commission of a crime, and can be for any amount; (see also 5.5).

It is to be noted that the county courts can deal with any debt cases (*i.e.*, a claim for a certain, or "liquidated", amount of money) even though the sum involved is greater than that laid down as the normal upper limit, provided that the parties themselves agree to this. The county courts must also deal with any cases which for one reason or another are transferred to them by the High Court. And they hear appeals from civil as well as criminal cases heard in magistrates' courts.

Undefended divorce cases

County court cases concerning family matters are begun either by issuing a summons (as with domestic cases in magistrates' courts; see 5.2) or by lodging a petition. Since 1981 county courts have been able to grant divorces, but only in undefended cases. Even in undefended cases, however, the petitioner must still appear personally in court; unlike a petitioner in England, he or she cannot get a divorce by post. On the other hand, legal aid remains available here to cover all divorce cases whether defended or undefended (see 3.3). In 1987 there were 426 divorce cases disposed of by the seven county court divisions; nearly a third of all divorce decrees were granted in the county courts as opposed to the High Court.

Civil bills

Other county court cases are usually begun by the plaintiff, or the plaintiff's solicitor, issuing a document called a civil bill (see Appendix 4). The civil bill is a way of proceeding which is peculiar to Ireland and dates back to mediaeval times. It is more straightforward than the procedures used in county courts in England. It requires much less resort to "interlocutory" (that is, preliminary) proceedings and there is no need for carefully worded pleadings (see 5.5 below). The case raised by the civil bill is dealt with by a judge sitting without a jury and the emphasis is on speed and cheapness. During 1987, 7,560 defended civil bills were dealt with by the county courts (6,986 ordinary bills and 574 Equity bills, the latter being reserved for the Equity business described in (3) above).

In all debt cases, if the defendant decides not to defend the civil bill or fails to return to the court the documents sent out attached to the civil bill, the county court judge can deal with the claim summarily relying on the case presented by the plaintiff and not hearing the defendant at all. In all other cases, even if the defendant does not appear for the trial, the plaintiff must call witnesses to prove his or her case and allow the defendant (if appearing) the opportunity both to question them and to call others.

Generally speaking, the proceedings are more formal than in magistrates' courts but less formal than in the High Court. Most of the cases, in any event, are undefended. It must also be remembered that at any stage the parties to a dispute can agree to sink their differences and settle the action between themselves. The judge usually delivers a judgment as soon as the parties have completed the submission of their arguments.

Appeals from a county court

A person aggrieved by a decision of a county court in the exercise of its "original" (that is, non-appellate) civil jurisdiction may appeal either by way of a full rehearing to the High Court or by way of case stated on a point of law to the Court of Appeal. The High Court can itself then state a case for the opinion of the Court of Appeal. Whichever path is followed the decision of the Court of Appeal is final. In 1987 there were 687 county court appeals to the High Court. (For details of appeal and case stated procedures, see 4.6; for the procedure known as judicial review, see 7.1.)

5.4 Circuit Registrars and the Small Claims Procedure

The small claims court is dealt with at this stage because it is the popular name given to a type of proceedings which in fact is a special county court procedure. The jurisdiction is exercised by officials called circuit registrars, four of whom were appointed under the Judicature (NI) Act 1978 to serve in the court circuits into which the province has been divided - the Northern, Eastern, South Eastern and South Western (see Table 2, page 8). The chief task of the registrars, who must be solicitors of at least six years' standing, is to deal with claims which are for less than £1,000. They also hear undefended county court claims for sums between £1,000 and £5,000 and they all frequently sit as deputy county court judges to hear other claims. If the value of the money or property claimed is between £500 and £1,000 the registrar will deal with the claim just as a county court judge would deal with a greater one, but if the value of the claim does not exceed even £500 then a much simpler procedure - known technically, though misleadingly, as "arbitration" - is followed. It is this type of hearing which is popularly called a small claims court.

Some types of dispute involving less than £500 cannot be resolved in a small claims court and must still be taken to the county court in the normal way. These "excepted proceedings" are disputes involving personal injuries, road accidents, libel or slander, a gift under a will or an annuity, the ownership of land, the property rights of married couples, and the matters referred to the county court from the High Court. Debt claims up to £500 can be brought either as a small claim or as a civil bill, but they must be treated as a small claim if either party so wishes. All other cases involving £500 or less *must now* be brought under the small claims procedure (unlike England, where the procedure is optional).

The 1988 report of the English civil justice review has recommended that the small claims procedure should be made available in cases involving up to £1,000 and that a self-contained set of small claims court rules should be prepared.

The current procedure

To make a claim in a small claims court the applicant sets out the details of the case on an application form (see Appendix 4) and sends it with two copies to a county court office. The fee is £5 for a claim not exceeding £75 and £12 for a claim between £75 and £500. A copy of the application form and a notice as to when and where the hearing is to take place will be returned to the applicant. Another copy is sent to the person against whom the claim is being made (the respondent) to find out if he or she intends to dispute the claim. Many claims will be "settled out of court" at this stage. But if the claim is not settled to the applicant's satisfaction it will be heard by the circuit registrar on the day given for the hearing.

The procedure at the hearing itself is intended for use by individual applicants without the need for legal representation; as things have turned out, however, lawyers are quite often present. Legal aid is not available. Compared with proceedings in a proper court, the hearing will be informal; it will sometimes be in private in a small room of the courthouse. If the parties agree, the circuit registrar may even decide the claim on the basis of written evidence only. Witnesses are usually required; there may be no witness box as such, but the swearing of a formal oath is usually demanded. If a witness is reluctant to attend, the party wishing to call the witness can oblige him or her to attend by applying to the registrar for a witness summons compelling attendance. Neither of the parties can (except rarely) recover their costs from the other in a small claims arbitration (except for the fee payable with the application form), so any travel expenses incurred by witnesses (the "viaticum") and the charge of any lawyers who are engaged for the case will have to be borne by the party calling the witness or employing the lawyer. So will the cost of engaging an expert (like a doctor) to report on some matter, but the registrar may ask for a report from an independent expert to clarify a technical point and the cost of this will be borne by the court office and not by the parties. The only occasion on which a circuit registrar may award costs to one party is where the other party's conduct has been unreasonable.

The circuit registrar's decision will usually be announced as soon as the hearing is over. It may be issued even in the absence of the losing party. If the losing party does not comply with whatever order is made, the winner can take the case to the Enforcement of Judgments Office (see 5.7). If one party wishes to appeal against the decision of a circuit registrar, he or she can only ask for a case to be stated to a High Court judge or apply to the High Court to have the arbitration set aside on account of the registrar's misconduct of the case. The rights of appeal are deliberately restricted so as to prevent undue consideration of what are, relatively speaking, fairly minor matters.

During 1987 a total of 9,636 applications were dealt with in the small claims courts. About four-fifths of these were claims by business or commercial organisations, usually in respect of non-payment of hire-purchase instalments or money owed for goods delivered or services rendered. The applications by private individuals were mostly in respect of consumer claims. The vast majority of small claims (95 per cent) were undefended, and Belfast accounted for 42 per cent of all small claims business.

5.5 Compensation for Criminal Injuries and Criminal Damage

It was pointed out in 2.1 and 5.1 that the law makes a basic distinction between civil wrongs and crimes. The former are acts for which private individuals can seek redress, whereas crimes are acts by which the state is offended. Even though one and the same act can constitute both a civil wrong and a crime the two forms of the misbehaviour are processed quite differently in the legal system. The victim of a civil wrong sues the performer of the act for damages; the state prosecutes and punishes him or her for the crime. In a perfect world both the victim and the state would be satisfied and the offender would pay his or her debt to the individual and to society alike.

For a number of reasons things may not work out so neatly, certainly from the point of view of the victim. In the first place the perpetrator of the act may never be caught; secondly, even if caught, the perpetrator may not be convicted because he or she is very young, mentally handicapped or immune from prosecution, or because the evidence is insufficient; thirdly, whether or not caught and convicted for the crime, the person may not be able to afford to compensate the victim. In these circumstances it would be unjust to expect the victim to bear the loss alone. For a very long time, therefore, the state has operated compensation schemes to which the victim of violent crime can have recourse, and these can be used even if no-one has been prosecuted or convicted for the crime.

In Northern Ireland, because of the heavy incidence of violent crime, there are two such schemes; each is long-established, though the legislation now applicable dates from 1977 for criminal damage and 1988 for criminal injuries. In addition there is a scheme for compensating persons whose property is damaged under the emergency powers legislation. (In England, under the Criminal Justice Act 1988, there is now a statutory scheme for compensation for criminal injuries, with claims being made to the Criminal Injuries Compensation Board, but the provision for property damage compensation - the Riot (Damages) Act 1886 - is different from and less extensive than that in Northern Ireland.)

It should be stressed that the claims made under all these schemes are civil, not criminal, claims. They are not like the compensation and restitution orders which can be made during criminal proceedings (see 4.6). If you think you are entitled to make a claim you should immediately contact a solicitor. Pay close attention to the time limits involved - the injury or damage must have been reported to the police within 48 hours - and bear in mind that help under the civil legal aid and legal advice and assistance schemes may be available to you (see 3.3) and that if your claim against the Secretary of State is successful, reasonable legal expenses will in any case be paid by the Northern Ireland Office.

Criminal injuries compensation

To qualify for compensation for personal injury resulting from a crime of violence in Northern Ireland the victim, or the relatives of a victim who has died from injuries received, must report the crime to the police within 48 hours and serve on the Secretary of State for Northern Ireland, usually within 28 days, a notice of intention to apply for compensation. This must fully and truthfully disclose all facts within the applicant's knowledge and belief which are material to the application. If such disclosure is not made, compensation can be refused outright; or if compensation has been paid and the Northern Ireland Office then discovers that full and true disclosure was not made, the Secretary of State can apply to a county court for reimbursement by the recipient. Within a further three months of serving the notice of intention to apply, the application itself must be made. These time limits may be extended in special cases, but no compensation can ever be paid if the application is more than three years after the injury was suffered.

A "criminal injury" for this purpose is defined as an injury or death which is directly attributable to a violent offence, the arrest of an offender or the prevention of an offence. "Injury" includes mental illness caused by reaction to a violent crime ("nervous shock"), but in most cases only if the mental illness is a serious one and the person was actually present when the crime was committed. A "violent offence" is defined quite broadly: it is not restricted to terrorist offences, so "ordinary" crimes such as street-mugging or causing injury during the course of a burglary are covered. Traffic offences are excluded, however, and where the violence has occurred within a household (*e.g.* wife-battering) certain conditions must be satisfied.

Although the coverage of the scheme is wide, there are many situations in which compensation will be refused or reduced because of the conduct or background of the victim. This will happen where the victim has been negligent or provocative, where there has been a failure to co-operate with the police, where the victim has at any time been a member of an unlawful organisation, or where the applicant or victim has a criminal conviction indicative of a certain character or way of life. There is also a general power to take into account any "relevant circumstances".

The Secretary of State - in effect the Criminal Injuries Branch of the Northern Ireland Office - decides what amount of compensation, if any, should be paid. The method of calculation differs according to whether the victim was merely injured or was killed. In the former case the compensation will cover pecuniary loss (that is, loss of earnings, less social security benefits, sick pay, pension money etc.), reasonable expenses and an amount for pain and suffering and for "loss of amenities" (the ability to enjoy life). A woman who has been raped, gives birth to and keeps a child conceived as a result of the rape is entitled to up to £5,000, but no compensation is payable for the maintenance of such a child. If the victim of a violent crime has died from injuries received, the compensation paid to the relatives will cover pecuniary loss and expenses, but instead of an award for pain and suffering and loss of amenities a bereavement sum of up to £3,500 is payable to the victim's husband or wife or (if the victim was under 18) to the parents. The Secretary of State has a discretion to "top up" an award made to a widow or widower. A compensation award will in no case be reduced because the applicant has already received money from an insurance company, but to help keep down administration costs the scheme does not allow compensation to be paid at all if it amounts to less than £400, while "nervous shock" is compensatable only if it is worth more than £1,000.

If the Secretary of State makes no decision within six months of an application having been lodged, the applicant may ask a county court for a declaration that the Secretary of State has had sufficient information and a reasonable time to come to a decision. Such declarations are in practice very rarely sought, but once obtained they will certainly speed things up. Much more importantly, any person who is aggrieved by a decision of the Secretary of State can appeal against it within 10 weeks to a county court. This is a matter on which there is no financial limit to a county court's jurisdiction. Further appeals lie to the High Court and the Court of Appeal, as in other cases where a county court exercises original jurisdiction (see 5.3). If someone is later convicted of the criminal offence which caused the criminal injury, the Secretary of State can apply to a county court for an order that this person must reimburse to the Secretary of State the whole or a part of the compensation already paid to the victim.

In the year ending 31st March 1988 there were 9,249 applications for criminal injuries compensation and almost £13 million was paid out. In 1987 there were 2,074 criminal injury appeals disposed of in Northern Ireland's county courts, a five per cent increase on the 1986 figure. Over 3,000 cases were outstanding - an indication that this area forms a very important part of the county courts' workload.

Criminal damage compensation

This scheme is a little more technical than the criminal injuries scheme. Except in relation to agricultural buildings and property, compensation for damage is available only if it has been caused by three or more persons unlawfully, riotously or tumultuously assembled together, or by an act committed maliciously by a person acting for an organisation engaged in terrorism. Compensation for unlawful removal of property (in other words, "looting") is restricted to situations where the removal takes place in the course of a riot causing more than £100 worth of damage to the building where the property was located.

To qualify for compensation a person must serve on the Secretary of State for Northern Ireland and the police, within 10 days of the damage being caused, a notice of intention to apply for compensation. This notice must fully and truthfully disclose certain facts. Within a further four months the application itself must be made.

The Secretary of State decides what amount of compensation, if any, should be paid. He has regard to all such circumstances as are relevant and in particular to the conduct of the applicant and whether all reasonable precautions were taken to reduce or avoid the loss. Again, anyone who at any time has been a terrorist or a member of an organisation engaged in terrorism is barred from recovering compensation, except that the Secretary of State may make an *ex gratia* payment in the public interest. No compensation at all is provided for the first £100 of any loss, and it cannot be paid for lost money or jewellery or for any loss for which the applicant has already received adequate compensation under a statute or at common law (as in a civil action for damages).

There are special provisions for dealing with situations where more than one person with an interest in property suffers loss through its damage or removal (*e.g.* when a house is mortgaged or a car is being bought on hire-purchase), but the provisions relating to appeals and reimbursement are the same as in the criminal injuries scheme (see above).

In the four years up to 31st March 1988 the number of claims for criminal damage compensation averaged 4,486 and the amount of compensation awarded was nearly £18 million per year.

Compensation under the emergency powers legislation

If any property is taken, occupied, destroyed or interfered with under the Northern Ireland (Emergency Provisions) Act 1978 (see 4.9), compensation must be paid by the Secretary of State. The only exception is that no person who has been convicted of a scheduled offence (see 4.1) or an offence under the 1978 Act has a right to compensation in respect of acts done in connection with that offence. Applications for compensation have usually to be submitted within four months of the act complained of. Failing acceptance of the amount offered as compensation, the claimant can appeal to a county court. The county court judge will process the application as if it were an equity civil bill (see 5.3), except that no limit applies as to the amount which can be claimed. In the years 1983-87 an average of £276,587 was paid by the Northern Ireland Office each year to people whose property had been damaged or requisitioned by the security forces.

It is also worth noting that since 1970 a non-statutory scheme has operated under which applications can be made to a Compensation Tribunal by employees who, having been in continuous employment for two years, have been dismissed by their employer or ceased employment voluntarily because of threats or other reasons directly attributable to civil disturbances. In the years 1984-86 some £66,000 was paid to a total of 65 applicants under this scheme.

5.6 Proceedings in the High Court

Unlike that of the inferior courts (magistrates' courts and county courts), the jurisdiction of the High Court is limited neither geographically nor by the value of the claim. If the matter is one which could also be dealt with in a magistrates' court or in a county court, the proceedings should be begun there because they will be cheaper and quicker; if they are begun in the High Court the judge can transfer them to a lower court and the plaintiff can be penalised as regards costs (see 3.4). The High Court can deal with any subject-matter, though for reasons of administrative convenience its business is roughly distributed between its three divisions as follows:-

(1)   *Queen's Bench Division*: claims for damages for personal   injury, or damage caused to a person's property or reputation (that is, tort claims); actions for breach of contract; actions concerning ships (Admiralty actions); all business not specifically assigned to another division (including various appeals);

(2)   *Chancery Division*: disputes concerning the distribution of a deceased person's property; difficulties arising out of the management of trust funds, including a charity's funds; the enforcement of mortgages and other securities; problems concerning partnerships and companies; bankruptcies; copyright; the supervision of contracts for the sale of land; the correction of deeds;

(3)   *Family Division*: petitions for divorce or nullity; property claims between married couples; disputes over a person's marital status or illegitimacy applications concerning the wardship, adoption or guardianship of persons under 18; applications for the right to carry out the terms of a person's will or to manage the property of someone who dies intestate (*i.e.* without having made a will); matters affecting mental patients.

The High Court in England is comprised of the same three divisions, but there are in addition informally organised subdivisions (*e.g.* the Companies Court and the Commercial Court). In Northern Ireland there is only one recognised subdivision, namely the Companies Court within the Chancery Division. The Restrictive Practices Court is a separate court in its own right, on the same level as the High Court. It operates for the whole of the United Kingdom, its members comprising five judges (including one Supreme Court judge nominated by the Lord Chief Justice of Northern Ireland) and 10 lay members, though usually only one judge and two lay members sit in any particular case. When it hears cases originating from the province - an extremely rare occurrence - appeals lie to the Court of Appeal of Northern Ireland.

It is also necessary to note the existence of so-called Divisional Courts, not to be confused with the courts of the three separate divisions. A Divisional Court is a court *within* a division and usually comprises two, or three, judges. It hears special appeal cases or deals with a particular type of case as a court of first instance. In England there are Divisional Courts within both the Queen's Bench Division and the Family Division; they hear appeals from magistrates' courts in, respectively, criminal and family law matters. The Divisional Court of the Queen's Bench Division also deals with applications for judicial review. It is mainly to deal with such cases that the Divisional Court of the Queen's Bench Division also exists in Northern Ireland. The decisions of Divisional Courts, being decisions of the High Court, are not as authoritative, in our system of precedent, as decisions of the Court of Appeal.

Proceedings in the High Court can be begun in a variety of ways, depending on the type of claim being made. We shall first of all look at a typical Queen's Bench action and then briefly consider actions in the Chancery and Family Divisions. It will be clear from the description of the Queen's Bench action that proceedings at a High Court trial can be rather formal and ponderous. Despite all the documentation, great emphasis is still laid on hearing the oral evidence of witnesses in the court-room. The system is designed to ensure that the plaintiff and the defendant feel satisfied that the trial in open court leaves no stone unturned in the dispute between them. It is an "adversarial" system, where the parties fight each other, rather than an "inquisitorial" or "investigative" system (like those on the Continent), where the court itself takes the initiative in seeking the truth. Partly on account of the delays and expense engendered by the present system, the review body on civil justice (see above, 5.1) suggests that the Lord Chancellor should consider introducing a no-fault scheme of liability for less serious road accidents. This would mean that insurance companies would pay out compensation automatically to people injured in such accidents regardless of whether the policy-holder was negligent or not.

Pleadings in a Queen's Bench action

Proceedings in the High Court can be begun in a variety of ways, depending on the type of claim being made. In the Queen's Bench Division the most typical claim is one made following an accident on the roads or at work. The claimant, who is called the plaintiff, sets the ball rolling by issuing a writ of summons, which warns the defendant that a claim is being made and states the general nature of that claim (see Appendix 4). This will be delivered by hand or posted to the defendant.

If the defendant wishes to have a chance to contest the plaintiff's claim he or she should, within 14 days, "enter an appearance" with the court by handing in or posting the appropriate document. If the defendant does not do this the plaintiff can obtain a judgment without further argument, provided it is proved that the writ of summons was properly delivered. This is called a judgment in default of appearance. Even after an appearance has been entered, the plaintiff may be so confident of the defendant's lack of defence to the claim (except perhaps as to the amount of compensation being claimed) that he or she will apply for what is called summary judgment, that is, judgment without a full-scale hearing. (In a few types of action, however, such as those involving libel, slander or fraud, it is not possible to apply for a summary judgment.) Another way in which cases can be brought to a conclusion without a full hearing taking place is if the defendant pays a sum of money into the relevant court office and the plaintiff, within three weeks, decides to accept this amount in settlement of the claim. This stops, or "stays", the proceedings. If a payment into court has been made but not accepted, the judge and jury must not be told about it in case it prejudices their decision on whether and to what extent the defendant is liable.

If the defendant enters an appearance and the plaintiff does not apply for summary judgment, the plaintiff should, within six weeks, send the defendant a document called a statement of claim, which specifies the precise facts and law on which the claim is based and asks for particular remedies. The statement of claim will say, for instance, where and how the accident occurred, why the defendant is liable and what injury was suffered. The defendant will respond to this, within three weeks, by sending to the plaintiff a defence. This document will deny most of the allegations made in the statement of claim and may well be accompanied by a counterclaim which makes allegations against the plaintiff. Within a further three weeks (14 days in England) the plaintiff produces a reply to the defence and, if necessary, a defence to the counterclaim. All these documents are called pleadings, and the general rule is that points not raised in the pleadings cannot be argued in court.

At this juncture the pleadings are normally "closed", though further documents can be served with the special permission of the court, and in most cases either side can apply to the court at an earlier stage to have the action tried without the exchange of any further pleadings. Pleadings are meant to serve the purpose of making each side aware, before the case comes to trial, of what exactly the other side is arguing. In practice, however, the lawyers drafting these documents often prefer to hedge their bets, so that when the case does come to court they will not be prevented from arguing a certain point just because it was not mentioned in their pleadings. It is therefore a widely held view that the system of pleadings does little to reduce the length and cost of a High Court action. As explained in 5.2 and 5.3, civil cases in magistrates' courts and county courts are not hampered in the same way. For a Northern Ireland case where the failure of the plaintiff's lawyers to plead certain points ultimately led to rejection of the plaintiff's case, see *Farrell* v *Secretary of State for Defence* (1980).

Interlocutory proceedings

Once the pleadings in a Queen's Bench action have been closed, the plaintiff can apply within six weeks to have the case set down for trial at a date some time in the future. But further pre-trial procedures can still be taken to ensure that when the case does reach the trial stage it will be dealt with as efficiently as possible. These further proceedings are called "interlocutory proceedings". Though well intentioned, they do add to the length, cost and complexity of the action. Examples are applications for the discovery of documents or for the serving of interrogatories: these help a party to prepare for the trial by giving access to certain vital papers or answers to important preliminary questions. The process known as an application for a summons for directions, where a party seeks a ruling from a judge on a preliminary point, is commonly used in England but is not known in Northern Ireland.

The decision-making process

If the case eventually comes to trial - and this will be many months or even years after the issue of the writ - it will usually be held in the presence of a judge sitting alone. Until June 1987 it was quite common for cases to be heard by a judge sitting with a jury (of seven persons), but the province has now adopted the English rule whereby trials without a jury are the norm unless special circumstances warrant otherwise. Only actions such as claims for libel will now be heard by a jury, or if the judge accedes to a particular application. Jury cases, not surprisingly, tend to last a little longer than non-jury trials. In 1987 the average durations were, respectively, 6 and 5 hours.

When a judge sits with a jury it is the judge's task to make sure that the trial is properly conducted and that the jury understands what law must be applied to the facts. The jury decides which version of the facts to believe, whom to hold liable, and what amount of compensation is to be paid. This power to decide what remedy to give distinguishes the role of the civil jury from the roles of the criminal jury (see 4.8) and the coroner's jury (see 6.3). However, if there is a need to carry out a detailed assessment of compensation to be paid, the matter will be referred to a Master (see 1.5). There are differing views over whether the use of juries in civil cases is a cause of higher compensation awards. In 1987 approximately 28 per cent of all judgments were for up to £5,000; 36 per cent were for between £5,000 and £10,000, and 36 per cent for more than £10,000.

On the whole there has been a downward trend in the number of full-scale civil trials since 1981; in that year the total was 112, whereas in 1987 there were only 89, of which 30 were jury cases. At present only about 3 per cent of all Queen's Bench cases lead to a full-scale trial; the remaining 97 per cent are settled before or during the course of the trial. In 1987 a total of 7,407 actions were initiated, with default or summary judgments being issued in 1,514 cases. In all, 3,407 Queen's Bench actions were set down for trial, over 3,000 of these being claims for negligence, nuisance, or breach of a duty imposed by statute. Nearly one third of the actions disposed of during 1987 had been set down for trial within the previous 12 months, but 14 per cent had been set down more than two years previously.

Actions in the Chancery and Family Divisions

High Court proceedings in the Chancery and Family Divisions may be just as cumbersome as those in the Queen's Bench Division, but because in such cases there is often little argument about the relevant facts giving rise to the action - the dispute being really about whether some legal rule applies - the legal procedures are sometimes speedier and more informal. Again, many such actions are settled out of court. Chancery actions - such as claims that a contract for the sale of a house should be enforced - are usually started by an originating summons, which does not then lead to an exchange of pleadings. The matter is heard in the absence of a jury by a Master (see 1.5) or by a High Court judge sitting in chambers (*i.e.* his own private rooms). Witnesses usually do not have to be present at the hearing because the evidence is presented in the form of written statements, called "affidavits", rather than as oral testimony. (Affidavits are documents sworn by the maker to be true in the presence of a Commissioner for Oaths. All solicitors are also Commissioners for Oaths.) During 1987 the number of proceedings begun in the Chancery Division was 2,586; 79 per cent of writs and summonses issued were mortgage suits brought by money-lending institutions; only 35 writ actions were actually disposed of in a full court hearing. Of all the proceedings begun, 155 were bankruptcy cases and 120 were Company Court cases (*e.g.* for winding-up orders).

An action in the Family Division, such as a request for a divorce, is usually begun by the petitioner lodging a petition with the court (see Appendix 4) and serving a copy of it on the respondent by having it handed over personally or posted. The petitioner must eventually be prepared to appear in open court to give an oral account of the grounds for the petition, though again there will be no jury. Many family actions are undefended, which obviously allows them to be processed more quickly and cheaply. What might delay the proceedings is the necessity for the judge to be satisfied that, when the parties to the action have children, the welfare of these children is being protected. There may also be some complications over the division of the family property, a matter which is usually dealt with by a master or judge in chambers. Applications by a married person for an award of money against his or her partner are made by originating summons and not by petition. During 1987, 1,794 divorce petitions were filed in the Family Division (two-thirds of them by wives); 1,453 decrees nisi were granted, more than 95 per cent of these being in undefended cases; a further 426 decrees nisi, it must be remembered, were granted in county courts.

Appeals

As well as its "original" (that is, non-appellate) jurisdiction, the High Court also functions as an appeal court, most notably for civil cases first heard in the county courts. In 1987 it disposed of 420 of these.

For cases begun in the High Court appeals lie directly to the Court of Appeal. The appeal takes the form of a full rehearing, without the re-examination of witnesses but usually with a word-for-word transcript of the evidence being placed before the judges. The Court of Appeal can overturn the decision on whether or not the defendant is liable, but it cannot recalculate the damages to be awarded. That issue has to be sent back to the High Court for retrial. The total number of civil appeals disposed of by the Court of Appeal in Northern Ireland during 1987 was 74; 46 of these were originally High Court cases, the others being a mixture of "cases stated" from inferior courts and tribunals.

There is then a further avenue of appeal, provided either the Court of Appeal or the House of Lords gives its leave, to the House of Lords. Only one or two such cases arise each year. An even rarer procedure is that provided for by the Administration of Justice Act 1969, whereby in certain cases there can be a direct appeal straight from the High Court in Northern Ireland to the House of Lords, by-passing the Court of Appeal. This "leapfrog" procedure is possible only if all the parties to the case consent and if the proposed appeal raises a question of law of general public importance involving either the construction of a piece of legislation or an issue on which the High Court is bound by a previous decision of the Court of Appeal or the House of Lords (see 2.4).

For the composition of the Court of Appeal and House of Lords, see 1.5; and for the procedure known as judicial review (not to be confused with appeal procedures strictly so called) see 7.1. The complete system of appeals for civil cases is represented diagramatically in Table 10.

Table 10. The appeal system for civil cases.

5.7 The Enforcement of Civil Judgments

The fact that a court order is issued in favour of the winner of litigation does not necessarily mean that he or she will receive the money (or whatever) from the other side. Sometimes the loser does not pay and has to be forced to do so. Ensuring that the loser of litigation complies with a court order can often be as difficult as obtaining that order in the first place. Since 1971, however, the task has been simplified through the creation of the Enforcement of Judgments Office, which is part of the Northern Ireland Court Service and under the overall control of the Lord Chancellor. It handles virtually all types of money judgments; the principal exceptions are most judgments issued in criminal proceedings and those against a spouse compelling the making of maintenance payments to the other spouse or to a child. The Office enforces civil judgments of magistrates' courts and county courts (including small claims courts) as well as the High Court. In England the judgments of each of these courts are enforced in different ways.

The person ordered by a court to pay money to another is called a judgment debtor; there is a duty to pay the money within a reasonable time of the judgment being delivered. If the person who is owed the money (the judgment creditor) thinks that more than a reasonable time has elapsed, he or she may get the Enforcement of Judgments Office to send the debtor a document called a notice of intent to enforce (see Appendix 4). This orders the debtor to pay up within 10 days. If the debtor still refuses to pay, the creditor may apply to the Office for actual enforcement of the judgment. This can cost quite a bit of money (*e.g.* £165 in respect of a £1500 judgment), so before good money is thrown after bad, the creditor should make sure that the debtor does in fact have assets out of which the value of the judgment can be realised. Money spent on enforcing a judgment is added to the amount owed by the judgment debtor, so that in the event of success the judgment creditor will get back the fees paid to the Enforcement of Judgments Office. Interest on the judgment debt is also payable.

In furtherance of an enforcement application the Enforcement of Judgments Office will interview the debtor to assess his or her means and will proceed to enforce the award in whichever of a number of ways it thinks fit. It may, for instance, make an order that property belonging to the debtor should be seized and sold, or an order that goods on premises occupied by the debtor should be deemed to be in the custody and possession of the Office, or an order that the debtor's earnings should be "attached" so that an employer must make periodical deductions from wages or salary and pay them directly to the Office on the creditor's behalf.

The Office may postpone enforcement if it thinks that the debtor's property ought to be administered for the benefit of all the creditors and not just those who have applied for enforcement. Or if the Enforcement Office thinks that enforcement within a reasonable time is impossible, it must issue a notice to that effect and, after hearing the parties, grant a certificate of unenforceability.

In these circumstances, or if the Office otherwise fails to extract any money from the debtor, the creditor is not allowed to resort to self-help and must come to terms with the fact that the judgment in his or her favour is worthless.

Against some of the Office's orders, such as an order for the transfer of possession of land or attachment of earnings, an aggrieved party may appeal to the High Court; against the rest an appeal may be made, on a question of law only, to the Court of Appeal. In both instances the decision of the court in which the appeal is heard is final.

During 1987 there were 10,527 applications for enforcement of judgments and 8,066 orders of enforcement were made. There were 1,006 certificates of unenforceability. A total of £2.5 million was recovered from debtors. Between 1985 and 1987 a Review Committee under the chairmanship of Master Hunter considered what changes should be made to the law and practice in this field. It recommended reforms in every respect: for example, forms should be simplified, an information booklet should be published, persons aggrieved by delay should be able to take the matter to the Director of the Northern Ireland Court Service, and decisions should always be appealable to the High Court and then, on a question of law, to the Court of Appeal. It remains to be seen if and when any of these proposed changes will be introduced.

6

Special Courts

6.1 Juvenile Courts

Juvenile courts are courts of summary jurisdiction which deal with persons aged between 10 and 16. They normally consist of a bench of three members, one of whom will be a resident magistrate acting as chairman; the others will be lay members, including at least one woman. The lay members are selected for cases by the clerk of petty sessions from panels appointed by the Lord Chancellor for each county court division. There are about 100 names on the panels, each of whom must retire at 70. Many of the lay panellists are in due course appointed Justices of the Peace (see 1.5). They will usually possess no legal qualifications but will have to attend training classes before assuming their responsibilities. The chairman of the court may sit alone, and has a casting vote if only one lay member is present; otherwise decisions are reached by majority vote.

The court generally sits in the same building as the district's magistrates' court, though it is a district court in its own right and usually sits at different times so that there is little chance of juveniles coming into contact with adult offenders or litigants. The proceedings are held in private, with only court officials, the parties to the case, the parties' representatives, bona fide representatives of the press, and other persons directly concerned in the case (such as parents) being present. Unless the court directs otherwise, no report or picture in any newspaper or broadcast can reveal the identity of any juvenile involved, in whatever capacity, in juvenile court hearings.

The jurisdiction of juvenile courts is mostly laid down in the Children and Young Persons Act (NI) 1968; procedure is governed by the Magistrates' Courts (Children and Young Persons) Rules (NI) 1969. It must be considered under two heads: proceedings relating to the care, protection or control of juveniles, and criminal proceedings. The Report of the Children and Young Persons Review Group (the Black Report) recommended in 1979 that future reform of the system should preserve a clear distinction between these two types of business. At the moment many people consider it to be unsatisfactory that care proceedings should be heard in the same forum as criminal proceedings.

Care, protection or control proceedings

Typical cases in this category (representing some 10 per cent of all juvenile court cases) are those involving youngsters who fail to attend school regularly or who are suffering or at risk because of a lack of parental care or because a member of their household has committed an offence directly linked to the safety of juveniles. Most of these cases are brought to court by one of the four Health and Social Services Boards, which will submit a report on the home surroundings, school record, physical and mental health and the character of the child or young person. In reaching its decision in any case, the juvenile court must take such reports into consideration in fulfilment of its statutory duties to have regard to the welfare of the juvenile and, in a proper case, to take steps to remove the juvenile from undesirable surroundings and to secure that proper provision is made for his or her education and training. The juvenile can be represented at the hearing, with the normal provisions as to legal aid and advice applying (see 3.3).

To deal with such cases, of which there were 1,054 during 1987, the juvenile court has the power to make a number of different orders. These include the following:

(a) *A fit person order.* This is an order sometimes referred to as a care order placing the juvenile under the care of someone who is willing to undertake that care and whom the court thinks is suitable. The fit person may be a relative or friend of the juvenile, but in the vast majority of cases the "person" will in fact be a Health and Social Services Board. It is the duty of these Boards to further the best interests of the child or young person within the limits of the facilities and services available. To allow the fit person to exercise proper care, the juvenile will sometimes be required to reside in that person's home or in a hostel run by the Health Board, but this requirement will usually be relaxed before the order expires (on the juvenile's eighteenth birthday).

(b) *A supervision order.* This is an order placing a child or young person under the supervision of a probation officer or some other person or body appointed for the purpose (including a Health Board). Again, the juvenile need not have to reside away from home during the life of the supervision order but in many cases will do so. The supervisor's function is to visit, advise and befriend the juvenile and where necessary help him or her to find suitable employment. The order can remain in force for up to three years.

(c) *A hospital or guardianship order.* These require the evidence of two medical practitioners to the effect that the juvenile is suffering from mental disorder warranting detention or special care. A hospital order entails specialised expert treatment as a resident in a hospital, while a guardianship order obliges the guardian to receive the patient into his or her care and make arrangements for the patient's training, recreation and od health. The duration of such orders is determined by the Health and Social Services Board, though in the case of hospital orders the juvenile court can restrict discharge of the patient during a specified period.

(d)   *A training school order.* Although training school orders can be made during care, protection or control proceedings, they are much more commonly made in criminal proceedings and are therefore described more fully below.

In addition to these four different types of order the juvenile court can require the juvenile's parent or guardian to enter into a promise, or "recognisance", to exercise proper care and guardianship. This means that the parent or guardian will forfeit some money if the promise is not fulfilled.

Criminal proceedings

Efforts are made to keep the number of criminal proceedings against juveniles to a minimum. If the police believe that a child or young person may be in need of advice, guidance or assistance they are required to inform the local social services office, and if they suspect children or young persons of the commission of some offence they often prefer to rely on informal words of advice or official cautions rather than bring the matter before a court.

Since 1975 the RUC have operated a Juvenile Liaison Scheme as an extension of the practice of cautioning, thereby enabling themselves to supervise informally those young persons who admit to having committed an offence but who have not been made to face a juvenile court. Nevertheless, despite such schemes, the number of criminal offences alleged against persons under the age of 17 each year is quite high. In 1987 there were 1,536 juveniles charged, including 1,092 for indictable offences. The rate of findings of guilt was 89 per cent. A total of 9,942 cases were referred to the Juvenile Liaison Scheme during 1987, of which over 5,000 were dealt with by administering an official caution or a juvenile warning.

There is a rule of law that a boy or girl under 10 years of age cannot commit a criminal offence: they are *doli incapax* (incapable of wickedness). Care proceedings may be taken in respect of such youngsters, but not criminal proceedings. A child, who in law is someone aged 10 to 14, is also presumed to be *doli incapax* but this time the presumption can be reversed by the prosecution, especially if the child is aware of what it means to be wicked. Children and young persons can be punished for committing criminal offences, though not in the same way as adults, and even the words "conviction" and "sentence" must not be used in relation to children and young persons dealt with summarily: the expressions "finding of guilt" and "order made on a finding of guilt" must be used instead. An exception is made when a child or young person is charged jointly with a person aged 17 or over: such charges must initially be heard by an ordinary magistrates' court and the ordinary terminology can be employed.

Any juvenile who has been arrested and charged may be released on police bail unless the charge is a very serious one, such as murder or manslaughter, or unless it is necessary in the juvenile's own interest to remove him or her from association with any reputed criminal or prostitute. If not so released, the police must detain the juvenile in a remand home until he or she can be brought before a magistrates' court. A remand in custody during the course of a hearing must also be to a remand home; it can be to a prison only if the court certifies that the juvenile is of so unruly or depraved a character that a remand home would not be a suitable place. Otherwise the same provisions concerning bail and legal aid and advice which apply to suspected adult offenders apply also to juvenile criminal proceedings.

A juvenile court can try juveniles summarily or can conduct preliminary investigations or preliminary enquiries into indictable offences (see 4.7) It can deal summarily with any indictable offence other than murder if it thinks that such a course is expedient and if the prosecutor and the child's parent or guardian, or the young person, consent. In such a case the juvenile court, on making a finding of guilt, may make any order which might have been made if the case had been tried by the Crown Court on indictment. It may therefore impose a much more serious sentence than an ordinary magistrates' court. Even after Crown Court trials the juvenile may be sent back to the juvenile court for sentencing.

Punishment

As in care proceedings, the juvenile court dealing with criminal proceedings must consider all medical and welfare reports relating to the juvenile and can choose from a wide selection of available remedies. The form of punishment most frequently administered is a fine. A juvenile can be fined for any offence other than murder, although a child cannot personally be made to pay more than £100 (including costs) or a young person more than £400. However, a parent or guardian may be ordered to pay the fine instead. In 1987 there were 999 fines imposed on juveniles. The court may also order the payment of up to £2,000 in compensation to the victim of the offence, issue an absolute or conditional discharge (that is, make a finding of guilt but exact no immediate punishment), or bind over the juvenile or a parent to be of good behaviour (that is, require good behaviour as a condition of withholding punishment). The court may also make any of the first three orders which were outlined above in respect of care proceedings. In addition it can impose the following:

(a)   *A probation order.* This places the juvenile under the supervision of a probation officer for a period between six months and three years and requires the juvenile to lead an honest and industrious life during that time. Under the proposed Treatment of Offenders (NI) Order 1989 a court will be able to attach an extra condition to a probation order whereby the probationer is required to attend at a specified place for up to a maximum of 60 days. If a probation order is breached, the juvenile may then be dealt with as if found guilty of the original offence for which he or she was placed on probation. If a young person (aged 14 to 16) does not wish to be placed on probation then the juvenile court must resort to some other punishment. There are also some offences which by statute cannot be dealt with in this way. In 1987, 450 probation orders were made in respect of juveniles (a reduction of 19 per cent on the 1986 figure).

(b)   *An attendance centre order.* Such an order requires the offender to attend the centre at Millfield in Belfast for a fixed number of hours every Saturday. A session of physical education is usually followed by a lecture (*e.g.* on first aid), employment in handicrafts, or other instruction. A juvenile cannot be required to attend for a total of more than 24 hours, but a young person (aged 14 to 16) must attend for at least 12 hours. During 1987, 173 attendance centre orders were made.

(c)   *A training school order.* These orders demand the residence of the juvenile in one of the province's five training schools, the aim being to allow the juvenile to learn how to readjust to society at large and to grow accustomed to the habit of work or school. The order usually remains in force for three years but the manager of the school is required to review the pupil's progress at regular intervals and will release the pupil at any time after 12 months if he or she is considered to be ready to return to the community. The proposed Treatment of Offenders (NI) Order 1989 reduces the maximum and minimum detention periods to, respectively, two years and six months. The parents of a juvenile residing in a training school may be asked to contribute to his or her keep and at the end of the period the juvenile will continue to be supervised at home by a social worker. During 1987 there were 722 training school orders issued.

(d)   *Committal to a remand home.* If the court considers that no other method of dealing with a juvenile is suitable, it can commit a juvenile to a remand home for a period not exceeding one month (or six months for scheduled offences; see 4.1). The five training schools also serve as remand homes for this purpose. Committal is possible only if the offence involved is one which in the case of an adult would be punishable with imprisonment. There were 31 remand home orders in 1987.

(e)   *Detention in a young offenders centre or in prison.* This option, which is available only for persons aged at least 16, can be resorted to only if the court certifies that the young person is of so unruly or depraved a character that no other method of dealing with him or her is appropriate. If the offence involved is one which is punishable in the case of an adult with 14 years' imprisonment (or five years if it is a scheduled offence; see 4.1) the detention of the offender may be ordered to be in such place and for such time as the Secretary of State for Northern Ireland may direct. These include the "SoSP's" mentioned in 4.8. Otherwise the maximum permissible period of detention in a young offenders centre is three years less one day; the proposed Treatment of Offenders (NI) Order 1989 will increase this to four years. The only young offenders centres in Northern

Ireland are at Hydebank Wood in South Belfast and (for females) at Magilligan near Londonderry.

(f)   *A community service order.* At the time of writing these orders are available only for persons aged 17 or over. The proposed Treatment of Offenders (NI) Order 1989 will extend their availability to 16 year olds.

Appeals

The system of appeals against decisions of juvenile courts, whether in care proceedings or criminal proceedings, is the same as for appeals against decisions of magistrates' courts (see 4.6 and 5.2), with the difference that in criminal proceedings lay members from juvenile court panels are appointed to sit as assessors with a county court judge hearing any appeal.

6.2 Courts-Martial

Courts-martial are a relic from the days when in addition to the ordinary courts of law there were many other courts dealing with special matters. Ecclesiastical courts are another example, but they are too specialised to warrant expanded treatment in this book.

Courts-martial apply military law, a special body of rules addressed only to persons serving in the Army. They also apply a similar body of rules addressed to members of the Navy and Air Force. Auxiliary and reserve forces are affected as well, as are civilians employed by the armed forces abroad. The rules are published officially in the *Manual of Military Law*, but derive ultimately from Acts of Parliament and from Regulations issued under the Royal Prerogative (see 2.2). They provide for many internal disciplinary offences, but all offences under the criminal law of England are also offences under military law if committed by a member of the armed forces. Some very serious offences, such as murder, manslaughter or rape, must be tried in ordinary civilian courts if committed within the United Kingdom. Once a trial has occurred in one of the court systems there cannot be a second trial on the same or a similar charge in the other court system. In practice, in Northern Ireland as well as Great Britain, the vast majority of criminal offences committed by members of the armed forces during peacetime are tried in the ordinary way, or as scheduled offences, by the ordinary courts; only if the defendant has since been posted abroad, or if the incident did not in any way affect civilians, might a court-martial be held.

Ordinary soldiers and non-commissioned officers can be dealt with summarily by the commanding officer of the battalion or regiment for a number of minor military offences. The severest punishment which can be imposed is 60 days' military detention or the forfeiture of 28 days' pay. The accused is not allowed to have any form of representation at these summary hearings, but if the commanding officer intends a fine or detention the accused has the right to call for a court-martial.

Trials

More serious charges must be investigated to see if the accused should be sent for trial by court-martial. The decision is taken by the commanding officer after consideration of an "abstract", or summary, of evidence. This is evidence notified to the accused in proceedings comparable to committal proceedings in ordinary magistrates' courts (see 4.7), though without the accused being entitled to representation. At the court-martial itself there can be representation by a lawyer nominated from civilian life or by a regimental officer; representatives from the forces are often preferred because they are more familiar with service standards and jargon. Legal aid under the Northern Ireland criminal legal aid scheme is not available for military proceedings in the province, but a special Army scheme based on the English civilian scheme has been set up in its place. One consequence of this is that the army scheme does not ensure free legal aid: the accused may be compelled to contribute an amount depending upon his savings and annual income.

In peacetime there are two basic types of court-martial. One is a District Court-Martial, which consists of a bench of three officers usually presided over by a major or lieutenant-colonel. It tries ordinary soldiers and non-commissioned officers, with powers to imprison convicted defendants for up to two years. The other is a General Court-Martial, which has a bench of at least five officers presided over by a colonel or higher-ranking officer. It can try any member of the forces and impose any sentence prescribed by military law. The judges for General Courts-Martial are appointed for one case at a time, but the Presidents of District Courts-Martial (of whom there are five in the United Kingdom) are appointed on a long-term basis for a particular area. The accused has the right to object to a particular officer being appointed to hear his case. The trial of civilians in a court-martial must be before Crown servants rather than military officers (with the exception of the court's President). The courts sit at irregular intervals (every four to six weeks) and in makeshift courtrooms. Each year there are about 1,100 District Courts-Martial and between 30 and 40 General Courts-Martial throughout the United Kingdom.

Judge Advocates

No court-martial sits with a jury, but in serious cases the officers on the bench are assisted by a lawyer employed in the Office of the Judge Advocate General.

This is an independent civilian office with general responsibility for supervising the handling of legal matters affecting the armed forces. As well as the Judge Advocate General himself, and the Vice-Judge Advocate General, there are (for the United Kingdom) four judge advocates. These are barristers who function in a similar way to the advocates-general in the European Court of Justice (see 2.6); they sum up the evidence and advise the court on questions of law. On some matters the court is bound to follow the judge advocate's advice, but the actual decision in the case must be taken by a vote among only the officers on the bench.

As well as being continuously under the supervision of the Office of the Judge Advocate General, the proceedings of a court-martial can be subjected to the judicial review procedures described in 7.1, and writs of *habeas corpus* can be issued to put an end to any unauthorised detention. In addition, every finding of guilt and every sentence has to be confirmed by a higher ranking officer before it takes full effect; in Northern Ireland this confirming officer will be a brigadier. The confirming officer can refuse to confirm any finding and can reduce any punishment, but in practice this occurs very infrequently.

Reviews and appeals

The court-martial's decision will be to find the defendant guilty or not guilty. By way of punishment it can fine, detain or imprison; it cannot grant a conditional discharge, make a probation order or impose a suspended sentence. If the defendant wishes to query a finding of guilt or the punishment, he or she can first of all ask for a review by the Defence Council (a body which co-ordinates all the armed forces); there can also be a formal petition to the Defence Council. If still dissatisfied, the defendant can ask the Courts-Martial Appeal Court for permission to appeal there.

This Appeal Court was set up in 1951 and is staffed by all the English Court of Appeal judges and by such English, Northern Irish and Scottish judges as are nominated for the purpose. It usually sits in London as a bench of three judges, though it may in fact sit anywhere in the United Kingdom or even abroad. Its powers are similar to those of the Northern Ireland Court of Appeal (see 4.8), though it can order a retrial only where there is fresh evidence to consider (not where there has been a wrong decision of law or a material irregularity in the course of the court-martial), and unless the appellant is a civilian it cannot hear an appeal against sentence alone (in such cases it can only voice disquiet at the harshness of the sentence and hope that the particular Service Board will as a result reduce it). Only a handful of appeals are heard each year.

There is a further channel of appeal for either side to the House of Lords, but one of the two courts must first grant permission for this appeal and the Courts-Martial Appeal Court must certify that a point of law of general public importance is involved. The last such appeal was in 1968.

6.3 Coroners' Courts

In Northern Ireland coroners are today appointed by the Lord Chancellor from among barristers or solicitors of five or more years' standing. (In England they are appointed by local authorities.) Before 1959 doctors were also eligible to be appointed. Coroners are meant to act completely independently of the government, the police and the medical profession. At present there are seven in Northern Ireland, with eight deputies.

The chief function of coroners is to investigate unexpected, unexplained, violent or suspicious deaths. Formerly the investigations were carried out with a view to uncovering unsuspected homicide, but with the development of the police service and medical science one of the main objects today is the accurate ascertainment of the cause of death. To assist in determining the cause of death, the coroner can order a *post-mortem* examination to be carried out by a government-approved doctor, and this is done in more than half the cases investigated. If the investigation indicates that death was due to an unnatural cause the coroner will usually hold an inquest. An inquest can be held even though the death occurred abroad, provided the body is now lying within the coroner's area.

Inquests

There are nearly 3,500 investigations each year in Northern Ireland and inquests are held in about a fifth of these. They usually take place in recognised courthouses and do not normally involve a jury, but if it appears to the coroner that there is reason to suspect that the death occurred in prison, in an accident, or in circumstances prejudicial to the safety of the public, a jury of between seven and 11 persons must be summoned (In England a jury must also be summoned if the death results from an injury caused by a police officer in the purported execution of his duty.)

The purpose behind an inquest is to determine who the deceased person was, and how, when and where he or she came to die. It must be held in public. The coroner plays a more leading role than a judge would do in a regular court of law; the coroner decides which witnesses should be called, compelling their attendance if necessary, and takes an active part in examining them. The witnesses are under oath and may also be questioned by other interested parties. There is no absolute right for such parties to be legally represented in the proceedings, neither legal advice and assistance nor legal aid are yet available, and speeches cannot be made to the jury except by the coroner in his summing-up. The proceedings, in short, are more inquisitorial than adversarial (see 5.6).

Within five days of the end of the inquest the coroner must send the particulars of death to the appropriate registrar of deaths. Where the circumstances appear to the coroner to disclose that a criminal offence may have been committed the coroner must also, as soon as practicable, furnish the Director of Public Prosecutions with a written report of those circumstances, but neither the coroner nor the jury may express any opinions on questions of criminal or civil liability. Coroners are not judges in a trial, and nothing in proceedings before a coroner should prejudice proceedings which might be taken in another court; for this reason inquests are often delayed until any criminal proceedings connected with the death have run their course. Until 1981 the coroner or jury had to record the death in one of five ways: from natural causes, as the result of an accident or misadventure, by the deceased's own act (adding, if appropriate, "whilst the balance of his mind was disturbed"), by execution of sentence of death, or as an open verdict. This last verdict was used when none of the others was appropriate. Since 1981 coroners or juries in Northern Ireland have simply had to list their "findings", a procedure which ought to allow for more informative conclusions but which still precludes any verdict (such as is possible in England) of "unlawful killing". The jurors' conclusions need not be unanimous, provided not more than two of them dissent.

There cannot be any appeal against the decision at a coroner's inquest, but the proceedings can be made the object of an application for judicial review (see 7.1), which might lead to a new inquest if at the earlier one the coroner, for example, failed to call a jury when one should have been called, or failed to sum up the evidence to the jury. In December 1988 the Northern Ireland Court of Appeal ordered a new inquest to be held in respect of a so-called "shoot-to-kill" incident in 1982; at the first inquest the coroner had applied a rule of evidence which the Court of Appeal said was *ultra vires* (beyond the powers conferred by) the Coroners Act (NI) 1959. In England, but not in Northern Ireland, the Attorney-General retains a power to refer a coroner's inquest to the High Court, which can order a second inquest to be held.

Treasure trove

Coroners also have jurisdiction to hold inquests into the finding of treasure trove, which is property consisting substantially of gold or silver. If the property was deliberately hidden it qualifies as treasure trove and belongs to the Crown, which then usually makes an *ex gratia* payment of compensation to the finder and donates the treasure to a museum. If the property was merely lost, the finder, his employer or the owner of the land acquires a good title to it and can keep it. This type of inquest is very rare.

7

Tribunals

7.1 Tribunals in General and Judicial Review

In Chapters 4 and 5 we examined, respectively, the workings of the criminal and civil courts in Northern Ireland. These can be called ordinary courts of law. Elsewhere in the book we have mentioned what might be called special courts of law: the Judicial Committee of the Privy Council (see 1.4), the European Court of Justice (see 2.6), the Restrictive Practices Court (see 5.6), juvenile courts (see 6.1) and courts-martial (see 6.2). With coroners' courts, in the previous chapter, we encountered an institution which is called a court but which in fact differs markedly in its procedures and powers from all the other courts. At this point it is necessary to turn our attention to other institutions which do not bear the name of courts but which, like coroners' courts, officially adjudicate on certain issues and make pronouncements. These institutions are called tribunals. They constitute a most important sector in our legal system.

The vast majority of tribunals are created by legislation. Among the first to be established were those which settled disputes arising out of the pension, health and unemployment insurance schemes set up by the Old Age Pensions Act, 1908, and the National Insurance Act, 1911. Since then many hundreds of different kinds of tribunal have been formed throughout the United Kingdom, their proliferation during the last 30 years being largely attributable to the development of the welfare state. About 50 operate at the present time. Given this phenomenon it has been well said that today the ordinary law-abiding citizen is much more likely to have to confront a tribunal than a court of law. The number of cases dealt with by tribunals certainly far exceeds that disposed of at county court level or above.

There are many reasons why tribunals have become such popular institutions. On the whole they provide justice which is quicker, cheaper, less formal and more private. But essentially they are preferred because the conventional judicial system is ill-suited to dealing with their particular kinds of problems, notably those which arise in the administration of some complex statutory scheme. Judges cannot be experts in every walk of life or field of law; some issues demand a particular expertise possessed by other persons which it would be wasteful to ignore when disputes arise. There are also issues which are peculiarly factual in nature and for which it would be both unnecessary and inappropriate to have to resort to the traditional paraphernalia associated with courts of law. It has to be conceded, though, that there sometimes appears to be little logic in the way in which some issues are allocated to tribunals while other equally specialised issues are allocated to courts of law.

Tribunals are most often composed of three members, only the chairperson being legally qualified. The pernickety rules of etiquette and of evidence, so beloved by judges and professional lawyers, are for the most part ignored. Representation is usually permitted, but is often undertaken by someone other than a solicitor or barrister - something unheard of in the ordinary courts. Legal aid for representation (see 3.3) is generally not available as the objective is to "de-legalise" proceedings as much as possible. But the legal advice and assistance scheme can be used. Decisions are more frequently arrived at on the spot than in courts of law, and the costs are kept to a minimum. Courts do, however, still play a significant background role; they decide questions specifically reserved for them by the relevant legislation governing the administrative scheme involved, they deal with some appeals and they supervise tribunals by hearing complaints that they have denied one of the parties natural justice or have committed some elementary error of law (*e.g.* they have dealt with a case which they had no authority to deal with). It is this supervisory jurisdiction which is exercised through the granting of applications for judicial review and which has given rise to many of the developments in administrative law in recent years. The procedure outlined below would have been initiated in only a handful of cases a few years ago, but in 1987 there were 75 such cases in Northern Ireland.

Applications for judicial review

In general, the judicial review procedure can be brought against all persons or bodies exercising a judicial, quasi-judicial or administrative function. However, as far as courts of law are concerned, the superior courts (Crown Court, High Court and above) are exempt; only magistrates' courts and county courts are affected. The orthodox view is that the procedure is also unavailable in respect of some kinds of tribunal, namely those which are predominantly private bodies, like those involved when individuals are in dispute with trades unions, professional bodies or universities. But a recent House of Lords decision permitting the procedure to be used vis-à-vis the City Panel on Mergers and Takeovers has cast doubt on this view. Tribunals dealing with private disputes (often involving disciplinary matters) are called domestic, as opposed to administrative, tribunals. Many of them are set up voluntarily. Those which are established by statute, however, such as the Law Society's Disciplinary Committee, are subject to the judicial review procedure.

Permission to make an application for judicial review in respect of an administrative tribunal cannot be granted unless the applicant is deemed to have a sufficient interest "or standing", in the matter to which the application relates. The law on what constitutes adequate *locus standi* for this purpose is still in a state of flux, but in matters directly affecting the general public - such as the levying of rates - it seems that virtually any person may be justified in applying. The application for permission must be made to the High Court within three months of the proceeding complained of, unless the judge is satisfied that the granting of relief after this time would not cause hardship to, or unfairly prejudice, the rights of any person. If the application for permission is unsuccessful, an appeal can be lodged with the Court of Appeal. If permission to apply is granted, the judicial review application itself will usually be considered by one judge of the High Court, again with appeals lying to the Court of Appeal. In some cases, particularly those involving criminal matters, the High Court will sit as a court of two or even three judges; this is the Divisional Court mentioned in 1.3 and 5.6.

In an application for judicial review the applicant can seek a number of remedies: (1) *certiorari,* an order that a decision be quashed; (2) prohibition, an order that a body decline to deal with a matter; (3) *mandamus,* an order to compel the performance of some public duty; (4) an injunction, an order to stop acting in a certain manner; and (5) a declaration, an order clarifying someone's legal position or condemning an administrative decision as illegal. The first three of these used to be officially known as "prerogative orders" and are sometimes still referred to as such.

Injunctions and declarations can be obtained not only through applications for judicial review but also through the issuing of a civil bill (see 5.3) or a writ of summons (see 5.5). These conventional processes allow aggrieved persons to query even the private, domestic proceedings which cannot be subjected to judicial review, but the remedy will not be obtained as quickly, directly or cheaply. On the other hand the conventional processes are not so constrained by time limits, they do not require prior judicial permission, they allow for more effective emergency relief, and they provide for a fuller trial of all the issues.

Tribunals in Northern Ireland

Although for most purposes Northern Ireland constitutes an independent legal system with its own laws, courts and tribunals, there are still some fields of law which are uniformly administered either throughout the United Kingdom or at least throughout Northern Ireland, England and Wales. Many of these fields are ones which were never within the domain of the Parliament of Northern Ireland because they were excepted or reserved matters under the Government of Ireland Act, 1920 (see 1.2). Any tribunal system existing within such fields will be a nationwide system, so that a tribunal sitting in Belfast will apply the same laws and operate in the same way as a tribunal sitting in Birmingham.

Examples of this phenomenon are the banking appeal tribunals, the income tax tribunals (composed of Special and - from 1989 - General Commissioners of Income Tax), the VAT tribunals, the Misuse of Drugs Tribunal and the Performing Rights Tribunal (which determines certain copyright claims). All of these are supervised by the Council on Tribunals, set up in 1958 to keep under review the workings of most tribunals throughout Great Britain. If courts need to be involved in such fields, to hear appeals, answer referred questions, or exercise a supervisory jurisdiction, the courts of Northern Ireland will deal with proceedings originating within the province, but the tribunals will still remain part of the United Kingdom system.

Occasionally, as in the case of immigration appeal tribunals and the Foreign Compensation Commission (which deals with claims for compensation regarding British-owned property confiscated abroad), hearings will take place at centres in England even though some of the relevant facts relate to Northern Ireland. If courts have to be involved in these cases they may be English courts.

For most matters, however, Northern Ireland retains its own independent tribunal systems. The law the tribunals apply may well be virtually identical to the law in the rest of the United kingdom, and the procedures they adopt may also be indistinguishable, but they nevertheless constitute separate systems. They are not subject to the supervision of the Council on Tribunals. It would be impossible to examine here the jurisdiction and procedures of all such tribunals, but the remaining sections of this chapter describe those which are most prominent.

The tribunals dealt with in this chapter should be distinguished from the tribunals of inquiry set up on an *ad hoc* basis under the Tribunals of Inquiry (Evidence) Act 1921. These are created by resolution of both Houses of Parliament; they entrust to a judge the task of inquiring into some recent scandal or disaster. An example is the Widgery Tribunal of Inquiry appointed in 1972 to investigate the killing of unarmed demonstrators in Derry on so-called "Bloody Sunday".

7.2 Social Security Appeal Tribunals

These tribunals handle disputes over entitlement to contributory, non-contributory and means-tested social security benefits - such as unemployment benefit, disablement benefit or income support. Local social security offices can provide information as to the conditions to be fulfilled before you are entitled to any of these payments, many of which were altered by the changes to social security law introduced in April 1988. They can also explain what precisely to do if you disagree with the assessment of your entitlement; this section gives just an outline of what might happen in such a situation.

Claims for benefits

Most of the law concerning entitlement to social security benefits derives from the Social Security (Northern Ireland) Acts 1975-1988 and regulations made thereunder. The initial decision as to whether or not a claimant qualifies for a particular benefit is taken by an assessment officer working in the local social security office. This person considers the information passed on by the staff of the office and can ask for more to be obtained. Assessment officers do not make independent enquiries or interview the claimant but they are not, strictly speaking, employees of the DHSS; they are meant to be independent. They decide on eligibility for both contributory benefits (for which you help to pay through subscriptions to the national insurance fund deducted from your wages or salary), non-contributory benefits and means-tested benefits. Contributory benefits include unemployment benefit, invalidity benefit, maternity benefit, widow's benefit and retirement pensions. Non-contributory benefits include child benefit, pensions for people over 80, industrial injury benefit, disablement benefit, attendance allowance and invalid care allowance. The best known of the means-tested benefits is income support (formerly supplementary benefit) which is designed to provide income to people who are not in full-time employment and whose income, if any, whether from other benefits or from private resources, is not enough to meet their requirements (see the Income Support (General) Regulations 1987).

An assessment officer is under a legal duty to dispose of a claim, so far as is practicable, within 14 days of its being submitted. However, certain issues must be reserved for consideration by a different body, which may take longer than 14 days. For instance, the question whether a person satisfies the medical conditions relating to attendance allowance must be referred to an Attendance Allowance Board and the questions which of two people might be entitled to an invalid care allowance in respect of a particular invalid, or whether a person is "available for employment " or "receiving relevant education" as regards eligibility for income support must be decided by the Secretary of State for Social Services (*i.e.* by officials in his Department). These special matters have their own systems of appeal (for example, decisions on whether contribution conditions have been satisfied can be appealed to the High Court), but in ordinary cases the claimant can appeal against the decision of the assessment officer, within 28 days of its being sent out to the claimant, to a social security appeal tribunal. The appeal must be in writing - you simply fill in a form and return it to your local social security office - and will usually be heard by the tribunal a month or so later.

The tribunal hearing

The system for dealing with appeals in social security matters was reformed in 1984. Prior to then there were separate appeal procedures depending on whether the claim in question was for a benefit connected with the national insurance fund or for supplementary benefit. Under the Social Security (Adjudications) Regulations (NI) 1984, most of the features of the former national insurance local tribunals have been incorporated into the new tribunal system. Thus, a social security appeal tribunal will consist of a legally qualified chairperson, one member drawn from a panel representing employers and the self-employed, and another member drawn from a panel representing employees and the unemployed and possessing knowledge of local social conditions. The panels are officially appointed by the Department of Health and Social Services, but the chairpersons are appointed by the Lord Chancellor and the tribunals are meant to be, as well as to seem, completely independent of the DHSS. For this reason they do not sit on DHSS premises. Members of the public can attend tribunal hearings just as they can attend hearings in a court of law, though of course they rarely do so. If intimate personal or financial circumstances or public security considerations are involved, the chairperson can direct the hearing to be held in private.

The proceedings in a social security appeal tribunal are meant to be informal and uncomplicated. The chairperson has a wide discretion as to how to run things. With a little forethought a claimant ought to be able to conduct his or her own case (it is, after all, a personal problem and no-one knows all the circumstances better than the claimant), but research has shown that claimants stand a far greater chance of winning their cases if they are legally represented. At the very least claimants ought to ensure that they turn up in person at their hearings: cases can be dealt with in their absence but the vast majority of these will be lost.

Most controversially, legal aid is not available for people who are too poor to afford representation by a solicitor, although the legal advice and assistance scheme (described in 3.3) can make £50 worth of solicitor's help available short of actual representation; this would cover most of the cost of the paperwork involved in preparing a case for hearing. Alternatively, or additionally, a welfare rights worker, Citizens' Advice Bureau worker, friend or relative may be able to represent the claimant free of charge; in tribunals, unlike courts, there are no restrictions on who can act as an advocate. The Law Society has created a welfare lawyers scheme to help all claimants in a social security appeals tribunal. Some people believe it is a good thing that legal aid is not available for representation because otherwise the proceedings would be bound to become too legalistic; others hold that the denial of legal aid is blatant discrimination. The British Government's latest proposals on legal aid and advice entail removing from solicitors the power to give advice on social security matters under the green form scheme; the Government wishes advice centres to undertake this work instead.

A claimant can obtain reimbursement of travelling expenses and compensation for loss of wages incurred through attendance at a tribunal. Witnesses can be called and questioned by both sides, but a tribunal has no power, as a court of law would have, to compel the attendance of witnesses, the swearing of oaths or the production of documents. Whatever decision the tribunal comes to - whether it be unanimous or by a two to one majority (with the lay panel members perhaps outvoting the legally qualified chairperson) - it must be supported by written reasons. Important decisions will in due course be selected for publication and circulated to all other tribunal members in the province.

The social security appeal tribunal system is presided over by a President of Social Security Appeal Tribunals (who is also, coincidentally, the President of Medical Appeal Tribunals, which sit to deal with disputes over medical matters in cases of claims to industrial injury benefit). The role of the President is to ensure that chairpersons and panel members are adequately trained and informed, that procedures are kept fair and easy to understand, and that the arrangements for holding tribunals are properly made. In status and salary the President is of equal rank with county court judges.

Reviews and further appeals

All decisions in social security matters may at any time be internally reviewed by assessment officers; indeed, in income support cases a review takes place automatically whenever an appeal has been lodged and the original decision may be altered in a way which cures the appellant's grievance before the tribunal hearing takes place. Even after a tribunal hearing, if a further appeal is pending, reviews are still possible. They can occur if the decision was based on a mistake as to a material fact or if there has been a change of circumstances since the decision complained about was made.

From the decision of a social security appeal tribunal there is the opportunity of a full appeal, within three months, by either the claimant or the assessment officer, to a person called a Social Security Commissioner. But the permission of the local tribunal or of the Social Security Commissioner is needed for an appeal if the tribunal's original decision was unanimous, and in income support cases not only is the permission of the Commissioner required but the point at issue must be a question of law (not of fact). Commissioners have to be barristers of at least 10 years' standing, which also puts them on a footing with county court judges. The three Social Security Commissioners in Northern Ireland also act as chairpersons of medical appeal tribunals.

The Commissioner may or may not hold an oral hearing into the case, but he or she must always fully reconsider the case and give a decision in writing. A new decision can be substituted for that of the tribunal, or the case can be referred back to a tribunal with instructions as to how to determine it. Reports of Commissioners' decisions are regularly published, and precedents are sometimes cited to, and followed by, social security appeal tribunals. Another appeal can lie from the Commissioner, though only with permission and on points of unclear law, to the Court of Appeal; only one or two of these occur each year.

Reviews of social security decisions can be appealed against in just the same way as an ordinary decision of an assessment officer. Questions reserved for the office of the Secretary of State are also reviewable, but only by the DHSS itself. There is also a process known as setting aside, which can occur within 28 days of a decision if the decision-making body made an accidental error or a relevant document went astray in the post; the procedure is the responsibility of the body which took the original decision. The appeal, review and setting aside procedures must, of course, be distinguished from the judicial review procedure described in 7.1.

The Social Security Advisory Committee

This Committee was set up in 1980 when the supplementary benefit scheme was being substantially altered. It is an independent body with the task of advising the Secretary of State for Social Services and the Department of Health and Social Services for Northern Ireland on United Kingdom social security matters. Although the Chairman and the dozen or so members are appointed by the Secretary of State, they do not automatically toe the Government line when giving an opinion on social security issues, which they may do either at the government's request or on their own initiative. Most social security regulations, when they are at the drafting stage, have to be submitted to the Committee for its comments; before producing a report on the draft regulations the Committee usually undertakes a public consultation exercise. The Government must publish the report when it lays the regulations before Parliament for consideration.

7.3 Industrial Tribunals and the Industrial Court

Industrial tribunals deal with disputes relating to individual employment contracts. More general collective disputes (*i.e.,* those between employers and trade unions) are the concern of the Industrial Court and statutory bodies such as the Labour Relations Agency. Watchdog bodies with a role to play in matters concerning employment or industrial relations are outlined in the following chapter.

Industrial tribunals

Industrial tribunals have operated in Northern Ireland since 1965 and are now established under the Industrial Training (NI) Order 1984. Their procedures are governed by the Industrial Tribunals (Rules of Procedure) Regulations (NI) 1981. They are staffed by a President (Mr Maguire), two full-time and 11 part-time chairpersons, and approximately 130 lay members. They sit all year round in 11 different cities and towns in Northern Ireland. The chairperson and lay members are appointed by the Department of Economic Development, but of course they are meant to act completely impartially.

The various employment rights which industrial tribunals protect are enshrined in many different pieces of legislation and are subject to varying conditions and qualifications. The most frequently recurring types of case are those which concern redundancy, unfair dismissal, discrimination, maternity pay or activities on behalf of a trade union. One important employment right - that to a minimum period of notice of dismissal - is at present protected not by means of a complaint to an industrial tribunal but through an action in the civil courts.

Proceedings for a tribunal hearing are begun by the applicant sending an application to the Central Office of Industrial Tribunals (see Appendix 4). Many applications will then be automatically referred to the Labour Relations Agency (see 8.3) to see if the matter can be resolved with the help of one of its conciliation officers. If a tribunal hearing does eventually take place the evidence will be presented through the testimony of witnesses or the production of documents; written representations may also be made. The tribunal is expressly authorised to regulate procedure in whatever way is deemed best. The chairperson, who is legally qualified and sits with two lay persons with industrial relations experience, has considerable control over the strictness or otherwise of the procedure to be adopted. Proceedings are meant to be informal, but since 12 of the 14 hearing rooms in Northern Ireland are in fact county court rooms the atmosphere of informality is not always easy to engender.

The two sides can be legally represented at tribunal hearings but cannot obtain legal aid for this purpose. They will have to bear the cost themselves unless their representative is, for instance, a volunteer or appointed by a trade union. Legal advice and assistance, however, is still available to those who are financially eligible (see 3.3). Only in exceptional circumstances, as where one party has asked for a postponement of the proceedings or has been vexatious, will one of the parties be made to bear the other's costs. These should not in any event be very high.

Decision and challenge

The tribunal's decision may be given at the end of the hearing or reached later and notified to the parties. Written reasons must be given. If the tribunal decides that the applicant is in the right the particular remedy afforded will depend on the nature of the application. If it is in respect of redundancy or maternity pay the tribunal may assess the amount of payments due; if it concerns a claim of unfair dismissal the tribunal can order the reinstatement of the employee, or compensation, or both; if the complaint relates to discrimination an order can be issued requiring the discrimination to be stopped. A register of all decisions is open for general public inspection at the Central Office of Industrial Tribunals.

There are three ways of challenging an industrial tribunal's decision: there can be a review by the tribunal itself, a judicial review by the High Court (see 7.1), or an appeal to the Court of Appeal by way of case stated on a point of law (see 4.6). There is no Employment Appeal Tribunal in Northern Ireland such as there is in England. In each of these cases care has to be taken to make the challenge within the specified time limit. There is no appeal, as there is in social security cases, to a higher tribunal or to a Commissioner. If an industrial tribunal makes an award of money to one of the parties, and that party proves unwilling to pay, the award may be enforced through an application first to a county court, and then, if necessary, to the Enforcement of Judgments Office (see 5.7).

In 1987-88 there were 1,933 tribunal applications referred to the Labour Relations Agency. As many as 1,245 of these were resolved through that office; only some 588 cases were actually heard in an industrial tribunal.

The Industrial Court

The Industrial Court for Northern Ireland, which is the counterpart of the Central Arbitration Committee in Great Britain, was provided for by the Industrial Courts Act 1919 but was not actually constituted until 1964, when it was required to give effect to the Terms and Conditions of Employment Act (NI) 1963. As in the case of tribunals, a sitting of the Court comprises one independent chairman (the President of the Court) plus two lay members selected from panels representing both sides of industry. The President of the Court is currently the same person as the President of Industrial Tribunals (as well as being a county court judge).

The jurisdiction of the Industrial Court is fairly limited. It deals with failure to comply with a recommendation made by the Labour Relations Agency for trade union recognition. Under the Equal Pay Act (NI) 1970 it can amend collective agreements, pay structures or wages orders whenever they contain discriminatory provisions applicable to men only or women only. Certain of the Court's decisions, while not in themselves enforceable in ordinary courts, lead to the incorporation of new terms into individual contracts of employment.

7.4 The Mental Health Review Tribunal

The Mental Health Review Tribunal has existed in Northern Ireland since 1962 and at present operates under the Mental Health (NI) Order 1986 (Part V and Schedule 3). The total membership of the Tribunal consists of legal members (appointed by the Lord Chancellor), medical members (appointed by the Lord Chancellor after consultation with the Head of the Department of Health and Social Services) and other persons (appointed in the same way as medical members) who have such experience in administration, such knowledge of social services or such other qualifications or experience as the Lord Chancellor considers suitable. At the moment the Tribunal comprises five legal members, five medical members and five other members.

One of the legal members acts as overall chairperson (currently Mr Fraser Elliott QC). The chairperson or one of the other legal members presides over each sitting of the Tribunal, which usually involves three members, one from each of the professional groups. For the purposes of any proceedings which are of a preliminary or incidental nature the Tribunal may consist of only one member.

The Tribunal exists to hear applications for discharge made by or on behalf of patients who are liable to be detained in a hospital under the Mental Health (NI) Order 1986 or under a restriction order issued by a criminal court. The 1986 Order updated the law in Northern Ireland on the detention, guardianship, care and treatment of patients suffering from mental disorder and on the management of the property and affairs of such patients. The Tribunal cannot itself instigate hearings about patients' cases, but does so only when applications in writing are made to it. As regards long-stay patients, Health and Social Services Boards (or, in the case of restricted patients, the Secretary of State) are under a duty to refer cases to the Tribunal at least once every two years. As regards restricted patients (those sent to hospital by order of a criminal court) the Tribunal now has powers concerning their absolute or conditional discharge.

During the year ending 31st March 1988, the Tribunal processed 68 cases. Of these, all but 11 had been dealt with at a hearing by the end of the year. Several cases were withdrawn or adjourned at the hearing stage; of the 48 cases fully considered, 36 of the patients were directed to remain in hospital. The cost of operating the Tribunal during 1987-88 was just over £20,000.

It should be noted that the Review Tribunal does not concern itself with the management of the property of mental patients. Prime responsibility for this lies with the Office of Care and Protection, an office within the Family Division of the High Court (which is also responsible for wardship, guardianship and adoption proceedings). At any one time about 1,600 people have property which is being managed by this office. It is the Master (Care and Protection) who decides whether any step needs to be taken to deal with a patient's property; if necessary the Master will appoint a Controller (formerly called a Committee) to manage a patient's affairs. A patient living in a hospital or other statutory accommodation can have small amounts of money managed by the Health Board on his or her behalf (unusually sums less than £1,200).

Hearings

When the Tribunal receives an application concerning a patient it sends a copy to the Health Board administering the hospital in which the patient is detained. The Board then forwards full information about the patient to the Tribunal, which in turn sends it to the patient with the exception of those parts which the Board considers should not be disclosed in the interests of the patient or for other specific reasons. The patient's nearest relative or guardian is also notified. On the day of the hearing the Tribunal may decide to release even the information not disclosed by the Board.

Procedures of the Tribunal are governed by the Mental Health Review Tribunal Rules (NI) 1986. Once an application for a hearing has been received, the Tribunal must give all parties concerned at least 14 days' notice of the date of the hearing. The Tribunal has a discretion to exclude any person from the hearing, but it may appoint some person to act as the applicant's or patient's authorised representative. Representation under the legal advice and assistance scheme (see 3.3) has been available since 1980. Patients and other parties to the hearing may be accompanied by other persons of their choice.

Before or during the hearing the medical member of the Tribunal must examine the patient to form an opinion about his or her mental condition. The Tribunal may interview the patient, and is required to do so if the patient so requests. Written arguments can be presented, in addition to the oral testimony of witnesses; the attendance of witnesses or the production of documents can be compelled as in a proper court of law, but the Tribunal has discretion to receive in evidence any documents or information which would not be admissible in such a court. It is an essential feature of the Tribunal that its decisions are based as much on its own observations and assessments of the patient's mental condition as on the opinions expressed by the patient, the doctor in charge or other interested parties.

Decisions and appeals

Decisions of the Mental Health Review Tribunal can be by majority vote. They must be communicated in writing, with reasons, within 14 days of the hearing, unless the Tribunal considers that this would adversely affect the health or welfare of the patient or other people.

The Tribunal has power to recommend the continued detention of a patient or, if it is satisfied that the patient is not suffering from mental illness or severe mental impairment or that discharge would not create a substantial likelihood of serious physical harm to the patient or to other persons, the Tribunal must order the patient's release (either immediately or on a future date). With a view to facilitating discharge on a future date the Tribunal may recommend leave of absence for the patient or transfer to another hospital.

The only way of appealing against a decision of the Review Tribunal is by requesting a case to be stated (see 4.6) for determination by the Court of Appeal. As only questions of law can be stated in this way, such appeals are rare. The substance of the law in this area is fairly clear: it is in its application to the facts, and in the ascertainment of those facts, that the difficulties lie. There can be no further appeal beyond the Court of Appeal. Of course, judicial review proceedings might also be available (see 7.1).

The Mental Health Commission

The Mental Health Commission was set up under the Mental Health (NI) Order 1986, largely as a result of one of the recommendations made in the Northern Ireland Review Committee on Mental Health Legislation (the MacDermott Committee), which reported in 1981. It has the duty of keeping under review not only the care and treatment of patients suffering from mental disorder but also the interests of staff concerned with the care and treatment of such patients. At present it has 12 part-time members, six of these being appointed for two years and the other six for four years; the members include two lawyers, two doctors, one psychologist, one social worker, two nurses and four lay persons. The current chairperson is a lawyer, Mr Henry Pierce.

The chief functions of the Commission are to make inquiries into any case where it appears to the Commission that there may be ill-treatment, etc. of any patient, to visit and interview in private patients detained under the 1986 Order, and to monitor the operation of the powers and duties placed by the Order on the Health Boards, the Department of Health and Social Services, the Secretary of State and persons running private hospitals. Where it thinks fit it may refer to the Mental Health Review Tribunal the case of any patient who is liable to be detained under the 1986 Order, but the Commissions's role is not confined to detained patients: it also covers voluntary patients and anyone else suffering from mental disorder. By April 1988 only one patient had been referred to the Tribunal.

The Mental Health Commission must publish a report on its activities in such form and at such intervals as the Head of the Department of Health and Social Services may direct. It can in turn be subject to investigation by the Commissioner for Complaints (see 8.1).

7.5 Tribunals Concerning Land, Rents and Planning

The Lands Tribunal

The Lands Tribunal for Northern Ireland was set up by the Lands Tribunal and Compensation Act (NI) 1964. Its rules of procedure are laid down in the Lands Tribunal Rules (NI) 1976, as amended. Unlike the Lands Tribunal for England and Wales it is technically not a tribunal at all but a proper court, although it is not always staffed by judges. Persons serving on it are barristers or solicitors of seven years' standing or persons experienced in the valuation of land. They do not work full-time for the Tribunal and are assisted by a registrar, an assistant registrar and a small clerical staff. There are at present only two members, one of whom is a county court judge (the President, Judge Rowland). The President's salary is £59,000, that of the other member is £45,800.

The Tribunal has its own courtroom and offices in the Royal Courts of Justice in Belfast, but in practice it sits in the county courthouse appropriate to the location of the land concerned whenever the parties prefer such a venue. Usually only one member of the Tribunal will hear each case, though very occasionally both members will sit if the case involves complex issues of law as well as difficult valuation issues; the President has a casting vote if the two members disagree. If a member is temporarily unable to perform his duties (because, say, of illness or personal interest in a case) a county court judge will usually be appointed to sit in his place.

The functions of the Lands Tribunal are varied, being derived from many different Acts of Parliament and touching upon more than 60 different matters. One of its most important tasks is to resolve disputes concerning the amount of compensation to be paid for the compulsory acquisition of land or for the injury caused to land by, for example, the making of roads. Another important function is the hearing of appeals and references concerning the valuation of land for rating and taxation purposes, a job which frequently entails deciding (and it is in this context that such decisions are usually made in Northern Ireland) whether a particular organisation is a charity or not. There is no public register of charities in Northern Ireland. The Tribunal must also deal with the renewal of business tenancies, the buying of ground rents, the extension of leases and the modification of legal obligations, such as rights of way, which impede the enjoyment of land. Parties, moreover, can agree to ask the Lands Tribunal to sit in private as an arbitrator in order to settle any dispute concerning the value, use or development of a piece of land.

Hearings are in public and legal aid is available for them. Decisions, together with reasons, have to be given in writing, unless the Tribunal is satisfied that no injustice or inconvenience would be caused by giving them orally. In 1987, 194 cases were referred to the Tribunal and decisions had to be made in 28 of them; the rest were settled by consent or withdrawn. Some of the written decisions are published and can be referred to in future cases as precedents. Copies of any past decision are available from the registrar whenever required, on payment of a small fee. The decisions are final as regards the determination of facts; the only appeal is within one week, by way of case stated on a point of law to the Court of Appeal (see 4.6). There are only two or three of these each year.

Rent assessment committees

Northern Ireland has a complex system for controlling the level of rents in the private housing sector. If on 1st October 1978 the dwelling was not let at a rent controlled under the Rent Restriction Acts, it still today cannot be subjected to control. But if the dwelling was so controlled it is now subject to the Rent (NI) Order 1978.

Under that Order the Department of the Environment for Northern Ireland will, upon application, register an increased rent if the net annual value of the dwelling is more than £60 or, when the NAV is less than £60, if the district council has certified that the dwelling meets certain standards. If either the landlord or the tenant disagrees with the registered rent, appeal against it can be made to a rent assessment committee.

The appeal is first of all sent to the Rent Officer who is an official independent of the government. He makes the necessary arrangements for a survey of the premises and for the determination of the issue by a rent assessment committee at a hearing. The committees are composed of members drawn from a Rent Assessment Panel of about 50 people (all appointed by the Department of the Environment) and they sit in the principal town of each district council area. The Rent Officer appoints one chairperson for each committee and usually one or two other members. At the hearing the landlord and tenant can be heard either in person or by being represented by a barrister, solicitor or any other authorised person. The proceedings resemble those at a social security tribunal (see 7.2), with no state legal aid being obtainable. In determining the appropriate rent the committee wil have regard to the report of its surveyor, its own inspection and the rents of comparable houses in the private sector and of those let by the Northern Ireland Housing Executive. These public sector rents in turn mostly depend at present on the age of the premises and the number of persons they can accommodate. The committee will disregard any improvements made by the tenant.

Rent assessment committees also hear applications for the reassessment of registered rents in cases where there has been a change in circumstances relating to either the dwelling-house or the tenancy. This is in effect the only way of challenging a rent assessment committee's original assessment of rent.

Up to December 1988 just over 9,000 rents had been registered in Northern Ireland and about 7,500 of these had been appealed to a rent assessment committee. There had been about 1,500 "change of circumstance" applications. Over half of the appeals have resulted in rents being reduced, but these reductions must be set against the increases in all rents decreed by the Housing Executive in recent years.

The Planning Appeals Commission

This is one of those bodies which, like rent assessment committees, does not call itself a tribunal but in fact operates in much the same way as those which do. It was established in 1973 under the Planning (NI) Order 1972.

In Northern Ireland all applications for planning permission must be made to the Department of the Environment. The Department has a duty to consult with district councils and other affected bodies but the decision whether to grant planning permission is for it alone to take. If the permission is refused, or granted subject to conditions, the applicant may appeal to the Planning Appeals Commission within six months (or such longer period as the Commission may allow).

The Commission consists of a Chief Commissioner and such number of other members as the Department of the Environment may determine. They are appointed by the Secretary of State for Northern Ireland. At present in addition to the Chief Commissioner there are five full-time and five part-time members. An appeal is generally heard by one Commissioner appointed by the Chief Commissioner, and the hearing usually takes place at a venue near to the location of the relevant land. The actual decision on the appeal, however, is taken by the Commission as whole.

As full reasons for the refusal of planning permission are not always given at the time when the refusal is first announced, the hearing before a Commissioner may be the applicant's earliest opportunity to discover what those reasons were. The Department consequently presents its case first at these hearings even though it is technically the respondent. No official rules have been made to govern the conduct of proceedings at a hearing but they are kept as informal as possible. Legal aid is not available. There is an alternative "written representation" procedure available to appellants which avoids the need for a hearing and is used for some of the straightforward appeals.

In 1987 there were 19,028 applications for planning permission and of those which were considered during that year some 90 per cent were granted. The Planning Appeals Commission dealt with 267 appeals in the year ending 31st March 1988 and allowed 26 per cent of these.

The Commission also has the duty of conducting public local inquiries to consider objections made against development plans and hearings or inquiries which may arise from planning applications which the Department of the

Environment judges to be of major significance. Normally one member of the Commission will conduct such an inquiry or hearing and will report to the Commission as a whole. Having considered the matter the Commission prepares its corporate recommendations and submits them to the Department of the Environment. It is the Department which makes the final decision. In 1987-88 the Commission made nine recommendations to the Department concerning public inquiries.

There can be no further appeal against a decision of the Planning Appeals Commission, only an application for judicial review (see 7.1).

8

Watchdog Bodies

It would be misleading to create the impression that the Northern Ireland legal system, any more than other legal systems, comprises only courts and tribunals. On the contrary, there are a number of "para-legal" bodies which devote their time to overseeing the administration of the law in Northern Ireland (or in the United Kingdom as a whole) and to making proposals for improvements. This chapter briefly describes the modes of operation of nine such bodies or sets of bodies. Some are accountable to Parliament, others are not; some have real powers to change matters, others may only advise. All act as watchdogs so that the general public may have greater confidence in the fairness and justness of the legal system in various fields.

Readers will perhaps be able to think of other bodies with a similar role in the Northern Ireland legal system, but there is not the space to describe them all in detail here. The role of the Lay Observer, *vis-à-vis* complaints against solicitors, was mentioned in 3.2 and the Social Security Advisory Committee was described in 7.2. In many other spheres there are lobbying organisations which try to keep the law in step with prevailing views in society; reference to a few of them has already been made in 3.1 under the heading "pressure groups".

8.1 The Ombudsmen

The term "ombudsman", which derives from Scandinavia, is used to describe both official (that is, government appointed) and unofficial positions. Industries such as banking and insurance have recently established their own unofficial ombudsmen (see 8.8), but these operate on a United Kingdom basis and have no separate or special role in Northern Ireland. There have also been calls for a prisons ombudsman.

In Northern Ireland there are two official ombudsman posts for the independent investigation of complaints about public maladministration. One is the Parliamentary Commissioner for Administration and the other is the Commissioner for Complaints. Dr Maurice Hayes currently holds both positions. He and his staff spend about a quarter of their time working on Parliamentary Commissioner cases and the rest on Commissioner for Complaints cases. In 1987-88 the cost of running the joint office was £317,000.

An annual report on the work of each of the two posts has to be submitted to the House of Commons at Westminster, where there is a Select Committee on the Parliamentary Commissioner for Administration.

It should be noted that in both instances the Commissioner's job is to examine the procedures by which administrative decisions are reached, not to assess the merits of those decisions in the absence of maladministration. The term "maladministration" does not mean simply "error"; it refers to action which has been influenced by improper considerations, which is totally unreasonable or which smacks of incompetence, malice, discrimination or neglect. The Commissioner, therefore, does not usually investigate complaints in respect of which the complainant has, or had, a right to take proceedings in a court of law, or to appeal to a tribunal, and for this purpose the Fair Employment Agency (see 8.2) and the Independent Commission for Police Complaints (see 8.7) are tribunals. Someone complaining about being refused unemployment benefit, for instance, must take the grievance to a social security appeal tribunal (see 7.2). Only if he or she is unhappy with the *manner* in which the claim was processed before or after the decision was made will a complaint to the ombudsman be allowable.

In 1988 the Policy Research Institute in Belfast was due to publish the results of research into the role and impact of the joint ombudsman office.

The Parliamentary Commissioner for Administration

The function of this ombudsman is to investigate written complaints about maladministration within any of the Northern Ireland government departments (see 1.4). Unlike the ombudsman in Great Britain, the Commissioner in Northern Ireland also has the power to investigate complaints about personnel matters in the civil service. The role was created by an Act of Parliament in 1969, two years after a similar post was established for United Kingdom government departments. As the Northern Ireland Office is a UK government department, complaints about it should be sent to the UK Parlamentary Commissioner for Administration, who is based in London, as should complaints about national public bodies such as the Post Office or the Office of Fair Trading.

Complaints about maladministration can be made by anyone who claims to have sustained injustice as a result of it. In the first instance the complaint should be made to a Member of Parliament who then passes it to the Commissioner, but, in practice, if the Commissioner receives a complaint which has not first been passed through an MP, he will refer it to an MP nominated by the complainant and ask the latter to sponsor it.

A complaint must normally be made within 12 months of the time when the aggrieved person first had notice of the matters alleged in the complaint. The Commissioner may, however, investigate a complaint made at a later date if he thinks there is a special justification for doing so. In all cases the Commissioner invites the comments of the body concerned, examines papers, and interviews persons privately. He then sends a report on his investigation to the Member of Parliament who sponsored the complaint, to the department concerned and to any person involved in the allegations made in the complaint. If the Commissioner finds that a complaint is justified, he seeks to obtain a settlement of the grievance on the complainant's behalf; this may involve the granting of an apology, the remedying of some situation or even the payment of compensation. But if no settlement can be reached the complainant cannot take the matter any further.

Many of the complaints received by the Commissioner fall outside his jurisdiction. In 1987 there were 207 complaints received (the highest annual number to date, of which only 30 came directly via an MP) but 156 had to be rejected at the screening stage. Reports were completed on 20 cases, of which seven concerned the handling of planning applications and a further six the social security system. Complaints of maladministration were upheld in 10 cases (five involving the DHSS, three the Department of the Environment, and two the Department of Economic Development); in two other cases the complaint was not upheld but the departments concerned were criticised.

The Commissioner for Complaints

The function of the Commissioner for Complaints is to investigate written complaints made directly to him by persons claiming to have suffered injustice through maladministration on the part of such bodies as Education and Library Boards, Health and Social Services Boards, district councils, the Northern Ireland Council for Nurses and Midwives and the Sports Council. The office was also created in 1969, and has a similar, but by no means identical, role to that of the Health Service Ombudsmen and the Local Ombudsmen in Great Britain. Among the matters which cannot be investigated are the conduct of legal proceedings, the actions of doctors and dentists, the behaviour of the RUC, and the financial interests of district councillors.

This kind of complaint does not have to be processed through a Member of Parliament, but it usually needs to be made within two months of the complainant getting to know of the action complained of, or within six months of the action itself, whichever is the earlier. Investigations are conducted in the same way as described for the Parliamentary Commissioner, with reports made to the complainant, the body concerned and any other person involved in the complaint. An important difference between the two procedures is that if the Commissioner for Complaints upholds a grievance but is unable to obtain a satisfactory settlement the complainant can then apply to a county court for compensation. And the Commissioner for Complaints may seek an injunction or declaration in the High Court to restrain a body from persisting in action which has been found to amount to maladministration. These remedies are not available in England.

In 1987, 285 complaints against local and public bodies were received by the Commissioner; 19 had to be rejected as falling outside his jurisdiction and a further 193 did not survive the preinvestigation screening stage. A total of 62 cases were investigated, with maladministration being established in nine of these. More than half of the investigations related to employment practices, such as delays in recruitment processes or in resolving pay problems. The most popular target for complaints is still the Northern Ireland Housing Executive, but since the Executive introduced its own internal complaints system in 1985, the number of cases involving housing matters which need to be examined by the Commissioner has dropped appreciably; in 1987, 85 of the 144 housing cases notified to the Commissioner were passed on to and dealt with by the Executive. Also in 1987 there were 15 investigations into the Education and Library Boards and 13 into the district councils.

8.2 The Fair Employment Agency

The Fair Employment Agency was set up by the Fair Employment (NI) Act 1976 (a Westminster statute) with the general functions of promoting equality of opportunity and eliminating unlawful discrimination on the grounds of religious belief or political opinion. For this purpose atheism and agnosticism are religious beliefs, but "political opinion" does not include an opinion which involves acceptance of the use of violence for political ends connected with Northern Ireland affairs.

The Agency comprises a Chairman (since its inception this has been Mr Robert Cooper) plus between five and 11 members, including three trade unionists and three representatives of employers. Although all its members are appointed by the Secretary of State for Northern Ireland, and despite being entirely funded by the Department of Economic Development (to the tune of £750,000 in 1988-89) the Agency is meant to be independent of the Government. It has recently expanded its staffing level to 32 employees. An annual report is submitted to the Secretary of State and presented to Parliament as a House of Commons paper.

In carrying out its primary functions the Agency works in conjunction with county courts rather than with industrial tribunals. As presently drafted the 1976 Act does not make inequality of opportunity or unlawful discrimination a criminal offence, and certain forms of employment, such as serving as a cleric, a schoolteacher or in a private household, are exempt from control. All other employers, provided they have more than 10 employees, come within the scope of the fair employment legislation. The exemption for schoolteaching is particularly controversial and the Agency keeps its desirability under constant review.

Equality of opportunity

To promote equality of opportunity the Agency invites employers to subscribe to a Declaration of Principle and Intent so that they can then have their names placed on a public register and be issued with a certificate describing them as an Equal Opportunity Employer. In May 1988 there were 9,471 organisations listed on the register. Unfortunately, one of the province's five

Education and Library Boards has refused to subscribe to the Declaration, as have 17 of the 26 district councils.

It is at present the case that organisations can to some extent sit back complacently, knowing that they need not introduce a proper equality of opportunity programme unless the Fair Employment Agency embarks on a time-consuming formal investigation and finds against them. This power to investigate is conferred by section 12 of the 1976 Act. It has been used much more frequently in the past three years than before. There have been 113 investigations altogether of which 63 were completed by May 1988. In 1986-87 the Agency investigated such bodies as Northern Ireland Railways, Ulsterbus-Citybus, the province's two universities, the Western Health and Social Services Board, six motor traders and eight insurance companies. If the Agency finds a failure to afford equality of opportunity it can determine what steps should be taken to secure it. It can also ask for undertakings from employers or give them directions; employers, if aggrieved by the Agency's directions or by a decision to remove their name from the register of Equal Opportunity Employers, can appeal to a tribunal known as the Fair Employment Appeals Board. This has only had to deal with three cases. If such an appeal is unsuccessful the Agency may apply to a county court for enforcement measures.

The Government has recently published proposals to strengthen the law on equality of opportunity. It wishes to require employers actively to practise equality of opportunity and to force all public sector employers and those private sector employees with more than 10 employees to monitor the religious composition of their workforces. Failure to do so is to be made a criminal offence (punishable with a fine up to £30,000) and will normally exclude employers from receiving government grants and business (this is the notion of "contract compliance"). The Agency already tries to ensure that employers realise their responsibility to create a climate of neutrality inside the workplace so that workers do not feel intimidated, but it also admits that there is a so-called "chill factor" which discourages some people from even applying for jobs in an environment where they might feel threatened.

Unlawful discrimination

To help eliminate unlawful discrimination the Fair Employment Agency can receive complaints from any person claiming to be a victim and investigate the matter. Even positive or reverse discrimination can be unlawful under the 1976 Act, though affirmative action programmes are not necessarily unlawful. The Agency sees itself as the guardian of fair practice, emphasising to employers the economic, social and industrial advantages which flow from fair and lawful practices in recruitment and promotion, etc.

A complaint of unlawful discrimination must be made within six months of the discrimination occurring, or within two months of the complainant getting to know of it, whichever is the earlier. As in cases of alleged sex discrimination, the burden of proof on the complainant is relatively easy to discharge. If the Agency finds that unlawful discrimination has taken place it is obliged to attempt to secure redress, though either side can appeal against the Agency's findings to a county court. Under section 42 of the Act investigations into individual complaints have to be curtailed if the Secretary of State for Northern Ireland issues a certificate that an allegedly discriminatory act was done for the purpose of safeguarding national security or protecting public safety or public order. The Fair Employment Agency is opposed to this provision and has often expressed concern at its possible misuse.

As with inequality of opportunity, in unlawful discrimination cases the Agency can institute an action in a county court if an employer fails to comply with an undertaking or with agency recommendations. The court can award the Agency damages and/or an injunction to get the discrimination stopped; damages received are passed on to the complainant, who personally incurs no legal expenses. The compensation can include an amount to cover injured feelings. Appeals from a county court decision lie to the Court of Appeal. During the year ending March 1988, 87 complaints were lodged with the Agency (of which almost two-thirds were from Roman Catholics); findings were reached in 45 cases, but in only three was discrimination found to have occurred.

Education, research and the future

As well as dealing with the two matters above, the Agency has a significant educational and research role. It visits employers to give training courses and advice on employment practices; it conducts seminars, shows videos and runs publicity campaigns. It promotes the Department of Economic Development's Guide to Effective Practice in Religious Equality of Opportunity in Employment; this indicates which policies and procedures should be adopted in order to create an equal opportunity environment within a workplace. The Agency's research has concentrated on identifying the factors which can influence the patterns and trends of employment in Northern Ireland; reports have been published for instance on occupational mobility, opportunities for school leavers and industrial location policy.

According to its latest annual report the Fair Employment Agency believes that during its existence there has been a significant improvement concerning fair employment in the public sector, some improvement in the private service sector, but too little improvement in manufacturing industry, "where the major problem areas are the long-established indigenous Northern Ireland industries and the smaller companies". The imbalance is most apparent when one looks at the figures for unemployment, which show that a Roman Catholic is 2.5 times more likely to be unemployed than a Protestant.

Dissatisfaction with current fair employment legislation led to the formulation in November 1984 of the so-called MacBride Principles, drawn up by a group of civil rights activists led by Sean MacBride, a Nobel Peace Price laureate. The Principles were inspired by the Sullivan Principles, which were designed to encourage responsible employment practices by American firms operating in South Africa. Several state legislatures in America have endorsed the MacBride Principles by threatening to disinvest from American companies which refuse to abide by them. The British government and the Fair Employment Agency have strongly condemned the Principles, claiming that several of them actually require conduct which is illegal under the 1976 Act. The Principles are supported, on the other hand, by the Fair Employment Trust, an unofficial body not to be confused with the Agency. In 1987 the Standing Advisory Commission on Human Rights (see 8.6) published a major report on fair employment and made 124 recommendations for change. These included calls for a prohibition on "indirect" discrimination, clarification of the scope for lawful affirmative action programmes and a new, more powerful body to replace the existing Fair Employment Agency.

In 1988, as mentioned above, the government announced its plans for reform. These involve the strengthening and restructuring of the Agency which is to be renamed the Fair Employment Commission. The Commission will be able to scrutinise job applications to all firms with more than 250 employees and all employers will have to review their employment practices every three years. Individual complaints of alleged religious discrimination are to be heard by a separate tribunal comparable to an industrial tribunal, with a right of appeal on a point of law to the Court of Appeal. The legislation to implement these proposals is expected to come into force during 1989. Meanwhile, as from March 1988, a fair employment support scheme has been introduced. Open to private sector employers with more than 25 employees, provided they have signed the Declaration of Principle and Intent, the scheme offers free consultancy advice and financial assistance of up to £5,000 for employers wishing to promote the active practice of equality of opportunity.

The Race Relations Acts in force in Great Britain do not apply in Northern Ireland, and the Commission for Racial Equality has no role in the province. It is, consequently, quite lawful for an employer to discriminate here on the basis of ethnic or national origins, just as there is no protection for discrimination against the handicapped, homosexuals or the elderly.

8.3 The Labour Relations Agency

The Labour Relations Agency was created by the Industrial Relations (NI) Order 1976. Like the Advisory, Conciliation and Arbitration Service (ACAS) in England, it is a body independent of government and operating under the direction of a Board comprising representatives of employers, employees and others. There are at present nine part-time members together with a full-time chairperson and Chief Executive (Mr Wilson Gamble), all appointed, after consultations, by the Department of Economic Development. A report on the Agency's activities is presented each year to the Department and can be obtained free of charge from the Agency's head office in Belfast. There are about 50 full-time members of staff employed there, with a small additional group based in Londonderry. The annual cost of running the Agency is approximately £1 million, which is granted by the government.

The Agency's chief tasks are to promote good industrial relations and to improve collective bargaining machinery. In fulfilment of these functions it involves itself in employment disputes in several different ways:

(1)   If the dispute involves groups of employers or employees the Agency can attempt collective conciliation; one of its conciliation officers meets with the parties and attempts to narrow their differences to vanishing point. During 1987-88 the Agency dealt with 117 disputes in this way and conciliated settlements were reached in 68 per cent of them; industrial action was avoided altogether in 67 per cent of cases, with a stoppage of work occurring in only 16 per cent.

(2)   If the dispute involves an individual's employment rights the matter will be referred to the Labour Relations Agency by the Central Office of Industrial Tribunals (see 7.3), unless it relates to a claim for redundancy payment. Again, a conciliation officer tries to arrive at a mutually agreed settlement, a service which is free and confidential; if a settlement cannot be reached the dispute can then go to an industrial tribunal. During 1987-88, 1,914 individual employment disputes were dealt with by the Agency and 69 per cent were determined without the need for a tribunal hearing; the vast majority related to claims of unfair dismissal.

(3)   If the conciliation process is unattractive or unsuccessful the Agency can try to resolve industrial disputes by referring them to independent arbitration; alternatively it can hold a formal inquiry into the issue, a step which does not require the consent of the parties and which occurs very rarely (though twice in 1986-87). During 1987-88 there were 14 arbitration hearings arranged by the Agency, with a further four being held privately but with Agency assistance.

(4)   If problems arise as to the non-recognition of a trade union by an employer the Agency can try to help by providing advice or conciliation or by issuing a report after making its own inquiries. During 1987-88, 15 such cases were dealt with.

(5)   The introduction of legislation on equal pay for work of equal value (see the Equal Pay (Amendment) Regulations (NI) 1984) has provided industrial tribunals with great problems in assessing whether different forms of work are indeed of equal value. The Labour Relations Agency assists the tribunals by maintaining a list of independent experts available to examine such claims.

(6)   To help nip industrial relations problems in the bud, the Agency provides expert advice on all aspects of employment relationships. At present it divides its specialist advisory assistance into a General Inquiry Service, a Short Term Advisory Service and an In-Depth Advisory Service. The assistance provided is confidential and free. In 1987-88, for example, advisory officers visited 643 organisations in response to requests for

advice and assistance; in-depth advisory assistance was supplied to 29 different projects. These were evenly split between the public and private sectors.

In addition to all this the Labour Relations Agency conducts reviews of industrial relations throughout whole industries, encourages industrial relations training, sponsors research and occasional papers, gives educational talks and issues codes of practice. A major survey of industrial relations in Northern Ireland was carried out in 1986-87. Codes of practice have so far been published on disclosure of information to trade unions for collective bargaining purposes, disciplinary practice and procedures, and time off for trade union activities. These have no actual legal force but are taken into account by industrial tribunals when deciding disputes. The Agency issues a twice-yearly newsletter and a series of very useful Information Notes, and has produced a regularly updated three-volume Encyclopaedia of Northern Ireland Labour Law and Practice.

8.4 The Health and Safety Agency

The Health and Safety at Work (NI) Order 1978 extended the protection of the health and safety legislation to all persons at work (except domestic servants in private households) and placed new basic duties regarding safety on employers, the self-employed, employees, and those manufacturing and supplying articles and substances for use at work. It protects not just persons at work but also the general public outside places of work. By virtue of the Reporting of Injuries, Diseases and Dangerous Occurrences Regulations (NI) 1986, new duties have been imposed concerning the reporting of accidents.

Northern Ireland has always had a much better industrial accident record than Great Britain, but to help with the implementation of the 1978 Order a Health and Safety Agency was established. The Agency is similar to the Health and Safety Commission in Great Britain but its role and functions differ in some important respects. Rather than having direct executive control over authorities responsible for enforcing health and safety legislation, the Agency has mainly advisory functions. It comprises 10 part-time members including its Chairman (Mr Harry Porter) and has a supporting staff of six. The members represent district councils and both sides of industry and are appointed by the Department of Economic Development. The cost of running the Agency in 1986 was approximately £110,000.

The Agency's general task is to promote health and safety at work. It fulfils this by making recommendations to appropriate Government departments, by arranging for research, training and the provision of information, and by issuing and approving codes of practice. The recommendations made to Government departments usually relate to regulations proposed by those departments or by the Agency itself for health and safety at work. The Agency cannot actually issue such regulations, but it must be consulted about their content. Its codes of practice have a semi-legal status in that a breach of them is some evidence of dubious practices but no offence in itself. One code covers the appointment of safety representatives, who are appointed by recognised trade unions and have a long list of specific functions in their place of work.

Responsibility for enforcement of the 1978 Order rests with the government departments which happen to be concerned with the particular work in question. Work on farms, for instance, is the responsibility of the Farm Safety Inspectorate of the Department of Agriculture, while work in factories, or in offices in the public sector, is the responsibility of the Health and Safety Inspectorate of the Department of Economic Development. The Agricultural Inspectorate issued 202 enforcement notices in 1986, while the DED's Inspectorate issued 91 such notices and undertook no fewer than 9,050 inspections.

Health and safety in shops, and in offices in the private sector, remains a matter for the environmental health officers of district councils. The recent rise in the number of small businesses in Northern Ireland has made this responsibility a heavy one. The Health and Safety Agency comments on the annual reports of these local enforcement agencies in its own annual reports, which are made to the Department of Economic Development and published.

Where prosecutions have to be brought for breach of safety regulations the Agency monitors the fines imposed to see if they are of real deterrent value. In 1986 the average fine in Northern Ireland rose to £280 but the Agency has complained that this is well below the average Great Britain figure of £472. As awareness of the importance of safety at work increases, and if the level of accidents at work remains high, it is likely that the average fine will rise significantly in the near future.

The Agency can recommend investigations and inquiries but cannot compel them or conduct them itself. It has commissioned research into some occupational diseases and has encouraged employers and trade unions to train personnel in good safety practices, though the Agency itself does not provide training. It has tried to promote safety at work through broadcasting short films on commercial television, as well as through publishing leaflets, conducting seminars, running competitions and issuing a bulletin (called "Health, Safety and You") describing recent developments in health and safety at work. It publishes guides to new legislation and a Construction Handbook (now in its third edition).

More particular advice about occupational health problems can be sought from the Employment Medical Advisory Service, a branch of the Department of Economic Development.

8.5 The Equal Opportunities Commission

The Equal Opportunities Commission for Northern Ireland was set up under the Sex Discrimination (NI) Order 1976 to work for the elimination of discrimination on the grounds of sex or marriage and to promote equality of opportunity between men and women generally. It consists of a full-time chairperson and chief executive (currently Mrs Mary Clark-Glass) and up to 12 other commissioners; all are appointed by the Department of Economic Development. The Commission issues an annual report to the Secretary of State, which is then published as a House of Commons paper. These reports present comprehensive surveys of the state of sex discrimination in Northern Ireland. The Commission is funded by the Department of Economic Development; in 1987-88 the grant was only £335,500, despite the secretariat numbering about 15 employees.

A particular duty of the Commission is to keep under review the workings of the Equal Pay Act (NI) 1970, the Sex Discrimination (NI) Order 1976, the Equal Pay (Amendment) Regulations (NI) 1984, and such parts of the health and safety legislation which require men and women to be treated differently. In this context discrimination can refer to one of two practices: treating a person of one sex less favourably than a person of the other sex solely because of the first person's sex, or treating a married person less favourably than a single person solely because the first person is married. It does not encompass less favourable treatment of single persons or homosexuals. Indirect discrimination, if intentional, is covered.

Research and education

As well as having power to submit proposals to the government for amending the legislation it reviews - most recently it issued critical comments on the proposed Sex Discrimination (NI) Order 1988 - the Commission has extensive powers covering research and education. Indeed, it spends nearly half of its budget on these activities. In campaigning for fairer treatment of women it is not satisfied with pious statements of intent concerning equal opportunities policies: it requires them to be matched with positive or affirmative action, which is not unlawful under the legislation. Employers, for instance, can legally train more women than men for occupations in which women have previously been underrepresented. The Commission's recent research projects include investigations into gender differentiation and sex-stereotyping in primary schools, the experiences of women in the professions, and the reasons for women who work in the retail sector being overrepresented in low-status occupations. The conditions of work of part-time employees are also monitored, since the part-time workforce in Northern Ireland is almost entirely female. Although women constitute 46 per cent of the entire full-time and part-time workforce, women's average earnings are still only 75 per cent of those of men.

In performing its functions the Equal Opportunities Commission publishes leaflets, booklets and reports (many of which are available free) and produces films, videos and posters. In 1986 it issued an informative factsheet entitled "Where Do Women Figure" and a guide to sexual harassment at places of work. In 1988 it published a booklet on how to make changes in the workplace so as to eliminate sexually discriminatory practices.

Enforcement

To fulfil its role as an enforcement body the Commission may initiate its own formal investigations into suspected instances of discrimination and may serve non-discrimination notices, which require the provisions of the 1970 Act and the 1976 Order, as amended, to be complied with; they are eventually enforceable in a county court. A register of non-discrimination notices is available for public inspection at the Commission's offices in Belfast. The Commission also has the sole right to initiate action in relation to persistent discrimination, discriminatory advertisements and instructions, or pressure to discriminate.

In the 12 months up to April 1988 the Commission received 729 complaints of discrimination; two-thirds of these related to employment issues such as discriminatory dismissals and involuntary reductions in hours of work; 49 complaints concerned the equal pay legislation and 92 concerned advertising. All but about five per cent of the complaints it receives are dealt with internally by EOC staff, the remainder being referred to solicitors. In 1987-88, 28 cases were taken to a court or tribunal (discrimination in the field of employment is dealt with by industrial tribunals, while other cases are heard by county courts); 16 of these were settled (four of them involving a joint claim). Of the 12 cases fought to a conclusion, a declaration of discrimination or an equality clause was obtained in six.

Under article 75(2) of the 1976 Order the Equal Opportunities Commission can provide personal and financial assistance to complainants in cases which are complex or involve a question of principle. This can be particularly valuable in employment cases, as the civil legal aid and legal advice and assistance schemes (see 3.3) do not provide for state-funded representation in industrial tribunals. In 1987-88 the Commission assisted 62 complainants in this manner. One such case is that involving 31 female police reservists, who complained that the Chief Constable of the RUC had discriminated against them in not renewing their contracts. The industrial tribunal dealing with this case referred it to the European Court of Justice, which delivered its judgment in May 1986 (*Johnston and others* v *Chief Constable of the RUC);* the decision led to a settlement payment of £1.2 million and resulted in the Sex Discrimination (Amendment) Order 1988, which changes the 1976 Order so as not in future to preclude judicial review of discrimination on grounds of national security.

In September 1986 the government issued a consultative paper outlining future strategy options for dealing with equality of employment in Northern Ireland. The Equal Opportunities Commission strongly criticised this paper for its superficiality and lack of understanding; it believed, together with women's organisations in the province, that the government's reform proposals would weaken, not strengthen, the anti-discrimination laws, especially in the private sector. Given the fact that the EOC's caseload has trebled since the first year of its existence, and that the law on sex discrimination is becoming ever more complex, the case for retaining a separate watchdog body for this field seems unanswerable.

8.6 The Standing Advisory Commission
on Human Rights

This Commission, set up under the Northern Ireland Constitution Act 1973, comprises 12 part-time members appointed by the Secretary of State for Northern Ireland. The current chairman is Sir Oliver Napier, a solicitor. The Parliamentary Commissioner for Administration and the Chairman of the Fair Employment Agency are *ex officio* members. The Secretariat contains a Secretary plus five supporting staff. The Commission's annual budget is not made public, but resources, it says, are stretched to the utmost. A report is presented to the Secretary of State every year, being published as a House of Commons paper.

The current statutory function of the Commission is to advise the Secretary of State on the adequacy and effectiveness of the law in preventing discrimination based on religious belief or political opinion, a less wide-ranging role than was originally envisaged in the White Paper preceding the enactment of the 1973 Act. The Commission has frequently pressed for its statutory remit to be officially widened so that it can examine and comment upon any aspect of the law affecting Northern Ireland and oversee other bodies or agencies whose activities impinge upon human rights. In 1984 the then Secretary of State gave a written undertaking that the Commission's statutory terms of reference would be amended so as to reflect more clearly its broad concerns, but to date no action has been taken on this.

Since its inception the Commission has regularly reviewed the operation of the law concerning public order and elections. Secretaries of State have specifically referred to it the topics of sex discrimination, homosexual law reform and family law. It played a significant role in getting the Fair Employment (NI) Act enacted in 1976. In recent years the Commission has declared itself anxious to give more attention to the social and economic aspects of human rights. It has looked closely at the topics of complaints against the police and the strip-searching of women prisoners, and in 1987 it issued a major report on discrimination and equality of opportunity in Northern Ireland. During 1988 it hopes to complete its work on arrangements for supporting the victims of crime, on plans for improving community relations, and on methods of recognising equal communal rights.

Despite its limited terms of reference the Commission has been encouraged by successive Secretaries of State to review the operation of the special legislation enacted as a result of the civil unrest in Northern Ireland. A constant watch has been kept on the workings of the Northern Ireland (Emergency Provisions) Acts and the Prevention of Terrorism (Temporary Provisions) Acts. An analysis has been made of matters such as the length of time persons charged with scheduled offences have been kept in custody between arrest and trial, and the length of periods of remand during a trial. The Commission has recommended the introduction of a statutory code governing the treatment of persons held in police custody (now projected in the Police and Criminal Evidence (NI) Order). Papers have been commissioned on the use of "supergrasses" as a method of prosecution and on the introduction of three-judge courts to try scheduled offences. Much to its disappointment, however, the Commission was not consulted about the right to silence legislation introduced in 1988.

The Commission has encouraged public discussion of whether a Bill of Rights is needed in Northern Ireland; its own view is that a Bill for the United Kingdom as a whole, based on the Council of Europe's Convention on Human Rights and Fundamental Freedoms (see 2.6), should be introduced as a matter of urgency. Advice is also given to the Government as to the implications of other international agreements such as the European Social Charter and the European and United Nations Conventions on Torture.

8.7 The Police Authority and the Independent Commission for Police Complaints

The Police Authority

The organisation of the police service in Northern Ireland has been briefly outlined in 1.5. We are here concerned with the accountability of the police. Up to 1970 the Royal Ulster Constabulary was exclusively accountable to the Minister of Home Affairs in the Northern Ireland Government, but following the civil disturbances in 1969 an Advisory Committee under the chairmanship of Lord Hunt recommended the establishment of a Police Authority, free of direct political influence, to monitor the RUC's activities. This was duly brought about by the Police Act (NI) 1970.

The Police Authority for Northern Ireland is composed of a chairman (currently Mr Tom Rainey), a vice-chairman, and between 14 and 20 other persons (at the moment thre are 18). All are appointed by the Secretary of State. The membership is meant, as far as practicable, to be representative of the whole community in Northern Ireland, and in particular there should be members representing the interests of district councils, public bodies (such as institutions of higher education), the legal professin, trade unions, agriculture, industry, commerce, and voluntary organisations concerned with the welfare of young persons. The members serve in a part-time capacity and hold office for three years, though their terms can be renewed. In England and Wales the police authorities are made up of local councillors (two-thirds) and justices of the peace (one-third). In Northern Ireland the feeling is that if elected representatives were appointed to the Authority it might quickly become partisan in its activities.

Functions

The main function of the Police Authority, according to the 1970 Act, is "to secure the maintenance of an adequate and efficient police force in Northern Ireland". This means that the Authority is ultimately responsible for providing buildings and equipment for the police and controlling expenditure on the service. The 1988-89 budget of the Authority amounts to some £380m, out of which the province's police stations have to be maintained and salaries paid to the force's 11,250 full-time officers, the 1,700 part-time reservists and the 3,000 civilian staff (telecommunication workers, vehicle maintenance officers, clerks, searchers, etc.). The Authority must also, subject to the Secretary of State's approval, determine the maximum number of persons of each rank which is to constitute the establishment of the force. In addition, it appoints all of Northern Ireland's traffic wardens.

The Authority appoints the senior officers in the RUC, that is, the 15 or so officers above the rank of chief superintendent (the Chief Constable, the Deputy Chief Constable, the Senior Assistant Chief Constables and the Assistant Chief Constables). It is also the disciplinary authority for such senior officers and can call upon any of them to retire in the interests of efficiency. In 1988 it considered the position of senior officers involved in the incidents investigated in the Stalker-Sampson report, but found none of them deserving of being disciplined. If the police are held liable to pay compensation in any legal proceedings (*e.g.* in a civil action for false imprisonment), it is the Police Authority which pays the money; it may also pay rewards to police officers for exceptional diligence or other specially meritorious conduct.

Under the Police (NI) Order 1987, the Authority has the duty to keep itself informed as to the manner in which complaints from members of the public against police officers are dealt with by the Chief Constable. Prior to 1987, if a complaint appeared to affect the public interest, the Authority could require the Chief Constable to refer it to a tribunal for consideration and report, but this was done on only one occasion (in the *Rafferty* case, 1980). Now, by virtue of article 8(2) of the 1987 Order, which has no equivalent in England, the Authority has the power to refer a matter not the subject of a complaint (see below) to the Independent Commission for Police Complaints, provided it appears to the Authority that it is in the public interest that the Commission should supervise the investigation of the matter. Under the 1970 Act the Authority can still require the Chief Constable to submit reports in writing on such matters as may be specified, but it is thought that this power has very rarely, if ever, been exercised.

It is vital to realise that the Police Authority is not meant to interfere with the way in which the police actually do their job. This is often put by saying that sole responsibility for operational matters within the force lies with the Chief Constable; section 6(2) of the 1970 Act states that the force shall be under his "direction and control". Needless to say, it is sometimes difficult to decide whether a matter relates to "direction or control" or to "adequacy and efficiency"; it is up to the Authority and the Chief Constable to agree where the dividing line should fall.

The Authority carries out most of its functions on a committee basis. Its Complaints and Public Relations Committee, for instance, meets once a month with the Deputy Chief Constable to monitor the handling of complaints. Its Consultative Committee on Public Order has to be consulted by the Secretary of State whenever he is considering whether to make an order under the Public Order (NI) Order 1987 prohibiting the holding of public processions or meetings. Under the proposed Police and Criminal Evidence (NI) Order the Authority will be under a duty to make arrangements for obtaining the views of the community on policing; this places on a more formal footing the contacts which the Public Relations Committee is already trying to develop through liaising with local consultative committees throughout the province.

It is to the Police Authority that the Chief Constable submits his annual report, but the Authority itself does not issue one. Instead it publishes a review of its activities every few years. In 1988, in an attempt to give itself a higher profile and enhance its flagging reputation, the Authority published "Working Together to Police Northern Ireland: Three Years of Progress". In 1987 it had a say in the content and eventual public release of "Professional Policing Ethics", the document popularly but inaccurately known as the new "code of conduct" for the RUC.

The Independent Commission for Police Complaints

The Independent Commission for Police Complaints for Northern Ireland was established by the Police (NI) Order 1987 and has been operating since 29th February 1988. It replaces the Police Complaints Board, which had existed since 1977 and which many observers felt was not effective enough. The equivalent English body is the Police Complaints Authority, created under the Police and Criminal Evidence Act 1984. The Commission must consist of a chairman, two deputy chairmen and at least four other members, all appointed by the Secretary of State. The members are appointed for a term of up to three years; they must not be present or former members of a police force in Britain or Ireland. The present chairman of the Commission is Mr James Grew, who is assisted by two deputies and five other members; all eight of these people are part-time and five of them have legal qualifications. There is a full-time secretariat of 15 people.

Junior officers

All complaints against RUC officers below the rank of Assistant Chief Constable must be recorded by the Chief Constable. Those which he feels are suitable for informal resolution may be dealt with accordingly; the remainder must be investigated formally by a member of the RUC or another United Kingdom police force appointed by the Chief Constable, and the complaint must be referred to the Commission. The Commission has a duty to supervise the investigation of serious complaints (*e.g.* those alleging that a police officer caused death or serious injury) and may supervise any other investigation if it considers this desirable in the public interest. The Commission must also supervise the investigation of any matter not the subject of a complaint provided that the Secretary of State or the Police Authority require it to do so, that the matter involves the alleged commission of a criminal offence or an offence against discipline by a police officer, and that supervision is desirable in the public interest.

The right to supervise investigations is one that the old Police Complaints Board did not have. It means that the Commission can veto the appointment of any particular investigator and impose requirements on how an investigation is to be conducted (who is to be interviewed, what forensic evidence is to be collected, etc.). The investigator's report must be submitted to the Commission, which will then tell the Chief Constable whether the investigation was or was not conducted to the Commission's satisfaction.

Until the Commission has issued a statement on a supervised investigator's report, no disciplinary charge or criminal proceedings can be brought against the officer involved in the complaint. The Chief Constable must send a copy of the investigator's report to the Director of Public Prosecutions if he thinks that the report indicates that an officer ought to be charged with committing a criminal offence. If the officer is not to be charged, or if the DPP has dealt with the question of criminal proceedings, the Chief Constable must decide whether to prefer disciplinary charges and inform the Commission accordingly. He must also send the Commission the investigator's report, and his decision about disciplinary charges, in cases where the investigation was not supervised. In all cases, after it has received the relevant information from the Chief Constable, the Commission can itself direct the Chief Constable to refer a case to the DPP and can recommend or, if need be, direct the preferment of disciplinary charges.

Police discipline is regulated by the RUC (Discipline and Disciplinary Appeals) Regulations 1988. Normally it is a purely internal matter, but when the Independent Commission for Police Complaints directs that it is desirable by reason of exceptional circumstances affecting the case, a tribunal may be set up to decide whether the accused officer is guilty of the charge or not. Usually the tribunal will comprise the Chief Constable as chairman and two members of the Commission. The standard of proof required for a finding of guilt is the same as in criminal proceedings, namely beyond all reasonable doubt.

Senior officers and reports

Complaints against senior RUC officers (those above the rank of chief superintendent) are the responsibility of the Police Authority rather than of the Chief Constable, but the Commission's rights of supervision are just the same. Once the Authority has received a statement from the Commission about the investigation, it must decide whether to refer the case to the DPP. Disciplinary charges will be heard by a tribunal consisting of a single person, assisted by one or more assessors, appointed by the Police Authority. In this context the Commission does not have any power to direct referrals to the DPP or the bringing of disciplinary charges.

The Commission must make an annual report to the Secretary of State and a report at least once in every three years reviewing the working of the complaints system. The Secretary of State can require the Commission to report on matters relating generally to its functions or the Commission itself can report to him on any matters which are grave or exceptional.

It remains to be seen how active the Independent Commission becomes. In 1987 its predecessor, the Police Complaints Board, received 2,376 complaints against police officers; 43 per cent of these were later withdrawn but 803 cases were fully considered. Some 286 of all cases related to persons arrested under the emergency laws, but 64 per cent were incapable of completion due to the complainant's failure to co-operate. Over four-fifths of the cases looked at by the Board were also referred to the DPP, who directed nine prosecutions. Disciplinary charges were preferred in 15 cases and disciplinary action short of charges was taken in 71 further cases. In the first 10 months of its operation the new Commission received 1600 complaints. The commonest type of complaint made is that the police assaulted someone.

8.8 Consumer Protection Bodies

There are several bodies whose job it is to look after the interests of consumers. Some of these are branches of Government at the central or local level; others are independent of Government but receive Government funding; a third group operates on an entirely voluntary basis.

The Office of Fair Trading

Of government bodies the most important is the Office of Fair Trading. This was established in 1973 and is the office in London from which the Director-General of Fair Trading carries out his various statutory responsibilities for the whole of the United Kingdom. These have been extended by the Consumer Protection Act and the Consumer Protection (NI) Order 1987. They include the collection of evidence relating to business practices which may adversely affect the economic, health, safety or other interests of consumers. He may refer such practices to the Consumer Protection Advisory Committee, which in turn can make recommendations to the Secretary of State for Trade and Industry on proposed regulation of these practices (*e.g.*, the banning of "no refund" notices). The Director-General also encourages trade associations to issue voluntary codes of practice to safeguard consumers' interests. He does not deal individually with complaints received directly from the public, except in so far as these alert him to a course of conduct detrimental to consumers as a whole, which he can then try to have altered, if necessary through court proceedings. In addition, most organisations giving credit to consumers can only do so if licensed by the Office of Fair Trading.

The Office of Fair Trading receives a lot of information from the local agencies which enforce legislation dealing with hygiene and with weights and measures (now called trading standards). In Northern Ireland the responsibility for supervising and enforcing trading standards (including trade descriptions) rests with the Department of Economic Development, while the control of food hygiene is part of the duties of the local district councils. These are the bodies which instigate prosecutions under the relevant legislation. The Office of Fair Trading publishes information concerning these responsibilities and providing general advice for consumers. Its pamphlets are available in advice centres and public libraries.

Local government is also responsible for the establishment of consumer advice centres. In Northern Ireland there are at present two such centres, in Belfast and Londonderry. Their job is to advise consumers rather than represent them or enforce consumer protection law (see 3.2).

The Monopolies and Mergers Commission

This Commission, also a government body, has existed in some form or other since 1948; it comprises between 10 and 27 members appointed by the Secretary of State for Trade and Industry and has its headquarters in London. It investigates and reports on proposed or actual trade practices and structures which are referred to it by the Secretary of State or, more commonly, by the Director-General of Fair Trading. The aim may simply be to examine the facts, or it may be to assess whether the action in question will operate against the public interest. In the latter event the Commission will have to take into account, amongst other things, the interests of consumers, the need to reduce costs and the importance of developing new manufacturing techniques.

The Commission's reports usually take several months to prepare as its investigations are thorough. It holds formal confidential hearings at which witnesses will be examined and interested parties represented by barristers. The reports are laid before Parliament and published but the government is not obliged to heed the recommendations. Among the practices condemned within the field of legal services have been the restrictions placed by the Law Society on advertising by solicitors and the rule whereby a Queen's Counsel cannot work in court without the assistance of a junior barrister; some changes in these practices were made as a result. Recently the Commission has done more work on mergers than monopolies, though the Competition Act of 1980 extended its role by enabling it to examine the costs and general efficiency of nationalised industries, provided that such matters are officially referred to it. In 1988 it investigated the pricing policies of ferry companies plying between Ireland and England.

The General Consumer Council

This body, functioning under the General Consumer Council (NI) Order 1984, came into full operation in April 1985. It replaced the Northern Ireland

Consumer Council, the Northern Ireland Electricity Consumers' Council and the Transport Users' Committee. It is independent of central or local government, although its members are appointed by the Department of Economic Development and it is funded by that Department. In 1986-87 the grant was £253,000.

The General Consumer Council consists of a part-time chairperson (Mrs Anne Dickson) and a deputy chairperson plus up to 16 other members. There is a supproting staff of eight employees. The members represent a wide range of organisations and interests, such as the trade union movement, advice centres, local authorities and women's groups. Together these representatives make up a central body of consumer opinion, watching over consumer interests and speaking on the consumer's behalf to government, nationalised and private industries, and commercial enterprises of all sorts. The Council liaises closely with the National Consumer Council (of which its chairperson is a member) as well as with the Consumer Councils for Scotland and Wales.

The Council has a general duty to promote the consumer interest. To this end it has powers to carry out research, provide information and investigate matters of consumer concern. It has particular responsibilities in the realms of electricity, transport, energy and food: it has special groups working in those areas, and electricity and transport matters are the only ones on which it will deal with individual complaints. Indeed it has a full-time member of staff to handle these. If consumers contact the Council to complain about other areas it will give basic advice or redirect the consumer to other bodies (see 3.1). The need for easily assessible consumer advice agencies in Northern Ireland is great; an official survey published in 1986 showed that the province had proportionally more consumer complaints than any other region in Britain; of those consumers who took some action on their complaint, Northern Ireland had the highest level of residual dissatisfaction.

The present Consumer Council or its predecessor has commissioned and published incisive reports on such matters as the cost of funerals, the small claims courts (see 5.4), the conversion of dwellings from town gas, and ferry services to and from Northern Ireland. It has also published a guide to fundamental consumer protection measures in Northern Ireland (entitled "Buying, Selling and Borrowing") and a booklet called "Patients' Rights", updated in 1986. (The National Health Service has its own statutory scheme to deal with complaints about the services of a general medical or dental practitioner, as well as established procedures for handling complaints about the services or treatment in hospitals.)

Unfortunately the General Consumer Council does not possess the power to compel other bodies to act on its views. It seeks to influence rather than to enforce. Through developing its consumer education service and publishing a full annual report (submitted to the Department of Economic Development) it makes consumers aware of their legal rights.

Not within the remit of the Consumer Council are issues concerning postal and telecommunications services. Consumers' grievances in these fields should be directed respectively to the Post Office Users' Council for Northern Ireland and the regional office of Oftel (the Office of Telecommunications), the new body set up in 1984 to monitor the now privatised telecommunications industry.

Registrar of Friendly Societies

The function of this official, who operates within the government's Department of Economic Development, is to supervise the activities of industrial and provident societies (such as co-operatives and housing associations), credit unions, friendly societies and trade unions. He visits these bodies and scrutinises their annual reports. He allows the public to search his registers for relevant information and he answers day-to-day enquiries. At the end of 1985 there were eight trade unions registered with chief offices situated in Northern Ireland (and having 35,000 members). Some 42 trade unions registered in Great Britain had also registered their rule-books in the province. At least six Northern Ireland trade unions are unregistered, including the Ulster Teachers' Union and the Ulster Farmers' Union.

Voluntary bodies

Of the purely voluntary organisations which act as watchdog bodies for all consumers the best known are probably the Consumers' Association and the National Federation of Consumer Groups. Both of these have members, though no groups, in Northern Ireland. The former publishes *Which?*, the magazine providing information about the range of products and services available to consumers. The National Federation of Consumer Groups is a body representing groups of consumers as well as individuals throughout the United Kingdom; it too provides information to its members concerning all aspects of consumer affairs.

Many private bodies exist to help consumers in relation to particular industries or professions. Trade associations, such as those for jewellers or manufacturers of electrical appliances, often run their own complaints machinery. The insurance industry, eager to polish up its tarnished image, has recently established an Insurance Ombudsman Bureau, described below. The Press Council can deal with complaints about newspaper practices, including those of the local and provincial newspapers in Northern Ireland, though someone who complains to it must give a written undertaking that he will not take out a civil action against the newspaper at some later date, and the Council is powerless to award any effective remedy to the complainant. People who believe they have been unfairly treated in television or radio programmes can write to the Broadcasting Complaints Commission. Complaints about advertisements in newspapers or the cinema can be made to the Advertising Standards Authority while the Independent Broadcasting Authority handles complaints about radio or TV commercials. Again, however, neither of these bodies can grant remedies.

The Insurance, Banking and Building Societies Ombudsmen

The Insurance Ombudsman's Bureau was set up in 1981 for the United Kingdom as a whole by a group of large insurance companies. (It has nothing to do with the ombudsmen offices described in 8.1.) There are now more than 250 members. If you are insured with one of these companies and have a complaint which is not dealt with satisfactorily by the company's own complaints procedure you can send your complaint, within six months, to the Insurance Ombudsman. He will look into the matter, if necessary ordering the firm to produce all the inter-office memos and files relating to your case. If some settlement cannot be arrived at, a formal adjudication will be made by the Insurance Ombudsman and the member firms have agreed to abide by his decisions in cases involving less than £100,000. There can be no recourse against any of the Insurance Ombudsman's decisions to the courts, but legal rights are otherwise unaffected by the scheme.

The office of the Banking Ombudsman was established in 1986. It deals with complaints against any member bank, provided not more than six months have elapsed since the last word on the subject by the bank involved. The Ombudsman can award up to £50,000, and if you accept the offer of compensation you cannot later take the matter to court. The building societies set up a similar scheme in 1987; membership of it is compulsory, therefore all the United Kingdom societies are covered. The Building Societies Ombudsman will investigate complaints about mortgages and other loans, savings accounts, cheques, direct debits, etc. Neither he nor the Banking Ombudsman, however, can look into complaints about an institution's commercial judgment, nor can the Building Societies Ombudsman deal with complaints about surveys carried out before a mortgage is granted. A Unit Trusts Ombudsman also exists.

8.9 Law Reform Agencies

As explained in chapters 1 and 2, the two main sources of law in Northern Ireland are legislation and case law. Case law is obviously an unsatisfactory medium for introducing changes in the law because by definition it comes into being only when persons choose to take matters to court, and judges have neither the time nor the authority to expound parts of the law which are not the precise subject of the litigation. Legislation is therefore the preferred medium for law reform and to help Parliament and the government in designing new legislation there exist various law reform agencies.

The Office of Law Reform

The most important such body for Northern Ireland is the Office of Law

Reform. This was originally constituted in 1965 as a separate branch of the Office of the Parliamentary Draftsman in Northern Ireland, that also being the year when the Law Commissions for England and Scotland, described below, were established. The Office's remit then was to consider matters within the legislative powers of the Stormont Parliament, while bodies such as the English Law Commission retained power to consider matters falling outside Stormont's legislative capacity. The Office initiated a survey of land law in Northern Ireland, and during its first five years was instrumental in having legislation enacted on, amongst other things, theft, compensation for criminal injuries, preliminary enquiries in committal proceedings, misrepresentations, the age of majority and the enforcement of judgments.

During the short existence of the first Northern Ireland Assembly in 1974, the Office of Law Reform in effect became a separate department of the Executive, but since the Assembly's demise the Office has functioned as a branch of what is now the Department of Finance and Personnel in the Northern Ireland Office. It has a director and one or two other members of staff.

The Office no longer publishes regular reports on its activities, but its role is to consider what changes should be made in any part of the law affecting Northern Ireland. The province is still a separate legal jurisdiction, so that whenever changes in the law of England are being considered, thought has always to be given to whether similar changes should apply in Northern Ireland. The office therefore devotes much of its time to examining the reports of other law reform bodies such as the English Law Commission. It also looks at suggestions for reform emanating from other common law jurisdictions, especially Canada, Australia and the Republic of Ireland. It reacts as well to proposals for reform put forward by pressure groups or dissatisfied individuals: the Law Society, for instance, has a parliamentary and law reform committee, which frequently submits ideas for change. The Office must inevitably work closely with the Office of the Legislative Draftsmen (see 2.2), commenting on draft legislation and making specific recommendations for new legislation. It is also involved in preparing consolidating Orders in Council, that is, Orders which bring together in one enactment the various provisions already relating to a certain topic without making any changes in the substance of the law. At the moment the Office is engaged in another major review of Northern Ireland land law (which remains significantly different from that in England).

The absence of a statutory independent law reform body specifically for Northern Ireland is widely lamented. In October 1988, however, the Government announced that it was appointing a Law Reform Committee to keep the civil law of Northern Ireland under review and to make recommendations for reform. This Committee is to comprise a part-time chairperson and six members and should be operational early in 1989.

The English Law Commission

Of the English law reform agencies which may have some impact on the law in Northern Ireland the most important is the Law Commission. This has offices in London and is chaired by a High Court judge (currently Sir Roy Beldam) with four full-time Commissioners appointed by the Lord Chancellor. It runs at a cost of over £2 million per year.

The Law Commission considers topics referred to it by the Lord Chancellor's Department or adjudged by itself to require attention. It is now working mainly on criminal law, family law, property law and landlord and tenant law. It normally issues working papers for general discussion before publishing final reports. These reports often include draft bills designed to show how the proposed changes in the law might be enacted. Since its establishment in 1965 the Commission (to March 1989), has produced 111 working papers and 175 reports (including 23 annual reports). The vast majority of reports have resulted in reforming legislation within two or three years. The Scottish Law Commission, which functions in a similar way, has also been very active.

In addition to proposing reforms the Law Commission makes suggestions for tidying up the statute book. It drafts Statute Law (Repeals) Bills and undertakes consolidation work (see 2.2). It was responsible, for example, for the Income and Corporation Taxes Act 1988 which, at over 1,000 pages is the largest statute ever enacted in the United Kingdom. By the end of 1988 the Commission hoped to produce a Criminal Code Bill, the culmination of its long-standing project to put into one code all of the important criminal law.

A core of 12 civil service lawyers are employed at the Commission, together with three draftsmen serving on secondment from the Office of Parliamentary Counsel. From time to time university academics and research assistants are also engaged. The Commission's librarian issues a quarterly bulletin called "Law Under Review", which gives up-to-date summaries of all Government law reform projects. In 1985, to underline further the Commission's commitment to practical law reform, a Standing Committee on Conveyancing was set up; this has focussed its attention on procedural reforms which would be of benefit to ordinary house buyers and sellers.

The Law Commission has no direct responsibility for law reform in Northern Ireland, but many of the changes which it succeeds in getting introduced in England are later made in Northern Ireland as a matter of course.

Other review bodies for the United Kingdom

Two other standing committees exist to review particular aspects of the law which are from time to time referred to them. They are the Law Reform Committee and the Criminal Law Revision Committee. The Law Reform Committee was appointed in 1952 as the successor to the Law Revision Committee, set up in 1934; it considers matters specifically assigned to it by the Lord Chancellor, assignments which in recent years have produced reports on, for example, rules of evidence in civil proceedings and the making, interpreting and revoking of wills. In all, 22 reports have been produced so far.

The Criminal Law Revision Committee was created in 1959 and has issued 14 reports, some of which have taken the form of very detailed examinations of large areas of the criminal law (such as theft and evidence). It is accountable to the Home Secretary rather than the Lord Chancellor. Like the Law Reform Committee it operates with part-time members and full-time secretariats; like the Law Commission both Committees now issue working papers or consultative documents.

On occasions a body is appointed by the government of the day to look into matters of specific or of general concern. The best example of the latter type are Royal Commissions, which conduct large-scale inquiries into affairs with wide-ranging social and legal implications. They are usually chaired by judges or high-ranking public servants. Recent Royal Commissions have included the Pearson Commission on Civil Liability and Compensation for Personal Injury (1978), the Benson Commission on Legal Services (1979), and the Philips Commission on Criminal Procedure (1981). Their reports extend to hundreds of pages and are based on considerable empirical research. An example of a less formal investigation is that known as the Civil Justice Review, conducted under the auspices of the Lord Chancellor's Department between 1985 and 1988; it looked into ways of improving the administration of the civil courts in England and Wales (see Chapter 5). Other government departments, or interdepartmental working parties, frequently issue green or white papers suggesting reforms.

APPENDIX 1

WHERE TO FIND MORE INFORMATION

There are two ways to look for further information concerning any of the topics dealt with in this book. You can consult the published literature, or you can try to contact a relevant person or body connected with the inquiry. In a small place like Northern Ireland, where it is not often economically feasible to publish information or commentaries on aspects of the legal system but where personal contacts are easy to establish, the second method of seeking information will usually be the more fruitful. Appendix 2 sets out the addresses and telephone numbers of a variety of bodies which will usually be very willing to help you with any such query.

As regards the published literature there are rather few books readily available on specific aspects of the legal system in Northern Ireland, and there is no other book at all on the legal system as a whole. Information is more commonly to be found in academic journals, official reports or pamphlets issued by public bodies. These are often difficult to track down. In such circumstances the most reliable source for information is the actual law purporting to govern the point in issue. Chapter 2 of this book explains how to search for these original legal sources, and Appendix 3 provides a few examples of them. In most situations, unfortunately, you will require a lawyer to make sense of these sources, even though they are intended to be understood by lay people.

Listed below are types of published information relevant to each chapter in this book. Pertinent legislation is listed as well as secondary reports and commentaries. Some items are relevant to more than one chapter. The more official the document, the more likely it is to be available only in a public or academic library, or on application to the body originally publishing it. Most of the books mentioned are primarily concerned with the English legal system but contain some information relevant also to Northern Ireland. Items marked with an asterisk are available from the Servicing the Legal System Office, Faculty of Law, Queen's University, Belfast BT7 1NN (tel: 245133 ext. 3597).

1. The History and Administration of the Legal System

Legislation

Government of Ireland Act 1920

Prison Act (NI) 1953

Police Act (NI) 1970

Prosecution of Offences (NI) Order 1972

Northern Ireland Constitution Act 1973

Northern Ireland Act 1974

Judicature (NI) Act 1978

Northern Ireland Act 1982

Probation (NI) Order 1982

Prison Rules (NI) 1982

Reports

Report of the Committee on the Supreme Court of Judicature of Northern Ireland (Chairman: Lord MacDermott) (1970); Cmnd. 4292.

Interim Report of the Joint Committee on Civil and Criminal Jurisdiction in Northern Ireland (1972); Cmnd. 5431.

Report of the Committee on County Courts and Magistrates' Courts in Northern Ireland (Chairman: Lord Justice Jones) (1974); Cmnd. 6892.

Annual Reports of the Chief Constable of the Royal Ulster Constabulary.

Annual Reports of the Prison Service in Northern Ireland.

Report of the Chief Probation Officer for Northern Ireland 1985-87.

Books and articles

Boyle, Hadden and Hillyard, *Law and State: The Case of Northern Ireland* (1974), updated by the same authors in *Ten Years On in Northern Ireland: The Legal Control of Political Violence (1980)*.

Calvert, *Constitutional Law in Northern Ireland: A Study of Regional Government* (1968).

De Smith, *Constitutional and Administrative Law* (ed. Street and Brazier, 5th ed, 1985), especially pp. 62-7.

Griffith, *The Politics of the Judiciary* (3rd ed, 1985).

*Hadfield, "Committees of the House of Commons and Northern Ireland Affairs"(1981) 32 Northern Ireland Legal Quarterly (hereinafter NILQ) 199.

*Hadfield, "The Northern Ireland Act 1982 - Do-It-Yourself Devolution" (1982) 33 NILQ 301.

Newark, "The Bringing of English Law to Ireland" (1972) 23 NILQ 3, and "Notes on Irish Legal History" (1947) 7 NILQ 121. Both of these articles are reprinted in *Elegantia Juris, Selected Writings of F.H. Netwark*, (SLS Legal Publications, 1973).

Pannick, *Judges* (1987).

The Ulster Yearbook (HMSO, 1985), Chapter 2 (Government), Chapter 3 (Justice) and Chapter 4 (Security and Protective Services).

2. The Branches and Sources of Northern Ireland Law

See also the works listed on pages 205-6 below

Books and articles

Bell and Engle, *Cross: Statutory Interpretation* (2nd ed, 1987).

Brown and Jacobs, *The Court of Justice of the European Communities* (2nd ed, 1983).

Cross, *Precedent in English Law* (3rd ed, 1977).

Dane and Thomas, *How to use a Law Library* (2nd ed, 1987), especially Chapter 9.

Farrar and Dugdale, *Introduction to Legal Method* (2nd ed, 1984).

Harris, *An Introduction to Law* (3rd ed. 1988).

Lee, *Judging Judges* (1988).

* Maguire, "The Reports of the Examiner of Statutory Rules for N.I. 1974-78" (1979) 30 NILQ 306.

Miers and Page, *Legislation* (1982).

*Paisley, *A Guide to EEC Law in Northern Ireland* (1986)

Williams, *Learning the Law* (11th ed, 1982).

Zander, *The Law-Making Process* (3rd ed, 1989)

3. Legal Services

Legislation

Costs in Criminal Cases Act (NI) 1968.

Solicitors (NI) Order 1976.

Crown Court Rules (NI) 1979, rules 7-18.

Rules of the Supreme Court (NI) 1980, Order 62.

County Court Rules (NI) 1981, Order 55.

Magistrates' Courts (Costs) Rules (NI) 1981.

Magistrates' Courts (Costs in Criminal Cases) Rules (NI) 1981.

Legal Aid, Advice and Assistance (NI) Order 1981.

Reports

Report of the Committee on Legal Education in Northern Ireland (Chairman: Sir Arthur Armitage) (1973); Cmd. 579.

Report of the Royal Commission on Legal Services (Chairman: Sir Henry Benson) (1979); Cmnd. 7648; chapters 40-42.

Report of the Review Body on Civil Justice (Chairman: Sir Maurice Hodgson) (1988); Cm. 394.

Report for the Committee on the Future of the Legal Profession ("A Time for Change") (Chairman: Lady Marre) (1988).

Annual Reports of the Law Society of Northern Ireland on the Civil and Criminal Legal Aid Schemes.

Annual Reports of the Legal Aid Advisory Committee.

Books and articles

*Allen, *The Cost of Going to Law* (SLS Legal Publications, 1982).

Bradney and others, *How to Study Law* (1986).

Consumers' Association, *Taking Your Own Case to Court or Tribunal* (1985)

Gifford, *Where's the Justice?* (1986).

*Greer, *The Legal Aid, Advice and Assistance (NI) Order* (1981).

Law Society of Northern Ireland, *A Guide to Legal Aid in Northern Ireland* (1988) (a pamphlet).

4. Proceedings in Criminal Courts

Legislation

Indictment Act (NI) 1945.

County Courts Act (NI) 1959.

Magistrates' Courts Act (NI) 1964

Criminal Law Act (NI) 1967.

Criminal Procedure (Committal for Trial) Act (NI) 1968.

Prosecution of Offences (NI) Order 1972.

Juries (NI) Order 1978.

Northern Ireland (Emergency Provisions) Acts 1978 and 1987.

Judicature (NI) Act 1978.

Crown Court Rules (NI) 1979.

Criminal Appeals (NI) Act 1980.

County Court (NI) Order 1980.

County Court Rules (NI) 1981.

Magistrates' Courts (NI) Order 1981.

Magistrates' Courts Rules (NI) 1984.

Treatment of Offenders (NI) Order 1989.

Reports

Annual Reports of the Lord Chancellor's Department: Judicial Statistics for England, Wales and Northern Ireland.

Northern Ireland Annual Abstract of Statisics (HMSO), Chapter 3 (Law and Order).

Report of the Commission to consider legal procedures to deal with terrorist activities in Northern Ireland (Chairman: Lord Diplock) (1972); Cmnd. 5185.

Report of a Committee to consider, in the context of civil liberties and human rights, measures to deal with terrorism in Northern Ireland (Chairman: Lord Gardiner) (1975); Cmnd. 5847.

Report of a Committee of Inquiry into Police Interrogation Procedures in Northern Ireland (Chairman Judge Bennett) (1979); Cmnd. 7947.

Report of the Royal Commission on Criminal Procedure (Chairman: Sir Cyril Philips) (1979); Cmnd. 8092.

Review of the Operation of the Northern Ireland (Emergency Provisions) Act 1978 (Chairman: Sir George Baker) (1984); Cmnd. 9222.

Books and articles

Barnard, *The Criminal Court in Action* (3rd ed, 1988).

*Boyle and Allen, *Sentencing Law and Practice in Northern Ireland* (1983).

*Doran, Criminal Procedure in Northern Ireland: Chapter 5 of *The Digest of Northern Ireland Law* (1988).

Gifford, Supergrasses: Use of Accomplice Evidence in Northern Ireland (1984).

*Jackson, "The Northern Ireland (Emergency Provisions) Act 1987" (1988) 39 NILQ 235.

Jardine, Craig and Geddis, *Fines and Fine Default in Northern Ireland* (Policy, Planning and Research Unit, NIO, 1986)

Jennings (ed.), *Justice Under Fire: The Abuse of Civil Liberties in Northern Ireland* (1988).

* Lavery, *Road Traffic Law in Northern Ireland* (1989).

NCCL, Civil Liberty: *The NCCL Guide to Your Rights* (4th ed. 1989).

Stannard, *Northern Ireland Supplement to Smith and Hogan, Criminal Law* (1984).

Street, *Freedom, the Individual and the Law* (5th ed. 1982).

* Valentine and Hart, *Criminal Procedure in Northern Ireland* (1989).

Walsh, *The Use and Abuse of Emergency Legislation in Northern Ireland* (1983).

5. Proceedings in Civil Courts

Legislation

Criminal Damage (Compensation) (NI) Order 1977.

Judicature (NI) Act 1978.

Rules of the Supreme Court (NI) 1980.

Domestic Proceedings (NI) Order 1980.

County Courts (NI) Order 1980.

Magistrates' Courts (Domestic Proceedings) Rules (NI) 1980.

County Court Rules (NI) 1981.

Magistrates' Courts (NI) Order 1981.

Judgment Enforcement Rules (NI) 1981.

Judgment Enforcement (NI) Order 1981.

Emergency Provisions (Compensation) (NI) Rules 1982 and 1988.

Magistrates' Courts Rules (NI) 1984.

Criminal Injuries (Compensation) (NI) Order 1988.

Reports

Annual Reports of the Lord Chancellor's Department: Judicial Statistics for England, Wales and Northern Ireland.

Report of the Enforcement of Judgments Review Committee (NI) (Chairman: Master J M Hunter) (1987).

Books and articles

Barnard, *The Civil Court in Action* (2nd ed, 1985).

*Greer, *Small Claims: The New Procedure in Nc :hem Ireland* (3rd ed, 1988).

*Greer and Mitchell, *Compensation for Criminal Damage to Property* (1982).

*Greer and Mitchell, *Compensation for Criminal Injuries to Persons in Northern Ireland* (1976 and supplement 1978).

* Steele, "Compensation for Loss of Employment through Civil Unrest" (1987) 38 NILQ 62.

*Valentine, *County Court Procedure in Northern Ireland* (1985).

6. Special Courts

Legislation

Coroners Act (NI) 1959.

Coroners (Practice and Procedure) Rules (NI) 1963 and Amendment Rules 1980.

Children and Young Persons Act (NI) 1968.

Magistrates' Courts (Children and Young Persons) Rules (NI) 1969.

Young Offenders Centre Rules (NI) 1982.

Reports

Report of the Children and Young Persons Review Group (Chairman: Sir Harold Black) (1979).

Books and articles

Caul, Pinkerton and Powell, *The Juvenile Justice System in Northern Ireland* (University of Ulster, 1983).

McBrien, "An Outline of British Military Law" (1983) Military Law and Law of War Review 13.

Northern Ireland Juvenile Courts Association, *Lay Panel Magazine*.

7. Tribunals

Legislation

Tribunals of Inquiry (Evidence) Act 1921.
Lands Tribunal and Compensation Act (NI) 1964.
Tribunals and Inquiries Act 1971.
Planning (NI) Order 1972.
Rent (NI) Order 1978.
Social Security Adjudication (NI) Order 1983.
Mental Health (NI) Order 1986.

Reports

Report of the Review Committee on Mental Health Legislation (Chairman: Mr Justice MacDermott) (1981).
Department of Health and Social Services for Northern Ireland, *Guide to Social Security Benefits and Related Services* (1987-88).
Annual Reports of the Social Security Advisory Committee.
Annual Reports of the Council on Tribunals.

Books and articles

Abel-Smith and Stevens, *In Search of Justice* (1968).
*Albeson and Douglas, CPAG's National Welfare Benefits Handbook (17th ed, 1988).
*Bateson and McKee, *Industrial Tribunals in Northern Ireland* (2nd ed, 1989).
*Graham, "Judicial Review: The New Procedures in Northern Ireland" (1980) 31 NILQ 317.
McKee, "A Personal View of the Work of Industrial Tribunals" (1986) 49 Modern Law Review 314.
Rowland, *CPAG's Rights Guide to Non-Means-Tested Social Security Benefits* (11th ed, 1988-89).
*Walsh, *Northern Ireland Guide to Supplementary Benefit and Family Income Supplement Decisions* (1988).
Welfare Rights News, a quarterly bulletin issued by the Belfast Law Centre.

8. Watchdog Bodies

Legislation

Parliamentary Commissioner Act (NI) 1969.
Commissioner for Complaints Act (NI) 1969.

Equal Pay Act (NI) 1970.
Fair Employment (NI) Act 1976 (and Bill, 1989).
Sex Discrimination (NI) Order 1976.
Industrial Relations (NI) Order 1976.
Health and Safety at Work (NI) Order 1978.
Police (NI) Order 1987.

Reports

Annual Reports of the following:
> Parliamentary Commisioner for Administration;
> Commissioner for Complaints;
> Fair Employment Agency;
> Labour Relations Agency;
> Health and Safety Agency;
> Equal Opportunities Commission;
> Standing Advisory Commission on Human Rights;
> Independent Commission for Police Complaints;
> Office of Fair Trading;
> General Consumer Council;
> Law Commission.

Reports by the Police Authority on its work: 1974, 1983 and 1988.
Triennial Review Reports by the Police Complaints Board: 1980, 1983 and 1986.

In addition to the above materials, which are relevant to particular chapters in this book, there are many publications which describe the workings of the entire legal system in England and which include much information that is also applicable to Northern Ireland. But it is unsafe to rely on such works unless the relevant passage specifically states that the position in Northern Ireland is the same as that in England. Even when the position is the same, the legal basis for it (*i.e.* the relevant statute or case law) may well be different. Perhaps the best book on the day-to-day workings of the English legal system is *The Law Machine*, by Berlins and Dyer (Penguin, 2nd ed 1986). This is based on a TV documentary series explaining how the legal system operates in practice. It is very readable, containing quite a lot of critical comment on the present state of affairs. Of the vast array of more technical works on the subject, suitable for law students, the best are perhaps those by Ingman, *The English Legal Process* (Financial Training Publications, 2nd ed, 1987), Smith and Bailey, *The Modern English Legal System* (Sweet and Maxwell, 1984) and White, *The Administration of Justice* (Blackwell, 1985).

There are also several books which, as well as touching upon the structure and personnel of the English legal system, concentrate on introducing the reader to different areas of substantive law. The more traditional of these works, again designed primarily for law students, dwell on topics such as the law of contract, the law of torts, criminal law and land law. They include the books by James, *An Introduction to English Law* (Butterworths, 11th ed, 1985) and Smith and Keenan, *English Law* (Pitman, 8th ed, 1986). A smaller work is that called *General Principles of Law*, by Newton (Sweet and Maxwell, 3rd ed, 1983). The introductory books geared more to the lay person tend, quite naturally, to dwell on those legal topics which are most likely to be encountered in everyday life. An excellent work of this kind is *The Penguin Guide to the Law*, by John Pritchard (Penguin, 2nd ed, 1985). It has sections on family law, housing law, employment law, consumer law and motoring law: there are dozens of helpful diagrams to explain various procedures. Also to be recommended are Harpwood and Aldridge, *GCSE Law* (Financial Training Ltd, 1987) and Dugdale and others, *'A' Level Law* (Butterworths, 1988). The National Federation of Consumer Groups and the Consumers' Association have published *A Handbook of Consumer Law* (3rd ed, 1989), which is one of the very few English books on the subject to include notes on the Northern Ireland position.

Two compendiums on English law are useful reference books if you want to look up a particular word or phrase: the Readers' Digest's *You and Your Rights: An A to Z Guide to the Law* (6th ed, 1983) and *The Oxford Companion to Law* by D. M. Walker (1980). The best value legal dictionary is probably *Mozley and Whiteley's Law Dictionary*, by Hardy Ivamy (Butterworths, 10th ed, 1988). Also worth consulting is a new book by A.W.B Simpson, *Invitation to Law* (Blackwell, 1988).

SLS Legal Publications (NI) also publish *The Digest of Northern Ireland Law*, the first five chapters of which appeared in 1988. It provides detailed information on specific aspects of Northern Ireland Law for legal advisers; Chapter 1 (Legal Services in Northern Ireland) covers a lot of the same ground as is dealt with in this book, though in less detail.

APPENDIX 2

USEFUL ADDRESSES

Advice Centres (selected)

Ashgrove Advice Centre
Garvaghy Road
Portadown
Co Armagh BT62 1ED
(Tel: 0762-331650)

Ballybeen Advice Centre
Dungoyne Community Centre
Dundonald BT16 OQE
(Tel: 02318-480578)

Ballynafeigh Community Advice Centre
291 Ormeau Road
Belfast BT7 3GG
(Tel: 645161)

Belfast Housing Aid
92 Victoria Street
Belfast BT1 3GN
(Tel: 245640)

Centre for the Unemployed
45/47 Donegall Street
Belfast BT1 2FG
(Tel: 243920)

Craigavon Independent Advice Centre
Craigavon
Co Armagh BT65
(Tel: 0762 24945)

Cregagh Advice Centre
Cregagh Community Centre
Cappagh Gardens
Belfast BT6 0ET
(Tel: 799849)

Derry Women's Advice Centre
7 London Street
Londonderry BT48 6RQ
(Tel: 0504-267672)

Divis Advice Centre
22 St Peter's Row
Belfast BT12 4RR
(Tel: 231394)

East Belfast Community Council
198-200 Albertbridge Road
Belfast BT5 4GU
(Tel: 51512)

Falls Community Council
89b Glen Road
Belfast BT11 8BD
(Tel: 621410)

Gingerbread (for single parents)
291 Ormeau Road
Belfast BT7 3GG
(Tel: 692690)

Glenbryn Welfare Rights Advice Centre
Alliance Road
Belfast BT14 7JF
(Tel: 721943)

Lenadoon Advice Centre
Horn Drive Community Centre
Horn Drive
Belfast BT11 9GS
(Tel: 301903)

Lower Falls Advice Centre
St. Peter's School
Raglan Street
Belfast BT12 4EG

Lower Oldpark Advice Centre
59 Lower Oldpark Road
Belfast BT14 6FN
(Tel: 740334)

Markets Advice Centre
Community Centre
Eliza Street
Belfast BT7 2AT
(Tel: 235969)

Newry Welfare Rights Centre
2 Bridge Street
Newry BT35 8AE
(Tel: 0693 - 67631)

North Belfast Resource Centre
Gateway House
242 Antrim Road
Belfast BT15 2AR
(Tel: 754513)

Omagh and District Advice Centre
6 Bridge Street
Omagh BT78 1BX
(Tel: 0662-3252)

Rathcoole Advice Centre
c/o Rathcoole Self-Help Group
22a The Diamond
Rathcoole
Newtownabbey
Co Antrim BT37 9BJ
(Tel: 365322)

Shankill Legal Advice Centre
Shankill Community Council
77 Shankill Road
Belfast BT13 1FD
(Tel: 325536)

Suffolk Advice Centre
116 Stewartstown Road
Belfast BT11 9JP
(Tel: 615642)

Tullycarnet Advice Centre
Kinross Avene
Tullycarnet
Belfast BT5 7GE
(Tel: 02318-480855)

Upper Springfield Resource Centre
195 Whiterock Road
Belfast BT12 7FW
(Tel: 328928)

Whitehead Advice Centre
Whitehead Community Centre
Islandmagee
Co Antrim
(Tel: 09603 - 460)

Women's Aid Federation
143a University Street
Belfast BT7 1HP
(Tel: 249041)

Advertising Standards Authority
Brook House
2-16 Torrington Place
London WC1E 7HN
(Tel: 01-580-5555)

Age Concern
128 Great Victoria Street
Belfast BT2 7BG
(Tel: 245729)

Alcoholics Anonymous
152 Lisburn Road
Belfast BT9 7AJ
(Tel: 681084)

Amnesty International
c/o Corrymeela House
8 Upper Crescent
Belfast BT7 1NT
(Tel: 325008)

Association of Local Authorities
6 Callender Street
Belfast BT1 5BN
(Tel: 249286)
(Telephone numbers for individual local authorities are listed under the name of the authority in the telephone directory.)

Automobile Association
Fanum House
Great Victoria Street
Belfast BT2 7AT
(Tel: 336242)

Banking Ombudsman's Office
Citadel House
5-11 Fetter Lane
London EC4A 1BR
(Tel 01-283-8866)

Belfast Consumer Advice Centre
6 Callender Street
Belfast BT1 5BN
(Tel: 328260)

Belfast Law Centre
7 University Road
Belfast BT7 1NA

Bryson House
28 Bedford Street
Belfast BT2 7FE
(Tel: 325835)

Broadcasting Complaints Commission
20 Albert Embankment
London SW1
(Tel: 01-630-1966)

Cara-Friend
PO Box 44
Belfast BT1 1SH
(Tel: 322023)
(also Londonderry 263120)

Central Office of Industrial Tribunals
2nd Floor Bedford House
16-22 Bedford Street
Belfast BT2 7NR
(Tel: 327666)

Central Services Agency
25-27 Adelaide Street
Belfast BT2 7FH
(Tel: 324431)

Charities Unit
Department of Finance and Personnel
Rosepark House
Upper Newtownards Road
Belfast BT4 3NR
(Tel: 02318-4567)

Child Poverty Action Group
4th Floor, 1-5 Bath Street
London EC1V 9PY
(Tel: 01-405-5942)

Children's Legal Centre
20 Compton Terrace
London N1 2UN
(Tel: 01-359-6251)

Committee on the Administration of
Justice
45-47 Donegall Street
Belfast BT1 2FG
(Tel: 232394)

Companies Registry
43-47 Chichester Street
Belfast BT1 4JD
(Tel: 234121)

Community Information Service
2 Annadale Avenue
Belfast BT7 3JH
(Tel: 640011)

Consumers' Association
14 Buckingham Street
London WC2N 6DS
(Tel: 01-839-1222)

Criminal Injuries Branch
Northern Ireland Office
Royston House
35 Upper Queen Street
Belfast BT1 6EA
(Tel: 249944)

Crossroads Care Attenders Scheme
Unit 8, Comber Road Industrial Estate
Newtownards BT23 4RX
(Tel: 0247-815978)

Cruse (Northern Ireland)
50 University Street
Belfast BT7 1HB
(Tel: 232695)

Department of Agriculture
Dundonald House
Upper Newtownards Road
Belfast BT4 3SB
(Tel: 650111)

Department of Economic Development
(Headquarters)
Netherleigh
Massey Avenue
Belfast BT4 2JP
(Tel: 63244)
(Addresses of local employment service offices and jobmarkets are listed in the telephone directory, under "Government, Department of Economic Development".)

Department of Education
(Headquarters)
Rathgael House
Balloo Road
Bangor
Co Down BT19 2PR
(Tel: 0247-66311)

Department of the Environment
(Headquarters)
Parliament Buildings
Stormont
Belfast BT4 3SS
(Tel: 63210)
(Addresses of the Department's district development offices and other branch offices are listed in the current telephone directory, under "Government").

Department of Finance and Personnel
(Headquarters)
Parliament Buildings
Stormont
Belfast BT4 3SW
(Tel: 63210)

and

Rosepark House
Upper Newtownards Road
Belfast BT4 3NR
(Tel: 02318-4585)

Department of Health and Social Services
(Headquarters)
Dundonald House
Upper Newtownards Road
Belfast BT4 3SA
(Tel: 650111)

(Local social security offices are listed in the current telephone directory, under "Government, DHSS"; or ring Freeline Social Security: 0800-616757)..

Director of Public Prosecutions Office
Royal Courts of Justice
Chichester Street
Belfast BT1 3JE
(Tel: 235111)

Employment Medical Advisory Service
Royston House
35 Upper Queen Street
Belfast BT1 6EA
(Tel: 233045)

Enforcement of Judgments Office
Bedford House
Bedford Street
Belfast BT2 7NR
(Tel: 245081)

Equal Opportunities Commission
Chamber of Commerce House
22 Great Victoria Street
Belfast BT2 2BA
(Tel: 242752)

European Commission Office
Windsor House
9-15 Bedford Street
Belfast BT2 7EG
(Tel: 240708)

The Extern Organisation
46 University Street
Belfast BT7 1HB
(Tel: 244003)

Faculty of Law
Queen's University
Belfast BT7 1NN
(Tel: 245133)

Fair Employment Agency
Andras House
60 Great Victoria Street
Belfast BT2 7BB
(Tel: 240020)

Family Planning Association
113 University Street
Belfast BT7 1HP
(Tel: 325488).

and

14 Magazine Street
Londonderry BT48 6HH
(Tel: 0504-260016)

Gamblers Anonymous
45-47 Donegall Street
Belfast BT1 2FG
(Tel: 249185)

General Consumer Council
Elizabeth House
116 Holywood Road
Belfast BT4 1NY
(Tel: 672488)

Health and Safety Agency
Canada House
22 North Street
Belfast BT1 1NN
(Tel: 243249, 243509)

Her Majesty's Stationery Office
(HMSO)
Government Bookshop
80 Chichester Street
Belfast BT1 4JY
(Tel: 234488)

The Home Office
50 Queen Anne's Gate
London SW1H 9AT
(Tel: 01-213-3000)

Howard League for Penal Reform
125 Kennington Park Road
London SE11
(Tel: 01-735-3773)

Institute of Professional Legal Studies
Queen's University
1 Upper Crescent
Belfast BT7 1NT
(Tel: 245133)

Independent Broadcasting Authority
70 Brompton Road
Knightsbridge
London SW3 1EY
(Tel: 01-584-7011)

Independent Commission for Police Complaints
Chamber of Commerce House
22 Great Victoria Street
Belfast BT2 7BA
(Tel: 244821)

Industrial Development Board for
Northern Ireland
IDB House
64 Chichester Street
Belfast BT1 4LE
(Tel: 233233)

Insurance Ombudsman Bureau
31 Southampton Row
London WC1B 5HJ
(Tel: 01-401-0591)

Irish Congress of Trade Unions
(Northern Ireland Committee)
2 Castle Arcade
Belfast BT1 5DG
(Tel: 242452)

Irish Council for Civil Liberties
4 Nassau Street
Dublin 2
(Tel: 0001-603762)

JUSTICE
(British section of the International
Commission of Jurists)
95a Chancery Lane
London WC2A 1DT
(Tel: 01-405-6018)

Labour Relations Agency
Windsor House
9-15 Bedford Street
Belfast BT2 7NL
(Tel: 321442)

and

3 Foyle Street
Londonderry BT48 6AL
(Tel: 0504-69639)

Land Registry
River House
48 High Street
Belfast BT1 2DR
(Tel: 233552)

Law Centres' Federation
Duchess House
18-19 Warren Street
London W1P 5DB
(Tel: 01-387-8570)

Law Commission for England and Wales
Conquest House
37-38 John Street
Theobald's Road
London WC1N 2BQ
(Tel: 01-242-0861)

Law Reform Commission of Ireland
Ardilaun Centre
111 St Stephen's Green
Dublin 2
(Tel: 0001-715699)

Law Society of Northern Ireland
90 Victoria Street
Belfast BT1 3GN
(Tel: 231614)

The Lay Observer
Room 407, Clarendon House
Adelaide Street
Belfast BT2 8NR
(Tel: 244300 ext. 2333)

Legal Aid Depatment
Law Society of Northern Ireland
Bedford House
16-22 Bedford Street
Belfast BT2 7FL
(Tel: 246441)

Legislative Draftsman's Office
Dept of Finance and Personnel
Stormont
Belfast BT4 3SW
(Tel: 63210)

Londonderry Consumer Advice Council
8 Custom House Street
Londonderry BT48 6AD
(Tel: 0504-261504)

Medical Appeal Tribunal
(President's Office)
Yorkshire House
5 Linenhall Street
Belfast BT2 8AA
(Tel: 235111)

MENCAP
(for mentally handicapped)
Segal House
4 Annadale Avenue
Belfast BT7 3JH
(Tel: 691351)

Mental Health Commission
Elizabeth House
116-118 Holywood Road
Belfast BT4 1NY
(Tel: 651157)

Money and Relationship Counselling
Room 59, 3rd Floor,
Scottish Mutual Building
16 Donegall Square South
Belfast BT1 5JH
(Tel: 240649)

Monopolies and Mergers Commission
New Court
48 Carey Street
London WC2A 2JE
(Tel: 01-831-6111)

Motor Insurer's Bureau
Aldermary House
Queen Street
London EC4N 1TR
(Tel: 01-248-4477)

National Association of Citizen's
Advice Bureaux
26 Bedford Square
London WC2
(Tel: 01-636-4066)

National Consumer Council
18 Queen Anne's Gate
London SW1H 9AA
(Tel: 01-222-9501)

National Council for Civil Liberties
21 Tabard Street
London SE1 4LA
(Tel: 01-403-3888)

National Federation of Consumer Groups
12 Mosley Street
Newcastle - upon - Tyne NE1 1DE
(Tel: 0632-618259)

National House Building Council
Bedford House
Bedford Street
Belfast BT2 7NR
(Tel: 245501)

Northern Ireland Advisory Committee on Telecommunication
Chamber of Commerce House
22 Great Victoria Street
Belfast BT2 7QA
(Tel: 244113)

Northern Ireland Association for the Care and Resettlement of Offenders
22 Adelaide Street
Belfast BT2 8GD
(Tel: 320157)

Northern Ireland Association of Citizens' Advice Bureaux
Newforge Lane
Belfast BT9 5NW
(Tel: 681117)
(Addresses of local CABx are listed in the telephone directory under the heading "Citizens' Advice Bureaux".)

Northern Ireland Association for Mental Health
Beacon House
84 University Street
Belfast BT7 1HE
(Tel: 328474)

Northern Ireland Commissioner for Complaints
Progressive House
33 Wellington Place
Belfast BT1 6HN
(Tel: 233821)

Northern Ireland Council for Voluntary Action
127 Ormeau Road
Belfast BT7 1SH
(Tel: 321224)

Northern Ireland Council on Alcohol
40 Elmwood Avenue
Belfast BT9 6AZ
(Tel: 664434)

Northern Ireland Council on Disability
2nd Floor, Scottish Provident Building
7 Donegall Square West
Belfast BT1 6JJ
(Tel: 328378)

Northern Ireland Court Service
Windsor House
9-15 Bedford Street
Belfast BT2 7EH
(Tel: 328594)

Northern Ireland Federation of Housing Associations
88 Clifton Street
Belfast BT13 1AB
(Tel: 230446)

Northern Ireland Housing Executive
The Housing Centre
2 Adelaide Street
Belfast BT2 8PB
(Tel: 240588)
(Addresses of district offices are listed in the telephone directory under "NIHE").

Northern Ireland Office and Northern Ireland Inormation Service)
Stormont Castle
Stormont
Belfast BT4 3ST
(Tel: 63011)

and

Great George Street
London SW1P 3AJ
(Tel: 01-233-3000)

Northern Ireland Parliamentary Commissioner for Administration
Progressive House
33 Wellington Place
Belfast BT1 6HN
(Tel: 233821)

Northern Ireland Transport Users Committee
55 Royal Avenue
Belfast BT1 1FX
(Tel: 244147)

NSPCC (Cruelty to Children)
16-20 Rosemary Street
Belfast BT1 1QD
(Tel: 240311)

Office of Care and Protection
Royal Courts of Justice
Chichester Street
Belfast BT1 3JF
(Tel: 235111)

Office of Data Protection
Springfield House
Water Lane
Wilmslow
Cheshire SK9 5AX
(Tel: 0625-525777)

Office of Fair Trading
Field House
15-28 Bream's Buildings
London EC4A 1PR
Tel: (01-242-2858)

Office of Law Reform
Department of Finance and Personnel
Permanent House
21-23 Arthur Street
Belfast BT1 4JL
(Tel: 327661)

Peace People
Fredheim
224 Lisburn Road
Belfast BT9 6GE
(Tel: 663465)

Police Authority for Northern Ireland
5th Floor
River House
48 High Street
Belfast BT1 2DR
(Tel: 230111)

Post Office Users Council for Northern
Ireland
Chamber of Commerce House
22 Great Victoria Street
Belfast BT2 7BA
(Tel: 244113)

Probation Board for Northern Ireland
306 Antrim Road
Belfast BT15 5AB
(Tel: 757631)

Rape Crisis Centre (Belfast)
PO Box 46
Belfast BT2 7AR
(Tel: 249696)

Rape and Incest Line
PO Box 220
Belfast BT7 1R
(Tel: Belfast 326803
Londonderry 260566)

Registrar General's Office
Oxford House
49 Chichester Street
Belfast BT1 4HL
(Tel: 235211)

Registry of Deeds
Oxford House
49 Chichester Street
Belfast BT1 4HL
(Tel: 235211)

Relate (formerly Marriage Guidance
Council)
76 Dublin Road
Belfast BT2 7HP
(Tel: 323454)

Royal Automobile Club
RAC House
65 Chichester Street
Belfast BT1 4JD
(Tel: 240261)

Royal Courts of Justice
Chichester Street
Belfast BT1 3JE
(Tel: 235111)
*(The telephone numbers of Crown, county
court and petty sessions offices are listed in
the telephone directory under
"Government"; enquiries concerning small
claims should be made to county court
offices.)*

Royal Ulster Constabulary (RUC)
(Headquarters)
Brooklyn
Knock
Belfast BT5 6LE
(Tel: 650222)
(The addresses of local police stations are

*listed in the telephone directory, under
"Police".)*

St Vincent de Paul Society
Eia House
244 Antrim Road
Belfast BT15 2AR
(Tel: 752561)

Samaritans
46 Stranmillis Road
Belfast BT9 5AD
(Tel: 324635)
*(Other Samaritan offices are listed in the
telephone directory.)*

School of Public Administration and Legal
Studies
University of Ulster at Jordanstown
Shore Road
Newtownabbey
Co Antrim BT37 0QB
(Tel: 365131)

Shelter (Northern Ireland)
23A University Road
Belfast BT7 1NA
(Tel: 247752)

Social Security Advisory Committee
New Court
Carey Street
London WC2A 2LS
(Tel: 01-831-6111)

Social Security Appeal Tribunals
(President's Office)
Clarendon House
9 Adelaide Street
Belfast BT2 8NH
(Tel: 249577)

Social Security Commissioners
Yorkshire House
5 Linenhall Street
Belfast BT2 8AA
(Tel: 235111)

Standing Advisory Commission on Human
Rights
55 Royal Avenue
Belfast BT1 1FX
(Tel: 243987)

Trading Standards Branch
Department of Economic Development
176 Newtownbreda Road
Belfast BT8 4QS
(Tel: 647151)

United Kingdom Immigrants' Advisory
Service
7th Floor
Brettenham House
Savoy Street
London WC2
(Tel: 01-240-5176)

Wages Councils (Northern Ireland Office)
Dept of Economic Development
Arches Centre
13 Bloomfield Avenue
Belfast BT5 5ND
(Tel: 732411)

Women's Centre
18 Donegall Street
Belfast BT1 2GP
(Tel: 243363)

Women's Information Group
115a Ormeau Road
Belfast BT7 1SH
(Tel: 628342)

Workers' Educational Association
(Northern Ireland district)
1 Fitzwilliam Street
Belfast BT9 6AW
(Tel: 329718)

APPENDIX 3

SAMPLE SOURCES OF LAW

(1) An Act of Parliament: the Fatal Accidents Act (NI) 1959

(2) An Order in Council: the Fatal Accidents (NI) Order 1977

(3) A statutory rule: the Lobster (Prohibition of Introduction) Order (NI) 1982

(4) A reported case: *Campbell* v. *Armstrong and others.*

(1) An Act of Parliament

Ch. 18   Fatal Accidents Act   1959.

1959. Chapter 18

An Act to amend the Fatal Accidents Act, 1846, by enlarging the class of persons for whose benefits an action may be brought thereunder; to provide for certain benefits to be left out of account in assessing damages in such an action; and for purposes connected with those matters.

[15th December, 1959]

Be it enacted by the Queen's most Excellent Majesty, and the Senate and the House of Commons of Northern Ireland in this present Parliament assembled, and by the authority of the same as follows:-

Extension of classes of dependants.
9 & 10 Vict., c.93

1. - (1) The persons for whose benefit or by whom an action may be brought under the Fatal Accidents Act, 1846, shall include any person who is, or is the issue of, a brother, sister, uncle or aunt of the deceased person.

(2) In deducing any relationship for the purposes of the said Act and this Act-

(a) an adopted person shall be treated as the child of the person or persons by whom he was adopted and not as the child of any other person; and subject thereto,

(b) any relationship by affinity shall be treated as a relationship by consanguinity, any relationship of the half blood as a relationship of the whole blood, and the stepchild of any person as his child; and

(c) an illegitimate person shall be treated as the legitimate child of his mother and reputed father.

(3) In this section "adopted" means adopted in pursuance of an adoption order made under the Adoption of Children Act (Northern Ireland), 1950, or any previous enactment relating to the adoption of children, or any corresponding enactment of the Parliament of the United Kingdom; and for the purpose of any proceedings under the Fatal Accidents Act, 1846, an adoption authorised by any such order made in England or Scotland may be proved by the production of any document receivable as evidence thereof in that country.

1950, c. 6.

(4) In section sixteen of the Law Reform (Miscellaneous Provisions) Act (Northern Ireland), 1937, there shall be substituted, for the words "wife, husband, parent or child" in paragraph (b) of sub-section (1), the word "dependants", and for paragraph (a) of sub-section (3) the following paragraph-

1 Edw. 8 &
1 Geo. 6,
c.9.

"(a) the expression "dependants" means the persons for whose benefit actions may be brought under the Fatal Accidents Acts (Northern Ireland), 1846 to 1959; and".

2. - (1) In assessing damages in respect of a person's death in any action under the Fatal Accidents Act, 1846, there shall not be taken into account any insurance money, benefit, pension or gratuity which has been or will or may be paid as a result of the death.

Exclusion of
certain benefits
assessment of
damages

(2) In this section -

"benefit" means benefit under the National Insurance Acts (Northern Ireland), 1946, or any corresponding enactment of the Parliament of the United Kingdom and any payment by a friendly society or trade union for the relief or maintenance of a member's dependants;

1946, c.21.
1946, c.23

"insurance money" includes a return or premiums; and

"pension" includes a return of contributions and any payment of a lump sum in respect of a person's employment.

3. - (1) This Act may be cited as the Fatal Accidents Act (Northern Ireland), 1959; and the Fatal Accidents Act, 1846, and this Act may be cited together as the Fatal Accidents Acts (Northern Ireland), 1846 to 1959.

Short title, etc.
27 & 28 Vict.,
c.95

(2) References in this Act to the Fatal Accidents Act, 1846, are references thereto as amended by and read together with the Fatal Accidents Act, 1864.

(3) The enactments set out in the Schedule are hereby repealed to the extent specified in the third column of that Schedule.

(4) This Act shall apply only to actions brought in respect of deaths occurring after the passing of this Act.

SCHEDULE

ENACTMENTS REPEALED

Section 3

Session or Year and Chapter	Short Title	Extent of Repeal
9 & 10 Vict., c.93	The Fatal Accidents Act, 1846	In section five the words "and stepfather and stepmother" and "and stepson and stepdaughter".
8 Edw. 7, c. 7.	The Fatal Accidents (Damages) Act, 1908	The whole Act.
1 Edw. 8 & 1 Geo. 6, c. 9	The Law Reform (Misellaneous Provisions) Act (Northern Ireland), 1937	In section fifteen, sub-sections (1), (2) and (4).
1948,c..232	The Law Reform (Miscellaneous Provisions) Act (Northern Ireland), 1948	In section three, in sub-section (5), paragraph (a).

(2) An Order in Council

1977 No. 1251 (N.I.18)

NORTHERN IRELAND

The Fatal Accidents (Northern Ireland) Order 1977

Laid before Parliament in draft

Made	*26th July 1977*
Coming into Operation	*6th August 1977*

ARRANGEMENT OF ORDER

Article
1. Title and commencement.
2. Interpretation.
3. Right of action for wrongful act causing death.
4. Persons entitled to bring the action.
5. Assessment of damages.
6. Assessment of damages: disregard of certain benefits.
7. Contributory negligence.
8. Consequential amendments and repeals, and transitional provisions.

SCHEDULES:

Schedule 1 - Consequential amendments.
Schedule 2 - Repeals.

At the Court at Buckingham Palace, the 26th day of July 1977

Present,

The Queen's Most Excellent Majesty in Council

Whereas a draft of this Order has been approved by a resolution of each House of Parliament:

Now, therefore, Her Majesty, in exercise of the powers conferred by paragraph 1 of Schedule 1 to the Northern Ireland Act 1974 **(a)** and of all other powers enabling Her in that behalf, is pleased, by and with the advice of Her Privy Council, to order, and it is hereby ordered, as follows:-

Fatal Accidents (NI) Order

Title and commencement

1. - (1) This Order may be cited as the Fatal Accidents (Northern Ireland) Order 1977.

(2) This Order shall come into operation at the expiration of a period of one month from the day on which it is made

Interpretation

2. - (1) The Interpretation Act (Northern Ireland) 1954 **(b)** shall apply to Article 1 and the following provisions of this Order as it applies to a Measure of the Northern Ireland Assembly.

(2) In this Order "dependant" means -

(a) the wife or husband of the deceased,
(b) any person who is a parent or grandparent of the deceased,
(c) any person who is a child or grandchild of the deceased, and
(d) any person who is, or is the issue of, a brother, sister, uncle or aunt of the deceased;
and "deceased" has the meaning given by Article 3 (2).

(3) In deducing any relationship for the purposes of paragraph (2) -

(a) an adopted person shall be treated as the child of the person or person by whom he was adopted and not as the child of any other person; and subject thereto,
(b) any relationship by affinity shall be treated as a relationship by consanguinity, any relationship of the half blood as a relationship of the whole blood, and the stepchild of any person as his child; and
(c) an illegitimate person shall be treated as the legitimate child of his mother and reputed father.

(4) In paragraph (3) "adopted" means in pursuance of a court order made in any part of the United Kingdom, the Isle of Man or any of the Channel Islands or by a foreign adoption within the meaning of the Adoption (Hague Convention) Act (Northern Ireland) 1969 **(c).**

(5) Any reference in this Order to injury includes any disease and any impairment of a person's physical or mental condition.

(a) 1974 c.28   **(b)** 1954 c.33 (N.I.)   **(c)** 1969 c.22 (N.I)

Fatal Accidents (NI) Order

Right of action for wrongful act causing death

3. - (1) If death is caused by any wrongful act, neglect or default which is such as would (if death had not ensued) have entitled the person injured to maintain an action and recover damages in respect thereof, the person who would have been liable if death had not ensued shall be liable to an action for damages, notwithstanding the death of the person injured.

(2) Every such action shall be for the benefit of the dependants of the person ("the deceased") whose death has been so caused.

Persons entitled to bring the action

4. - (1) The action shall be brought by and in the name of the executor or administrator of the deceased.

(2) If -
(a) there is no executor or administrator of the deceased, or
(b) no action is brought within six months after the death by and in the name of an executor or administrator of the deceased,
the action may be brought by and in the name of all or any of the dependants.

(3) Not more that one action shall lie for and in respect of the same subject matter of complaint.

(4) The plaintiff in the action shall be required to deliver to the defendant or his solicitor full particulars of the dependants for whom and on whose behalf the action is brought, and of the nature of the claim in respect of which damages are sought to be recovered.

Assessment of damages

5 - (1) In the action such damages may be awarded as are proportioned to the injury resulting from the death to the dependants respectively, and the amount so recovered after deducting the costs not recovered from the defendant, shall be divided among the dependants in such shares as may be directed.

(2) In paragraph (1) "directed" means -
(a) where the court seized of the proceedings consists of a judge sitting with a jury, directed by the jury; and
(b) in any other case, directed by the judge.
(3) In assessing damages payable to a widow in respect of the death of her husband in an action under this Order there shall not be taken into account the remarriage of the widow or her prospects of remarriage.

(4) If the dependants have incurred funeral expenses in respect of the deceased, damages may be awarded in respect of those expenses.

Fatal Accidents (NI) Order

(5) Money paid into court in satisfaction of a cause of action under this Order may be in one sum without specifying the dependants' shares.

Assessment of damages: disregard of certain benefits

6. - (1) In assessing damages in respect of a person's death in an action under this Order there shall not be taken into account any insurance money, benefit, pension or gratuity which has been or will or may be paid as a result of the death.

(2) In this Article -

"benefit" means benefit under the enactments relating to social security, including enactments in force in Great Britain, and any payment by a friendly society or trade union for relief or maintenance of a member's dependants;
"insurance money" includes a return of premiums; and
"pension" includes a return of contributions and any payment of a lump sum in respect of a person's employment.

Contributory negligence

7. Where any person dies as the result partly of his own fault and partly of the fault of any other person or persons, and accordingly if an action were brought for the benefit of the estate the damages recoverable would be reduced under section 2 (1) of the Law Reform (Miscellaneous Provisions) Act (Northern Ireland) 1948 (a), any damages recoverable in an action brought for the benefit of the dependants of that person under this Order shall be reduced to a proportionate extent.

Consequential amendments and repeals, and transitional provisions

8. - (1) Schedule 1 contains consequential amendments.

(2) The enactments in Schedule 2 are repealed to the extent specified in the third column of that Schedule.

(3) Without prejudice to any provision of section 29 of the Interpretation Act (Northern Ireland) 1954 (effect of substituting provisions) proceedings may be taken after the commencement of this Order in respect of a death occurring before that commencement as if this Order had then been in operation.

(4) In the application of the said section 29 to any appeal made by this Order, subsections (1) and (3) (a) shall have effect with the omission of the word "statutory" wherever it occurs.

(5) For the purposes of Article 5 (3), any proceedings taken under the enactments repealed by this Order and continued by virtue of subsection (2) (c) of the said section

(a) 1948 c.23 (N.I.)

APPENDIX 3

Fatal Accidents (NI) Order

29 are proceedings in an action under this Order.

N.E. Leigh,
Clerk of the Privy Council.

SCHEDULES

SCHEDULE 1   Article 8 (1).

CONSEQUENTIAL AMENDMENTS

Law Reform (Miscellaneous Provisions) Act (Northern Ireland) 1937 (c.9)

1. - (1) In section 14 (5) for "the Fatal Accidents Acts 1846 to 1908" substitute "the Fatal Accidents (Northern Ireland) Order 1977", and for "the said Acts" substitute "that Order".

(2) In section 16 (3) *(a)* for "the Fatal Accidents Acts (Northern Ireland) 1846 to 1959" substitute "the Fatal Accidents (Northern Ireland) Order 1977".

Statute of Limitations (Northern Ireland) 1958 (c.10)

2.- (1) In sections 9B and 9C for "the Fatal Accidents Act 1846", wherever occurring, substitute "the Fatal Accidents (Northern Ireland) Order 1977".

(2) In section 9D (6) for "section 1 of the Fatal Accidents Act 1846" substitute "Article 3 (1) of the Fatal Accidents (Northern Ireland) Order 1977".

Fatal Accidents Act (Northern Ireland) 1959 (c.18)'

3. In section 1 (4) there shall be made the amendment specified in paragraph 1 (2).

County Courts Act (Northern Ireland) 1959 (c.25)

4. In section 99 (3) for "the Fatal Accidents 1846 to 1908" substitute "the Fatal Accidents (Northern Ireland) Order 1977".

Carriage by Air Act 1961 (c.27)

5. In section 3 for "in Northern Ireland" substitute "in Article 3 (1) of the Fatal Accidents (Northern Ireland) Order 1977".

Fatal Accidents (NI) Order

Mineral Workings (Offshore Installations) Act 1971 (c.61)

6. In section 11 (2) for "in Northern Ireland" substitute "in Article 3 (1) of the Fatal Accidents (Northern Ireland) Order 1977".

Carriage by Railway Act 1972 (c.33)

7. In section 3 (4) after "Northern Ireland" insert "references to the Fatal Accidents Act 1846 and section 3 of that Act shall be construed as references to the Fatal Accidents (Northern Ireland) Order 1977 and Article 4 (3) of that Order and", and for "section 2 of the Fatal Accidents Act (Northern Ireland) 1959" substitute "Article 6 of that Order".

Petroleum and Submarine Pipe-Lines Act 1975 (c.74)

8. In section 30 (1) for "and Northern Ireland" substitute, "and in Article 3 (1) of the Fatal Accidents (Northern Ireland) Order 1977".

Animals (Northern Ireland) Order 1976
(S.I. 1976/1040 (N.I. 13))

9. In Article 12 for "the Fatal Accidents Acts (Northern Ireland) 1846 to 1959" substitute "the Fatal Accidents (Northern Ireland) Order 1977".

Limitation (Northern Ireland) Order 1976
(S.I. 1976/1158 (N.I. 18))

10. In Article 3, the amendments made in sections 9B, 9C and 9D of the Statute of Limitations (Northern Ireland) 1958 by paragraph 2 (1) and (2) above.

APPENDIX 3

Fatal Accidents (NI) Order

Article 8 (2).   SCHEDULE 2

REPEALS

Chapter	Short Title	Extent of repeal
99 & 10 Vict. c. 93	Fatal Accidents Act 1846	The whole Act.
27 & 28 Vict., c. 95	Fatal Accidents Act 1864	The whole Act..
1 Edw. 8 & 1 Geo. 6 c.9	Law Reform (Miscellaneous Provisions) Act (Northern Ireland) 1937	Section 15(3)
1948 c.23	Law Reform (Miscellaneous Profvisions)Act (Northern Ireland) 1948	Section 2(4) In section 6 the definition of "dependant".
159 c.18	Fatal Accidents Act (Northern Ireland) 1959	In section 1, subsections (1) to (3). Section 2. In section 3, in subsection (1) the words from "and the" onwards, and subsections (2) and (4).
1967 c.35	Adoption Act (Northern Ireland) 1967	Section 27(2).
1973 c.38	Social Security Act 1973	In Schedule 27, paragraph 111.
S.I. 1976/1158 (N.I. 18)	Limitation (Northern Ireland) Order 1976.	In Schedule 1, paragraph 1

EXPLANATORY NOTE

(This Note is not part of the Order)

This Order consolidates the Fatal Accidents Acts (Northern Ireland) 1846 to 1959, and enactments amending them, with one major change of substance. The change is the addition of a provision (Article 5 (3)) requiring a widow's remarriage, or the prospects of her remarriage, to be left out of account in assessing damages payable to her in respect of her husband's death.

(3) A statutory rule

1982 No. 98

FISHERIES

Lobsters (Prohibition of Introduction) Order (Northern Ireland) 1982

Made	*30th March 1982*
Coming into operation	*1st May 1982*

The Department **(a)** of Agriculture, in exercise of the powers conferred on it by section 13 (1) of the Fisheries Act (Northern Ireland) 1966 **(b)** and of every other power enabling it in that behalf, hereby makes the following Order:

Citation and commencement

1. This Order may be cited as the Lobsters (Prohibition of Introduction) Order (Northern Ireland) 1982 and shall come into operation on 1st May 1982.

Interpretation

2. In this Order -

"lobsters" means fish of the species *Homarus americanus* or *Homarus gammarus;*

"the prohibited waters"means waters within British fishery limits which are adjacent to Northern Ireland and all tidal waters (whether forming part of the sea or not) within Northern Ireland.

Prohibition

3. A person shall not introduce into the prohibited waters any live lobsters or any young thereof taken from outside the prohibited waters.

Sealed with the Official Seal of the Department of Agriculture for Northern Ireland on 30th March 1982.

(L.S.)   N.E. Morrison
                                          Assistant Secretary.

(a) Formerly Ministry: see Northern Ireland Constitution Act 1973 (c. 36) Sch. 5 para. 8(1)
(b) 1966 c.17 (N.I.)

Lobsters (Prohibition of Introduction) Order (NI)

EXPLANATORY NOTE
(This note is not part of the Order)

This Order prohibits the introduction into the prohibited waters of live American lobsters (*Homarus americanus*) and European lobsters (*Homarus gammarus*) or the young thereof taken from outside the prohibited waters. The prohibited waters are waters within British fishery limits which are adjacent to Northern Ireland and are not nearer to any point on the baselines from which the breadth of the territorial seas adjacent to Great Britain or the Isle of Man is measured than to any point on the corresponding Northern Irish baselines and all tidal waters (whether forming part of the sea or not) within Northern Ireland. Under section 13(3) of the Fisheries Act (Northern Ireland) 1966 the Department may, on the application of any person, issue to that person a permit exempting him from the prohibition imposed by Article 3 of the Order. The Department may attach such conditions to a permit as it thinks proper.

A person who contravenes this Order is guilty of an offence under the Fisheries Act (Northern Ireland) 1966 and is liable on summary conviction to a fine not exceeding £500.

(4) A reported case   [1981]

CAMPBELL v. ARMSTRONG AND OTHERS[1]

Highway - Negligence - Vehicle struck large stones on verge of road - Whether highway out of repair - Whether duty of care arises - Road (Liability of Road Authorities for Neglect) Act (Northern Ireland) 1966 (c.11), ss.1,2.

The plaintiff's son was killed while a passenger in a motor car driven by the defendant which crashed when it struck a large stone or stones which had fallen on to the grass verge bordering the road from a stone wall which marched alongside it. The defendant joined the Department of the Environment, the road authority as a third party. In a preliminary issue to determine if the Department is liable to indemnify the defendant against the plaintiff's claim or make contribution to it,

Held that a highway is not out of repair because stones lie on its grass verge and the operation of removing such stones does not amount to repairing it. Accordingly there is no liability on the roads authority arising from the Roads (Liability of Road Authorities for Neglect) Act (Northern Ireland) 1966. There is also no liability on the roads authority under the neighbour principle in *Donoghue v Stevenson* [1932] A.C.562 as that principle does not extend the liability of a highway authority for non-feasance beyond the 1966 Act.

The following cases are referred to in the judgment:

Donoghue v. *Stevenson* [1932] A.C.562.

Forsythe v. *Evans* [1980] N.I. 230

Haydon v. *Kent County Council* [1978] Q.B. 343;[1978] 2 W.L.R. 485; [1978] 2 All E.R.97

Hedley Byrne and Co. v. *Heller & Partners* [1964] A.C. 465; [1963] 3 W.L.R. 101; [1963] 2 All E.R.575.

Hereford and Worcester County Council v. *Newsman* [1975] 1 W.L.R. 901; [1975] 2 All E.R. 673.

Home Office v. *Dorset Yacht Co.* [1970] A.C. 1004; [1970] 2 W.L.R. 1140; [1970] 2 All E.R. 294.

Lagan v. *Department of the Environment* [1978] N.I. 120.

PRELIMINARY ISSUE. The facts appear sufficiently from the judgment of Kelly J.

R.L. McCartney Q.C. and *M.A. Morrow* for the defendant.*R.D. Carswell Q.C.* and *B.F. Kerr* for the Department of the Environment.

---

1. In the Queen's Bench Division before Kelly J; January 22, March 13, 1981

N.I.   **Campbell v. Armstrong & Ors. (Q.B.D.)**   **Kelly J.**

Cur.adv.vult.

KELLY J. The pleadings in this action raise a point of law for determination as a preliminary issue. It concerns the civil liability of a highway authority for injury loss and damage caused by obstructions on the grass verge of a road maintainable by the authority.

The facts out of which the action arises can be stated shortly. On the 21 October 1977 the plaintiff's son was killed while a passenger in a motor car driven by the defendant which crashed when overtaking another car on a straight stretch of the Aughnacloy-Castlecaulfield road, County Tyrone. While overtaking the other car, part of the defendant's vehicle went on to the grass verge bordering the road and one or more of its wheels struck there a large stone or stones which had fallen on to the verge from a stone wall which marched alongside it.

The plaintiff as administratrix of her son's estate sues the defendant for damages under the Fatal Accident Order 1976 (sic) and the Law Reform (Miscellaneous Provisions) Act (Northern Ireland) 1937 alleging negligent driving. The defendant denies negligence and brings in as third parties to the action claiming indemnity or contribution against them, the Department of the Environment for Northern Ireland (hereinafter called "the Department") who is admittedly the road authority responsible for maintaining the roadway and grass verge in question and William Montgomery Buchanan who is the owner of the stone wall. This preliminary issue does not, however, concern the second-named third party.

It is the Department who disputes in law the defendant's claim that being the body responsible for the inspection maintenance repair and control of the grass verge and negligent in that duty in failing to keep it free of the stone or stones the Department is liable to indemnify the defendant against the plaintiff's claim or make contribution to it. The submission of the Department is that they cannot be made liable in damages.

I consider first their possible liability in damages for a breach of statutory duty. In this, one is drawn at once to the statutory duty of a highway authority in respect of obstructions on its roads contained in section 2 of the Roads (Liability of Road Authorities for Neglect) Act (Northern Ireland) 1966 which reads:

"2. (1) If an obstruction occurs in a road from accumulation of snow or from the falling down of banks on the side of the road, or from any other cause, the road authority by whom the road is maintainable shall remove the obstruction.

(2) If a road authority fail to remove an obstruction which it is their duty under this section to remove, a court of summary jurisdiction may, on a complaint made by any person, by order require the authority to remove the obstruction within such period (not being less than twenty-four hours) from the making of the order as the court thinks reasonable having regard to all the circumstances of the case."

But anyone who has suffered loss and damage from a breach of this section is stopped from embarking on a civil claim for damages by the clear prohibition of sub-section 6 of the section, which states;

"(6) it is hereby declared that nothing in this section shall operate to confer on any
person a right of action in tort against a road authority for failing to carry out
any duty imposed on them under this section."

A civil remedy in damages against a road authority is of course earlier given by
section 1 of the same Act, which states:

"1. (1) Any rule of law which operates to exempt a road authority from liability
for non-repair of roads is hereby abrogated."

but the language of section 1 has been held to confine the remedy to cases of strict
non-repair of the highway (see *Lagan v. Department of Environment* [1978] N.I. 120,
124). Following this, it seems to me that it cannot be seriously argued that a highway
is out of repair because stones lie on its grass verge or that the operation of removing
a stone or stones from it amounts to repairing it.

This view is reinforced by dicta of Cairns L.J. in *Hereford and Worcester County
Council v. Newman* [1975] 1 W.L.R. 901 and of Lord Denning M.R. in *Haydon V Kent
County Council* [1978] 2 W.L.R. 485. Cairns L.J. said at page 910:

"In relation to a highway I am of opinion that in ordinary speech nobody would
speak of the mere removal of an obstruction from the highway as being in itself a
repair. I respectfully agree with Lord Widgery C.J. in saying that if a builder chose
to dump tons of rubble on a footpath thus rendering it impassable, it would be an
abuse of language to say that the highway authority had allowed the footpath to
become out of repair.

It is I think striking that in all the Highway Acts from 1835 to 1959 repair and removal
of obstructions are separately dealt with ...

I consider that a highway can only be said to be out of repair if the surface of it is
defective or disturbed in some way."

Lord Denning M.R. in *Haydon's* case said at page 491:

" 'Repair' means making good defects in the surface of the highway itself ..."

and at page 492:

"An 'obstruction' to a highway occurs when it is rendered impassable, or more
difficult to pass along it by reason of some physical obstacle. It may be obstructed
without it being out of repair at all. If a tree falls across a road, it may not injure
the surface at all, it may even straddle it without touching the surface, the road is
then 'obstructed' but it is not out of repair ...

'Maintain' does not, however, include the removal of obstructions, except when the
obstruction damages the surfaces of the highway and makes it necessary to remove
the obstruction so as to execute the repairs."

The Act of 1966 does not therefore by any of its provisions give a civil remedy in the circumstances of this case and that appears to exhaust any possible remedy under statute.

Has the Department also immunity from civil liability at common law? It seems to me it has. Misfeasance cannot arise on the facts, but the defendant sought to apply the neighbour principle of *Donoghue* v. *Stevenson* [1932] A.C. 562 as a means of relief, encouraged no doubt by such well-known dicta as:

"The criterion of judgment must adjust and adapt itself to the changing circumstances of life; the categories of negligence are never closed." (Lord MacMillan in *Donoghue* v. *Stevenson* (supra) at page 619) and

"English law is wide enough to embrace any new category or proposition that exemplifies the principle of proximity." (Lord Devlin in *Hedley Byrne & Co. Ltd.* v. *Heller & Partners Ltd.* [1964] A.C. 465, at page 531).

But I think it is wise before any new application or expansion of the neighbour principle is attempted to heed the caution expressed by Lord Diplock in *Home Office* v. *Dorset Yacht Co. Ltd.* [1970] A.C. 1004. At page 1060 in a reference to Lord Atkin's neighbour principle, he said:

"Used as a guide to characteristics which will be found to exist in conduct and relationships which give rise to a legal duty of care this aphorism marks a milestone in the modern development of the law of negligence. But misused as a universal, it is manifestly false.

The branch of English law which deals with civil wrongs abounds with instances of acts and more particularly, of omissions which give rise to no legal liability in the doer or omitter for loss and damage sustained by others as a consequence of the act of omission, however reasonably or probably that loss or damage might have anticipated."

Immunity from civil liability for non-repair of highways continued after the decision in *Donoghue* v. *Stevenson* in 1932. There is no reported decision that I know of, thereafter, to show that the neighbour principle was successfully applied in a case of non- repair, up to the time when statutory exemption from liability for non-repair was cancelled in England by the Highways (Miscellaneous Provisions) Act 1961 and by the Act of 1966 here. And since the passing of the 1966 Act, despite the comparatively confined meanings given to "non-repair" and "failure to maintain" in section 1 (see *Lagan* v. *Department of the Environment* (supra)) no reported case has applied the neighbour principle to extend the liability of a highway authority for non-feasance outside that section. Therefore the acts of omission on the part of a highway authority would seem not to give rise to a cause of action for damages if they fall outside the highway authority's duty under section 1 on the principle, presumably, that where there is no duty to act, an omission to act gives no remedy.

And there may be sound reasons of public policy for refusing to expand the statutory duty of a road authority outside strict repair. I have stated possible considerations in a judgment in *Forsythe* v. *Evans, Charges Brand & Co. Ltd.,* v. *The Department of the Environment* [1980] N.I. 230 (an issue concerning the civil liability of a road authority in respect of injury caused by icy roads) some of which I think are in point here. In the

N.I.   **Campbell v. Armstrong & Ors. (Q.B.D.)**   **Kelly J.**

instant case it seems to me quite unreasonable that a duty of care should arise that obliges a road authority to inspect grass verges and free them from obstructions for the unnimpeded passage of traffic, vehicular or pedestrian.

I hold that the defendant's statement of claim does not disclose a cause of action by the defendant against the Department. I give judgment for the first Third Party, the Department, against the defendant, with costs.

Order accordingly

Solicitors for the defendant: *Wilson & Simms*
Solicitors for the Department of the Environment: *Crown Solicitor*

W.D.T.

APPENDIX 4

SPECIMEN LEGAL FORMS

APPENDIX 4
SPECIMEN LEGAL FORMS

**Rep. 5
GREEN FORM**

THE LAW SOCIETY OF NORTHERN IRELAND

SOLICITOR'S REPORT ON LEGAL ADVICE AND ASSISTANCE GIVEN UNDER
THE LEGAL AID, ADVICE & ASSISTANCE (NORTHERN IRELAND) ORDER, 1981

Key Card

PLEASE USE BLOCK CAPITALS

Surname   Forenames   Mr./Mrs./Miss

Address

CAPITAL   CLIENT   £

TOTAL SAVINGS and OTHER CAPITAL   SPOUSE £

                                       TOTAL   £

(A)

INCOME

State whether in receipt of Family Credit/Income Support.

YES/NO   If answer is YES ignore the rest of this Section.

(B)

Total weekly Gross Income

    Client   £

    Spouse   £

    TOTAL   £

Allowances and Deductions from Income

    Income tax   £   **(C)**

    National Health Contributions, etc.   £   **(D)**

    Spouse   £   **(E)**

Dependent children and/or
other dependants   Number   **(F)**

    Under 11   £

    11 but under 16   £

    16 " " 18   £

    18 and over   £

LESS TOTAL DEDUCTIONS   ➡

TOTAL WEEKLY DISPOSABLE INCOME   £

TO BE COMPLETED AND SIGNED BY CLIENT

I am over the compulsory school-leaving age.

I **have/have not** previously received help from a solicitor about this matter under the Legal Aid and Advice Schemes.

I am liable to pay a contribution not exceeding.   £

(G)

I understand that any money or property which is recovered or preserved for me may be subject to a deduction if my contribution (if any) is less than my Solicitor's charges.

The information on this page is to the best of my knowledge correct and complete. I understand that dishonesty in providing such information may lead to a prosecution.

Date ....   Signature ....

JF 6627

No. 29/4

STATEMENT OF MEANS OF AN APPLICANT FOR LEGAL AID IN A CRIMINAL CASE UNDER PART III OF THE LEGAL AID, ADVICE AND ASSISTANCE (NORTHERN IRELAND) ORDER 1981

If you wish to obtain legal aid in a criminal case you must first complete this form which will be used to determine whether you are entitled to legal aid.

WARNING. IF, IN COMPLETING THIS STATEMENT, YOU KNOWINGLY MAKE ANY FALSE STATEMENT OR FALSE REPRESENTATION YOU WILL BE LIABLE TO PROSECUTION AND IF FOUND GUILTY COULD BE FINED £100 OR IMPRISONED FOR UP TO 3 MONTHS OR BOTH.

PLEASE COMPLETE IN BLOCK CAPITALS.

1.   Surname (Mr/Mrs/Miss/Ms) _____

2.   Other names _____

3.   (a) Date of Birth _____   (b) National Insurance No (if known) _____

4.   Permanent address _____
_____

5.   If staying at temporary accommodation state address _____
_____

6.   Name and address of solicitor requested (if known) _____
_____

7.   State whether married/married, living apart/single/widowed/divorced *(delete as appropriate)*

8.   Are you currently receiving

    (a)   Supplementary benefit?   (Yes/No) _____

    (b)   Family Income Supplement?   (Yes/No) _____

NOTE—
IF YOU ARE RECEIVING SUPPLEMENTARY BENEFIT OR FAMILY INCOME SUPPLEMENT YOU NEED NOT ANSWER ANY FURTHER QUESTIONS ON THIS FORM. YOU MUST, HOWEVER, READ AND SIGN THE DECLARATION AT THE END.

9.   State occupation or profession _____

10. State whether you are employed/self employed/unemployed *(delete as appropriate)*

11. If you are employed state

    (a)   Whether full-time or part-time and

    (b)   Name and address of your employer   (a) _____   (b) _____

_____

12. What is your average weekly take-home pay (ie earnings after deductions of Income Tax and National Insurance? £ _____

13. If self-employed state annual net income £ _____

14. Is your spouse employed? (Yes/No) _____ or self-employed? (Yes/No) _____
If either answer is Yes state his/her

    (a)   Occupation _____

P.T.O.

(b)　Name and address of employer _____

_____

(c)　Approximate weekly earnings £ _____

15.　Do you or your spouse have any other income?　(eg interest from investments or rents received)
(Yes/No) _____

If the answer is Yes give details and amounts (including names of banks, Building Societies, etc from which interest is received, and state type of benefit, pensions etc received).

_____

_____

_____

16.　Do you or your spouse have any savings, money, property or other goods of value?　(Yes/No) _____

If Yes give details _____

_____

_____

17.　Have you any dependants?　(Yes/No) _____

If Yes give details (including names, ages and addresses if different from your own).

_____

_____

_____

18.　State the amount you pay per week for

　　　(a)　Rent　　　　　　　　　　　　　£ _____

　　　(b)　Rates　　　　　　　　　　　　　£ _____

　　　(c)　Mortgage　　　　　　　　　　　£ _____

　　　(d)　Board and lodging charge or contribution for keep　£ _____

19.　Do you have any other exceptional expenses which you feel should be taken into account?
(Yes/No) _____

If the answer is Yes give details _____

_____

_____

20.　If you are under 18 state the name and address of your parent or guardian

_____

_____

21.　If you are under 18 are your parents willing to assist you financially in providing you with legal aid?
(Yes/No) _____

DECLARATION

I declare that to the best of my knowledge and belief the above particulars are true and I understand that the Court may require the Department of Health and Social Services to enquire into my means before or after the granting of a Criminal Aid Certificate.

Signature _____　　Date _____　　　　　C8375253 15m 7/82 D gp 191

MAGISTRATES' COURTS (NORTHERN IRELAND) ORDER 1981
(Article 20(1), (2) and (3); Rule 8)

Summons to Defendant to answer Complaint

[Title as in Form 1]

WHEREAS a complaint has been made before me that on the (date)
at (place)
in the said petty sessions district and county court division, you, the said
defendant

THIS IS TO COMMAND YOU to appear as a defendant on the hearing of the
said complaint at (place)   on (date)
, at (time)
before a magistrates' court for the said county court division.

This   day of   19

                              Justice of the Peace
                              [Clerk of Petty Sessions]

To the said Defendant

MAGISTRATES' COURTS (NORTHERN IRELAND) ORDER 1981
(Articles 20 and 45; Rules 8 and 44(1))

**Summons to Defendant to answer Complaint charging an Indictable Offence
specified in Schedule 2 to the Order**

[Title as in Form 1]

WHEREAS a complaint has been made before me that on (date)
at (place)
in the said petty sessions district and county court division you, the said defendant,

THIS IS TO COMMAND YOU to appear in person as a defendant on the hearing of the
said complaint at (place)   , on (date)
at (time)   before a magistrates' court of the said county court division.

This   day of   19   .

Justice of the Peace
[Clerk of Petty Sessions]

Notice under Article 45 of the said Order of 1981

The [following] offence(s) [that is to say—]

for which you are hereby summoned to appear before the court [is] [are] [an]
indictable offence(s) specified in Schedule 2 to the said Order which may be dealt
with summarily by a resident magistrate in accordance with Article 45 of that Order.

The purpose of this notice is to inform you that the above offence(s) [is] [are] [an]
offence(s) for which you have a right to be tried by jury and which may be dealt with
summarily by a resident magistrate only with your consent, and if you do so consent,
only where the prosecutor also consents.

The resident magistrate may, however, even if you consent and the prosecutor
also consents to the summary trial of [any of] the above-mentioned offence(s), decide
that for any of the reasons specified in Article 45(1) of the said Order, it is inexpedient
to deal with any such offence(s) summarily.

FORM OF INDICTMENT

THE QUEEN v.

Court of Trial:

  Date:

CHARGE(S)

charged with the following offence(s):—

FIRST COUNT

STATEMENT OF OFFENCE

PARTICULARS OF OFFENCE

SECOND COUNT

STATEMENT OF OFFENCE

PARTICULARS OF OFFENCE

FORM 125

Claim No.

Application for Arbitration (Small Claims)

Order 26, Rule 3

Applicant: Full name and postal
address in BLOCK CAPITALS

(put your full name and address here)

Respondent: Full name and postal
address in BLOCK CAPITALS

*(the full name and address of the person
you are claiming against goes here)*

Take notice that I the above named Applicant intend to apply to the Circuit
Registrar

at   *(put name of court – see list on page 60)*   for arbitration in respect

of my claim for £

(insert particulars of claim)

*(here insert the amount claimed and short details of your claim –
see examples given on page 12)*

Date:

Signed: ....
Applicant

___

FOR OFFICE USE ONLY

NOTICE OF HEARING

This Application will be dealt with by the Circuit Registrar when he sits

at

on

The Circuit Registrar's sitting will start at

Chief Clerk

SC1   Date:

ORDINARY CIVIL BILL

No.

In the County Court for the Division

of

Between

of

in the County of

Plaintiff

and

of

in the County of

and Division of

Defendant

By The County Court Judge/Recorder

The sittings at which this civil bill is intended to be dealt with will commence on the   day of   19 and will be held at

The defendant therefore is hereby required to appear at the aforesaid Court at the hour of   on the   day of   19 to answer the plaintiff's claim for

Costs and outlay if paid within fourteen days from date of service £

NOTE—Costs and outlay if paid after fourteen days from service will be payable at a higher scale.

Dated this   day of   19

Signed

Solicitor for the Plaintiff

Address

A & S DONALDSON (N.I.) LTD. Law Stationers, Lisburn

19   . No. 12345

In The High Court of Justice in Northern Ireland

QUEEN'S BENCH DIVISION

ALBERT MOUSEPARTNER

v.

PERCY VERE and JOSEPH SMITH

WRIT OF SUMMONS

GENERAL FORM

We accept service hereof on behalf of Percy Vere, one of the within named Defendants.

Dated the   day of   19

Signed:

       Holbrook, Willoughby & Griffiths,
       1 Snob Lane,
       Belfast 1.

            Lowe, Snow & Co.,
            Solicitors,
            7 Donegall Square East,
            Belfast 1.

A. & S. Donaldson (N.I.) Ltd. Law Stationers, Lisburn

In the High Court of Justice in Northern Ireland

DIVISION

19   No. 12345

Between

ALBERT MOUSEPARTNER

Plaintiff

and

PERCY VERE and JOSEPH SMITH

Defendants

ELIZABETH THE SECOND, by the Grace of God, of the United Kingdom of Great Britain and Northern Ireland and of Our other realms and territories Queen, Head of the Commonwealth, Defender of the Faith:

To   Percy Vere, of "The Beeches", Weyford, and
         Joseph Smith

of   "Fag End", 1 Butt Lane, Weyford, both

in the County of Down

We command you, that within 14 days after the service of this writ on you, inclusive of the day of service, you do cause an appearance to be entered for you in an action at the suit of

ALBERT MOUSEPARTNER

and take notice that in default of your so doing, the plaintiff may proceed therein, and judgment may be given in your absence.

WITNESS, The Right Honourable ROBERT LYND ERSKINE, BARON LOWRY, Lord Chief Justice of Northern Ireland, the   day of

19

Note:—This writ may not be served later than 12 calendar months beginning with the above date unless renewed by order of the Court.

DIRECTIONS FOR ENTERING APPEARANCE

The defendant may enter an appearance in person or by a solicitor either (1) by handing in the appropriate forms, duly completed, at the Central Office or Chancery Office (as appropriate), Royal Courts of Justice, Chichester Street, Belfast BT1 3JF, or (2) by sending them to that Office by post. The appropriate forms may be obtained at H.M. Stationery Office, Chichester House, Chichester Street, Belfast BT1 1PS.

The Plaintiff's claim is for damages for personal injuries, loss and damage sustained by him by reason of the negligence of the first Defendant and/or the second Defendant in or about the driving, management and control of motor vehicles.

G. Bull

If the Plaintiff sues, or the defendant is sued, in a representative capacity, this must be stated in the endorsement of claim.

(Signed) ....

And £   (or such sum as may be allowed on taxation) for costs, and also, if the plaintiff obtains an order for substituted service, the further sum of £
(or such sum as may be allowed on taxation). If the amount claimed and costs be paid to the plaintiff or his solicitor within 14 days after service hereof (inclusive of the day of service), further proceedings will be stayed.

This paragraph should be deleted if the plaintiff's claim is not for a debt or liquidated demand only.

This writ was issued by Lowe, Snow & Co.,

of 7, Donegall Square East, in the City of Belfast,

Solicitor for the said plaintiff whose address is

5, Council Flats, Weyford, in the County of Down

OR

This writ was issued by the said plaintiff who resides at

and (*if the plaintiff does not reside within the jurisdiction*) whose address for service is

APPENDIX 4

* IN THE HIGH COURT OF JUSTICE IN NORTHERN IRELAND

FAMILY DIVISION

* Delete as appropriate

* IN THE COUNTY COURT FOR THE DIVISION OF

THE PETITION OF

1. On the   day of   19

the petitioner

was lawfully married to

(hereinafter called "the respondent") at

2. The petitioner and respondent last lived together as husband and wife at

3. The petitioner/respondent is domiciled in Northern Ireland.

4. The petitioner is by occupation a

and resides at

    The respondent is by occupation a

and resides at

5. There are no children of the family, now living, except

6. No other child, now living, has been born to the petitioner/respondent during the marriage (so far as is known to the petitioner) except

7. There are or have been no other proceedings in any court in Northern Ireland or elsewhere with reference to the marriage (or to any child of the family) or between the petitioner and respondent with reference to any property of either or both of them

except

8. There are no proceedings continuing in any country outside Northern Ireland which are in respect of the marriage or are capable of effecting its validity or subsistence

except

9. No agreement or arrangement has been made or is proposed to be made between the parties for the support of the petitioner/respondent (and any child of the family)

except

10. The said marriage has broken down irretrievably.

11.

12. Particulars

PRAYER

The petitioner therefore prays:

(1)   That the said marriage be dissolved.

(2)   That the petitioner may be granted custody of

(3)   That the   may be ordered to pay the costs of this suit.

(4)   That the petitioner may be granted the following ancillary relief:

    (a)   an order for maintenance pending suit and thereafter

        a periodical payments order

        a secured provision order

        a lump sum order

    (b)   a periodical payments order

        a secured provision order   }   for the children of the family

        a lump sum order

    (c)   a property adjustment order in relation to

Signed _____

The names and addresses of the persons to be served with this petition are:

Respondent:

Co-Respondent (adultery case only):

The Petitioner's address for service

Dated this   day of   19

Address all communications for the court to:

      The Master (Probate and Matrimonial)
      Royal Courts of Justice
      Chichester Street
      Belfast BT1 3JF.

NOTICE OF INTENT TO ENFORCE A MONEY JUDGMENT
JUDGMENTS ENFORCEMENT (NORTHERN IRELAND) ORDER 1981

BETWEEN:

Plaintiff/Applicant

Defendant/Respondent

To: [1]

of [2]

TAKE NOTICE that you owe [3]
the sum of £ [4]   together with interest at the rate of [5]   per cent per
annum which is the amount due on foot of a judgment given against you in the above matter
and a copy of which is attached.

YOU HAVE 10 DAYS from the date of this notice within which to pay that amount at the
*address given below. If you do not pay proceedings will be taken to enforce the judgment
against you.

Dated [6]   day of   19

Signed ....

Applicant/Duly Authorised Person/
Applicant's Solicitor

*Address ....

....

....

REQUISITION
The Chief Enforcement Officer, Enforcement of Judgments Office.
    Please issue and serve the above Notice of Intention to Proceed on
[1]
at [2]
which is the present address of the said [1]
to the best of my/our knowledge, information and belief.

Signed ....
    Creditor/Solicitor(s) for Creditor

Dated ....

NOTES
[1] Full name of debtor.
[2] Full postal address of debtor.
[3] Full name of creditor.
[4] This figure should represent the balance of all monies due and payable under the
    judgment at the date of signing.
[5] Insert the rate of interest prescribed by the relevant rule of court. Interest is not
    chargeable where the sum due and payable under the judgment does not exceed £200 or
    the judgment is for a penal sum for securing principal and interest.
[6] Leave blank.

APPENDIX 4

ORIGINATING APPLICATION TO AN INDUSTRIAL TRIBUNAL

<table>
<tr>
<td>

UNDER ONE OR MORE OF THE FOLLOWING ACTS OR ORDERS

CONTRACTS OF EMPLOYMENT AND REDUNDANCY PAYMENTS (NI) 1965

EQUAL PAY ACT (NI) 1970

SEX DISCRIMINATION (NI) ORDER 1976

INDUSTRIAL RELATIONS (NI) ORDERS 1976 TO 1982

</td>
<td>

For Official Use

Case Number	

CONTRACTS OF EMPLOYMENT AND REDUNDANCY PAYMENTS ACT (NI) 1965

EQUAL PAY ACT (NI) 1970

SEX DISCRIMINATION (NI) ORDER 1976

INDUSTRIAL RELATIONS (NI) ORDERS 1976

</td>
</tr>
</table>

IMPORTANT: DO NOT FILL IN THIS FORM UNTIL YOU HAVE READ EXPLANATORY LEAFLET 1TL 1(NI) ALL QUESTIONS MUST BE ANSWERED.

To:- The Secretary of the Tribunals
Central Office of the Industrial Tribunals
2nd Floor, Bedford House, Bedford Street
Belfast BT2 7NR

Telephone: 227666

1. I hereby apply for a decision of a tribunal on the following question (State here question to be decided by the tribunal and the Act(s) and/or Order(s) appropriate to your case).

....

....

....

(The grounds of your application should be stated in paragraph 14 overleaf)

2. My name (Surname in block captials first) is Mr/Mrs/Miss ....

Address and telephone number ....

OR title (if company or organisation) is ....

3. Date of Birth .... National Insurance No...........................

4. If your employment has ended have you claimed unemployment/supplementary benefit? ....

5. If you are a member of a trade union please state name of organisation ....

....

6. If a representative has agreed to act for you in this case please give his name and address below:-

Name ....

Address and telephone number ....

7. (a) Name of respondent(s) (in block capitals) ie the employer, person or body against whom a decision is sought ....

Address(es) and telephone number(s) ....

....

IT1(NI) (Rev)

7. (b) Respondent's relationship to you for the purpose of the application (eg employer, trade union, employment agency, employer recognising the union making application, etc)

....

8. Place of employment to which this application relates or place where act complained about took place.

....

Occupation or position held/applied for, or other relationship to the respondent named above (eg user of a service supplied by him) ....

10. Employment began on.........................and (if appropriate) ended on ....

11. Basic nett wage................Basic gross wage.............Other pay or remuneration ....

12. Normal basic weekly hours of work:- ....

13. (In an application under the Sex Discrimination (NI) Order 1976) Date on which action complained of took place or first came to my knowledge ....

....

14. The grounds of this application are as follows:-

15. (If dismissed) If you wish to state what in your opinion was the reason for your dismissal, please do so here.

....

....

16. If dismissed and the tribunal decides that you were unfairly dismissed, what remedy would you prefer? (Before answering this question please consult leaflet 1TL 1 (NI) for the remedies available and then write ONE only of the following in answer to this question: reinstatement, re-engagement or compensation)

....

Signature .... Date........................

FOR OFFICIAL USE

Issuing Office	Received at COIT	Initials

INDEX